Beyond Management

Taking Charge at Work

Mark Addleson

First published 2011 by
PALGRAVE MACMILLAN

Palgrave Macmillan in the UK is an imprint of Macmillan Publishers Limited,
registered in England, company number 785998, of Houndmills, Basingstoke,
Hampshire RG21 6XS.

Palgrave Macmillan in the US is a division of St Martin's Press LLC,
175 Fifth Avenue, New York, NY 10010.

Palgrave Macmillan is the global academic imprint of the above companies
and has companies and representatives throughout the world.

Palgrave® and Macmillan® are registered trademarks in the United States,
the United Kingdom, Europe and other countries.

ISBN 978–0–230–30816–9

This book is printed on paper suitable for recycling and made from fully
managed and sustained forest sources. Logging, pulping and manufacturing
processes are expected to conform to the environmental regulations of the
country of origin.

A catalogue record for this book is available from the British Library.

A catalog record for this book is available from the Library of Congress.

10   9   8   7   6   5   4   3   2   1
20   19   18   17   16   15   14   13   12   11

Printed and bound in Great Britain by
MPG Group, Bodmin and King's Lynn

For Rob and Kate (a.k.a. Dan and The P) –
they have always been beyond management

Contents

LIST OF FIGURES

Acknowledgments

Many people—friends, colleagues, and others—have had a hand in shaping this book. Dana Dolan generously read the final version and offered careful, detailed comments. She also asked me to remind readers who have the stamina to tackle the chapter notes that there is another book there (I have the impression she thinks it is the more interesting one!). Jessica Heineman-Pieper, Tony Joyce, Art Kleiner, Mark Leheney, Eric Meyer, Neil Olonoff, and Bill Tulloh all went beyond the call of duty and/or friendship in reading and commenting on typescripts.

Working with Jennifer Berger was a spur to start putting fingers to keyboard. Jeff Conklin introduced me to wicked problems many years ago and things have gone downhill ever since. My consulting colleagues, Scott Brumburgh, Christiane Frishmuth, and Mikaela Seligman, have tried very hard to keep me focused—against my natural impulses—on practical matters; as has Raj Chawla, to whom I owe a special thank you for his encouragement as well as his friendship. From the Hermanus crew, who adopted us during Cape winters, I want to thank Beth and Noel Hunt, of Hemingway's Bookshop, for their company and encouragement.

On the publishing side, John Wright, literary agent, very generously guided me through the process of creating a prospectus, then Stephen Rutt at Palgrave Macmillan was kind—or, I'd like to think, wise—enough to take the manuscript. I am grateful to all who have helped turn words and a few images into a handsome volume, in particular, Eleanor Davey-Corrigan at Palgrave Macmillan, and Keith Povey with Nick Fox, who, as editors, enabled me to handle the hurdles of the important final phases. Ioana Belcea did the marvelous drawings for Chapter 11. How fortunate I am to have a gifted iconographer as a neighbor.

I'm especially privileged to work with bright, experienced graduate students, my real teachers. Their enthusiasm and willingness to run with half-baked ideas brought this book to life.

Lastly, but certainly not leastly, I am deeply grateful to Jen, companion and advisor on this and many other journeys. *Beyond Management* would not have seen the light of day without her wisdom, humor, patience, and care.

MARK ADDLESON

The author and publishers are grateful to the following for permission to reproduce copyright material as indicated:

Figure 6.1 "Two pictures of factory-work, ca. 1930" (p. 66)
Source: "Behind the Scenes in the Machine Age," 1931, a film produced by the Women's Bureau of the United States Department of Labor.

Figure 6.2 "Diagram of an organizational network" (p. 68)
Source:Valdis Krebs (www.orgnet.com/decisions.html). Reproduced with permission.

Figure 8.1 "Work practices" (p. 101)
Source: Adapted from Etienne Wenger, *Communities of Practice: Learning, Meaning and Identity*, p. 63. Used by permission of Cambridge University Press. Copyright © 1998 by Etienne Wenger.

"Manifesto for Agile Development" box (p. 113)
Source: The Agile Alliance (agilemanifesto.org). Reproduced with permission.

Figure 9.1 "The waterfall model" (p. 115)
Source: Adapted from a diagram by Paul Hoadley. Used with his permission.

Figure 11.1 "Letting go!" (p. 139)
Drawn by Ioana Belcea. Used with her permission.

Figure 11.2 "A delicate balance" (p. 147)
Drawn by Ioana Belcea. Used with her permission.

Figure 15.1 "A pyramid-maze puzzle" (p. 206)
Source: Based on a puzzle marketed by Loncraine Broxton. Used with permission of the Lagoon Trading Co. Ltd.

CHAPTER 1

The end of the line

Talk about a revolution

Management is dead, but don't take my word for it. Peter Drucker saw this first. He begins *The Practice of Management*, the book that made him famous, with a bold prediction: "management will remain a basic and dominant institution perhaps as long as Western civilization itself survives".[1] What a surprise, then, to find him administering the last rites to management a little more than 40 years later: "as we advance deeper into the knowledge economy, the basic assumptions underlying much of what is taught and practiced in the name of management are hopelessly out of date . . . As a result, we are preaching, teaching, and practicing policies that are increasingly at odds with reality and therefore counterproductive."[2]

For most of his long and illustrious career, Drucker, who had a large following, wrote about how to be a good manager, maintaining that management is fundamental to a prosperous and progressive society. Toward the end of his career, "the father of modern management" turns his back on the profession he helped to establish, warning that management has run its course. He now says that management practices are *counterproductive*, meaning they do the *opposite* of what you want. Intended to make organizations more efficient and more profitable, this is an admission that they are actually *disorganizing*. What should we make of this dramatic reversal?

Prolific writer that he was, it is relatively easy to keep track of Drucker's intellectual journey and see why he made this U-turn. You might say it was simply a matter of putting two and two together, although doing the math needed someone not only well versed in management but also attuned to what was happening in the world of work.[3] By the 1960s, noticing industrial work was on the wane, he coined the expressions "knowledge work" and "knowledge worker" to describe professionals in the nascent information technology (IT) industry. What Drucker saw, and what knowledge workers know instinctively, is that management is all right for organizing factories. Factories run with the regular rhythm of machines, but old-style factory-work had been solitary, repetitive, mindless, with workers little more than automatons. Knowledge-work is an entirely different story.

Manufacturing jobs have all but disappeared, "off-shored" to countries where labor is cheap, productive, and, for lack of regulations, exploitable. The rest of us—administrators, bankers, consultants, designers, entertainers, IT specialists, journalists, lobbyists, musicians, nurses, restaurateurs, secretaries, social workers, trainers, and writers—are knowledge workers, as are janitors, landscape crews, and plumbers. Knowledge workers organize themselves. With a common interest in what they are doing, they cooperate, share knowledge, learn from one another, assign tasks, and make decisions while they work. Using management tools and techniques to organize knowledge-work makes a mess of work, which we've been doing for half a century or more.

As pretty much everyone is a knowledge worker nowadays, we'd better do something about this. The question is what. Drucker only hints at knowledge-work being a game-changer. He doesn't explain why or tell us how to deal with the fact that management practices are ubiquitous and deeply entrenched. What is wrong with "old" management? What does "new" management look like in the age of knowledge-work? And how do we remove the old and replace it with the new? Here are three large gaps that need filling, and I plan to fill them. To offer a way forward I'll pose four questions, answering a what, a why, a couple of wheres, and a how. What is knowledge-work? Why don't management and knowledge-work mix? And, once we know where management is deficient and where to look for new practices, how do we replace the old with the new? So, if you follow my story, you'll understand and be able to respond to the growing disillusionment with management.

Having lived in the shadow of management for generations, almost everyone still seems to take it for granted that when it is a question of getting the best results from work you turn to management for answers.[4] True, there is some disagreement about exactly how to get the best results; for example, whether the usual measures of managers' performance, to which their compensation is often tied, contribute to an unhealthy emphasis on short-term outcomes.[5] But, leaving aside serious criticism from the Left, disagreements about the substance of management, over how to manage organizations, are generally mild. The most common complaint is that something or other is missing; that there isn't enough emphasis given to, say, processes as opposed to structures.[6] Such complaints invariably come with the assurance that the problem can be fixed, with the promise that, when fixed, management will once again be in good shape, and with the claim by the critic that he has just the tool to put things right.

Lately, we've been hearing a different kind of objection from mainstream writers much like Drucker, who are dissatisfied with management and doubtful about its future. Gary Hamel is one; convinced that management has passed its sell-by date yet evidently not ready to toss it all away (he makes a handsome living as a management consultant, so this is probably not surprising). Writing in the *Harvard Business Review*, an establishment stronghold, he maintains that "management, like the combustion engine, is a mature technology that must now be reinvented for a new age." What is needed is a "management revolution . . . no less momentous than the one that spawned modern industry."[7] This probably sounds like the kind of hyperbole we've come to expect from management gurus, but Hamel is dead right and, I'm sure, realizes that redoing management from scratch involves a far-reaching agenda that calls for profoundly political action.

How seriously should we take Hamel and other agnostics? Having held an orthodox line, we can be certain that their past disagreements with management have been relatively mild, probably over practices, and that they've come to their new positions only after some soul searching. Agnosticism covers principles as well as practices and, if their status in the profession isn't a good enough reason to pay attention to what they're saying, there is another compelling one. They speak for a very large group who are fed up with standard management methods. Actually, there are two groups.

One is the workers caught up in "change management" initiatives, confused and disheartened by a maelstrom of internal organizational changes that they're unable to make head or tail of. In the course of a restructuring, reorganization (a "reorg"), downsizing, or merger, divisions are renamed, sales teams which were organized by product are reorganized by region, new mission statements and organizational (org) charts appear magically on the walls and the web, and they have new job descriptions. What is the point of it all? When the smoke finally clears little has changed. With the old systems and procedures still in place, everyone continues to work as they did before, with one important difference: some of their colleagues have been fired and those who still have jobs feel insecure and anxious about theirs. Is this an improvement and, if so, why and for whom?

Then, there are managers at all levels, in all kinds of organizations, who, when they talk frankly about their work, will tell you they, too, are frustrated. Often referring to their subordinates' lack of commitment and/or accountability, they'll say they aren't getting the results they want. They blame poor teamwork for slippage that includes missed deadlines and projects that are over budget and may tell you that the tools and techniques they've learned to rely on, from performance measures to IT systems, don't work as they're supposed to. I've heard a few managers say that they've run out of ideas about what to do and I'm certain there are many, many more who feel the same way.

If you are in either group, dissatisfied with what you see and wanting to do something about it, you are a potential activist for change and this book is meant for you. The same goes for management consultants and organization development practitioners who advise organizations about change. I've written the book to explain what is going on and what you can do about it. And, even if you're not in one of these groups, there is every reason for you to take an interest, make a stand, and become an activist. Whether it is the work of medical professionals, county maintenance workers, volunteer community organizers, soldiers, financial brokers, or structural engineers, how we manage (i.e. organize) the work we do affects all sorts of people in different ways, so we need to see to it that we do it properly.

Whenever people want to accomplish anything they need to organize, whether they are arranging a wedding reception, publishing a book, drilling an oil well, or even if it is just two of them trying to schedule lunch. At work, ordinary human acts of organizing are surrounded by dense, almost impenetrable layers of procedures and jargon held together by pseudo-science. What we call "management" is a morass of rules, regulations, and rigid structures that spring from a command-and-control mentality, coupled with an obsession for measuring and an insatiable appetite for data. This is because, as a so-called "science," management is meant to be empirical and objective, which means that when it comes to making decisions, "hard data" or "facts" are supposed to trump whatever it is that decision-makers think, feel, believe, and value. These trappings of science and weasel-words like "efficiency" (translation: "nothing matters except the bottom line") are like a protective covering that makes it difficult to see that management is actually about people organizing to get things done with other people.

There are many who'll argue that doing things the management way— the MBA way, with all those rules, structures, systems, and data—is the right way and possibly the only way to organize work. And you may think you have every reason to believe them. They seem to speak on good authority. After all, they have hundreds, if not thousands, of business books, and untold numbers of consultants, not to say all the programs at management schools, to back up their story.[8] But, unwrapping management practices, I want to peel away the protective layers, so you can see work, especially knowledge-work, in a way that management books don't tell you about and see how people actually do it. You'll also see why, underneath the pseudo-science and impressive language of "scorecards," "value propositions," "human capital," and "data mining," management is a cause of widespread dissatisfaction at work as well as a source of organizational breakdowns. You'll go further too. If you're an activist, or want to become one, you will find out what you can and should do about this unacceptable state of affairs.

The problem we're up against, which Drucker saw, is that management cannot be transplanted from the industrial age, where it began, into the age of knowledge-work, from steam power and smokestacks to smoke-free offices. Today's good management, whether taught in business schools or learned on the job, consists of practices devised in a world dominated by machines for running factories with production lines. But, the work most people do today, like renewing run-down urban communities, selling office equipment, designing software, educating children or adults, organizing labor unions, and providing financial aid to support international development work, isn't at all like factory-work. Knowledge-work marks the end of the production line, which means, too, it is the end of the line for management.[9]

Once you understand that management practices are playing havoc with knowledge-work and understand why, it is relatively easy to see what you ought to do. Even when you want to, though, it is quite another thing to accomplish the change. Bureaucracy, hierarchy, aggressive competition, and bottom-line accounting, some of the ideas and practices that are bad for knowledge-work, are so much part of the scene that is difficult to conceive of workplaces without them. Replacing management means tinkering with the vitals of society and challenging an ideology that has become a matter of faith. This takes a strong stomach. If it was easy to do, we would have eliminated the worst practices by now. It is going to take a change of heart, seeing work through new eyes, with new values, to replace management; but I won't have done my job unless you know why it's worth the effort and I can point you to the kinds of collaborative workplaces that are right for knowledge-work, where people are committed to doing good work and are accountable to one another for doing it.

We may be a long way from where we ought to be, but, on the upside, we don't have to look far, or hard, to find practices that support knowledge-work. The right ones could not be closer. Scientific advisors drafting a policy document on climate change, a mother taking her kids to after-school activities, or teens going to movies with their friends organize; so do you and I. Organizing is an important part of life. We all know about it and know how to do it. Organizing is collective work, which is why knowledge workers participate in networks, establish groups, and form teams. And, whether they do it face-to-face, on the phone, or, nowadays, online, on social networking sites or texting, organizing is, unquestionably, a grass-roots effort. At work, what we are after, in fact, are ordinary, every-day ways of organizing that have served human beings well, all over the world, for thousands of years before management appeared on the scene roughly a century ago. Let me tell you, briefly, how I plan to help you find and—if you're an activist—get into your "new" work practices.

The story in outline

Oscar Wilde is supposed to have said that there are two kinds of people: those who divide the world into two kinds of types of people and those who don't.[10] In writing about work, management, and organizing I find it helpful to make distinctions, which surely means I'm the dividing kind. For now I'll talk about some of the distinctions that are central to my story, leaving others for later. The story begins with two ways of getting work done. One is "management," which is familiar. The other I'll call "organizing." I'll also describe and contrast two kinds of work: "factory-work," which is physical, repetitive, solitary, and often quite mindless; and "knowledge-work," which on every count is just the opposite. Invented for organizing factory-work, we now use management to organize knowledge-work—and the results are entirely unsatisfactory.

The view from the top

The word "management" covers the things managers do, like making plans and giving directions to subordinates. It also refers to the managers themselves—the people with titles such as "vice president," "director of operations," or "district supervisor."[11] Perhaps it is less obvious that there is a third way of thinking about "management": as point of view or per-spective. Here, management is a particular way of looking at organizations and the human activities we call "work." I probably don't have to explain why I think of it as the "view from the top."[12] In the view from the top there are organizations: *things* that have to be run efficiently. It is management's job to do this by "directing resources." These include "cap-ital" (machines and other replaceable assets) and "workers" (or nowadays "human capital"). "Managing work" means one or more people at the very top of the organization, who are not actually doing the work, are in charge, delegating authority through a "chain of command," telling people what to do, when, and how, or, quoting a standard definition of management, "planning, coordinating, and controlling" everything and everyone below them.

The view from practice

Writing about how the view from the top influences the way we see and organize work, I'll contrast it with the "view from practice." This is the view you have when you are actually doing your work, in the trenches so to speak, intimately involved with colleagues or clients and aware of what they are doing, saying, and even what they are thinking and feeling, as you make plans together and talk to one another about what you want to accomplish. Figure 1.1 is a summary of these distinctions, the main ones I use to tell my story. Management, the view from the top, historically is tied to factory-work. It takes a view from practice to understand knowledge-work and to see how knowledge workers organize their work.

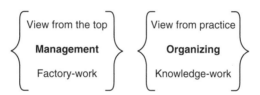

Figure 1.1   Two perspectives on work

Around organizations only the management view (the left-hand side of Figure 1.1) carries real weight. The result is we miss what is most important about knowledge-work: the organizing knowledge workers do as they work. With their view from the top, managers are preoccupied with documentation, data, directives, deliverables, deadlines, and dollars. These—what I'll call the "six Ds" for short—have very little to do with work and don't get anything done. If knowledge workers weren't, themselves, constantly organizing, nothing could or would get done. But you don't see this from the top. You need the view from practice. Once you have it, it's quickly apparent that management is incompatible with knowledge-work. So it is time to shine a spotlight on knowledge workers: to see what the work of organizing is all about, how they do it, and why management practices hinder rather than help them.

CHAPTER 2

Getting into work

Breakdowns large and small

Business books have a similar, simple agenda. They tell you how to manage people and organizations successfully. When it comes to how to run the whole operation, they have a similar, simple recipe. They start with the premise (often left unsaid) that organizations consist of two separate sets of activities—management and work—and then concentrate on management alone. Work and workers hardly feature. Managers ("above") plan, budget, schedule, and coordinate activities; and workers ("below") follow those plans and schedules. Managers need data and tools to solve problems. This data comes up, from below, in reports, databases, and the like. Workers need "incentives"—both "carrots" and "sticks"—to persuade them to work hard. These come down from above.

As there are enough business books to fill a decent-sized public library, you'd think, by now, we would be quite good at doing what they say can be done if you take their advice. Organizations, running like clockwork, producing excellent bottom-line results, would be providing first-rate services and top quality products to highly satisfied customers. In each you'd find a homogeneous work culture and contented employees committed to a shared vision and common mission. In short, in the hands of capable managers and inspirational leaders, everyone and everything would be performing at its peak. Does this sound like your organization? I'm confident in saying that it is not like any I know in the business, government, or nonprofit worlds, because, apart from that fact that it doesn't make sense to separate doing the work from organizing or managing it (it isn't practical), the cast of one-dimensional characters—managers, executives, supervisors, leaders, administrators, workers, and so on—in the idealized and romanticized abstractions these books call "organizations" lacks all traces of humanity. This begs two questions. What planet are the writers from? And what, exactly, are they trying to tell us?

Ironically, the parodies of organizations, their managers, leaders, and work, in Scott Adam's *Dilbert* cartoon strip or the TV comedy *The Office* seem infinitely more real than the paragons of rationality you find in business books or articles. Take the people. Some are imaginative and others dull; some visionary, others short-sighted; some kind, others cruel; some cooperative and helpful, others competitive and perverse; some seem to have an insatiable desire for more power, recognition, or money (possibly all three), while others, in spite of their grumbling, are more or less content with their lot. As satire often depends on highlighting one character's distress (e.g. Dilbert's) at another's attitudes or actions (his pointy-haired boss), or on exposing awkward and sometimes disastrous relationships, there's no mistaking that work life is social and, as such, is complicated.[1] It is also impossible to overlook the fact that organizations are punctuated by breakdowns, both big and small, or that these two sets of factors—the social complexity of work and the breakdowns—are related.[2]

Though management books seldom mention breakdowns, in real life they range from the largely inconsequential—disagreement over what color Post-it notes to use for urgent as opposed to normal tasks—to debacles on a scale that are sometimes quite breathtaking, especially when you consider the amount of money spent and how little, if anything, there is to show for it. To highlight some of these breakdowns, large and small, I've chosen examples which illustrate that they are not confined to one type of organization, but are as prevalent in government agencies, say, as they are in businesses or nonprofits.

Large-scale breakdowns

It is easy to find examples of large-scale breakdowns, as some make it into the media. Many, such as failed mergers, often don't become public and remain dirty secrets of management. Software projects, costing hundreds or even thousands of millions of dollars are abandoned when, eventually, it becomes clear they aren't going to meet a client's requirements and the provider's promises.[3] Bank collapses in the last few years have once again brought to light the irresponsible and careless strategies and self-serving actions of executives of institutions whose reputations and business depend on prudence, responsibility, and trust. The question of how to prevent future attacks like those in 2001 on the World Trade Center and the Pentagon led to the United States Congress authorizing the creation of a Department of Homeland Security. Surely it doesn't need a formal inquiry to agree that consigning more than 30 huge, bureaucratic, often competing departments and agencies, with their own internal schisms and rivalries, to one enormous bureaucratic structure adds up to a fiasco: one which won't make employees any more willing, or able, to share information.

In the same vein, consider projects which, when completed, are next to useless. These aren't exactly the Ford Edsels of their time, because the Edsel ran. It just wasn't appealing enough to sell in numbers that would have made it profitable.[4] I'm thinking of programs and projects which don't work out at all, like large-scale management interventions, including mergers, that don't have discernible benefits; or development-aid programs that don't deliver anything resembling development or poverty relief.[5] Time and again, development agencies, employing highly qualified people at generous salaries, compile data and formulate policies using sophisticated equipment and complex models. Then they spend vast sums of money, but in ways that do hardly any good for the poor and destitute in the countries they are "assisting." When these projects reach their completion dates, or exhaust their budgets, they are over, no matter what they've accomplished. The expatriots staffing them, who are getting ready to move on to the next assignment on their schedule, pull out, often leaving a vacuum, but without so much as either a thought for what they've left behind or a care about what will follow.[6] What major accomplishments can you point to after more than half a century—not to say the billions of dollars spent— of "managing development"?

Smaller-scale breakdowns

I'm especially interested in the countless, smaller-scale breakdowns that happen every day at work that are hard to find unless you are on hand—inside organizations, involved in the work—to see them. These breakdowns often pit management against workers, so it isn't unusual for each to blame the other: the "higher-ups" or "the people in charge" are blamed for bad planning and unrealistic budgets; "the workers" or "the team" are blamed for poor performance or a lack of commitment; and they blame one another for "poor communication." "Couldn't *they* see what would happen?" "Don't *they* know what is going on?" "Didn't *they* know what they were supposed to do?"

I'd put strategic interventions like business process reengineering into this category. They hardly ever have identifiable, longer-term benefits, but are usually incredibly disruptive and can ruin the lives of people who are swept away on the premise of "improved performance." Then there are equally pointless "restructurings." For some reason one misguided restructuring is rarely enough. It is nearly always followed by another, and possibly yet another, each abandoned before the plans have been fully implemented, presumably because they weren't going anywhere. With each one, employees ask: "why"? And, when it's over, they say: "nothing has changed." While a restructuring is in progress, they wait anxiously to see whether they'll have their jobs at the end of it. After experiencing the ups-and-downs, not surprisingly they are deeply prejudiced against "change management," which seems to achieve nothing more than a pervasive mood of resignation and apathy combined with the fear that those who survived will "get it" in the next round.

Most of the breakdowns associated with dysfunctional teams fall into this category too. They occur frequently and are usually, but not always, on quite a small scale. As a rule, knowledge workers interact and cooperate to get things done and, more and more, are organized in teams: sales teams, project teams, design teams, customer service teams, and planning teams, as well as "red" and "blue" teams, or "alpha" and "beta" teams (the kinds of names given to groups of administrative staff set up to handle particular functions, such as "accounts receivable" or "benefits"). Usually, these are teams only in name.[7] "My project group never functions as a real team" is a common complaint, which is hardly surprising, as competition is the prevailing ethos at work and people are rewarded for competing, not for collaborating. Moreover, they are seldom accountable to each other, especially when they belong to separate departments or divisions and report to different bosses who manage their units like private fiefdoms and expect "their" employees to follow their own, separate, sometimes personal, agendas and meet their particular goals and requirements.[8]

Breakdowns with tragic consequences

Breakdowns can have tragic consequences. Astonishingly, the United States government spends more on its military than virtually all other governments in the rest of the world *combined*. You might expect, therefore, that the U.S. military would be very good at supplying soldiers in the field with whatever they need, when they need it.[9] After the United States invaded Iraq in 2003, however, there were reports of serious deficiencies in organizing:

> Soldiers and Marines on the ground soon found themselves short of even water and food. According to the GAO,[10] the military lacked more than 1 million cases of Meals Ready to Eat. Soldiers ran short of the non-rechargeable lithium batteries needed to operate 60 different communications and electronic systems, systems that are critical to

tracking targets or allowing soldiers under fire to talk to one another. Many soldiers and Marines not only didn't have armor on trucks or Humvees, they didn't even have spare tires. The tire shortage was so severe that . . . [they] were forced to strip and abandon expensive, and otherwise perfectly good, vehicles because they had no way to replace flats.[11]

While shortages of any kind can be dire for soldiers, the failure to get them items like batteries and tires is especially puzzling. After all, some of these aren't highly specialized, made-to-order products. It might be possible to pick them up at a local store if there was one nearby. It's easy to understand why soldiers in the field would want their comrades in logistics units to do their jobs carefully and conscientiously, to stay focused on what they're doing, and to check to see that others down the line have responded to everything they've initiated or requested. In other words, that those who are responsible for organizing, recognize their responsibilities and take them seriously and organize well. If they did this, wouldn't there be fewer breakdowns? And, isn't good organizing what we all wish for? Isn't good organizing integral to what we consider good work? Shouldn't we expect that anyone organizing anything does the best he or she can? If we are organizers, shouldn't we take responsibility for doing it well? And, shouldn't we be prepared to hold one other to account and have them do the same to us if this is what it takes to make sure we do it well?

Systematic disorganization

If we know what it takes to do a good job, why do efforts to organize work often fall woefully short? As you see, writing about breakdowns almost inevitably brings up the twin questions of what causes them and what you can do to tackle them or, ideally, to prevent them.

A standard response is that organizations are complicated, lots can go wrong, and to avoid breakdowns you should learn the lessons of management books and follow the advice of consultants. You should work at getting the structure right; coming up with a better strategy; improving processes; enhancing communications; paying more attention to plans; and using new tools. Charting work processes will help you to reengineer your workplace; while information technologies, which enable you to move data around, will make everyone more efficient. Whatever the advice, however, two things don't change. One is the basic belief that management will see to it that everything gets done properly. The other is the touching faith that, whatever goes wrong, management will find a way to put it right.[12] Like the whole story of management told in business books, these assumptions don't ring true. Clearly, they rule out the possibility, which is precisely the one I want you to consider, that, whether the problem is, say, team members not cooperating or employees of intelligence agencies not sharing what they know, management itself—the practices—are a primary source of work breakdowns.

When deep-seated beliefs give rise to practices that are wrong for the work at hand, they lead to *systemic breakdowns*. Three examples are competition, bureaucracy, and hierarchy. These are believed to be necessary for efficiency; but all are obstacles to sharing knowledge and to collaboration. When cooperation is high on your agenda, as it must be for knowledge workers, you don't want any of them.

Systematic breakdowns, though related, are a little different. These are caused by misguided actions, or poorly designed tools and structures, which are considered "sound management," but prevent knowledge workers from doing a good job and/or solving their problems. Examples include: structures intended to make large organizations manageable that contribute to a "silo mentality"; a dependence on data, even when "numbers" can shed little light on the issues at hand; long, convoluted chains of command that make it difficult to reach the right people when you need to talk to them; frequent changes in personnel, who take their experience and tacit knowledge with them when they are promoted or rotated through the organization; and the use of consultants and other outside "experts" who don't know enough about what is going on to offer sensible advice. You'll find these practices in organization after organization, which makes the breakdowns they cause systematic.

"Systematic disorganization" may sound like a contradiction, because one word suggests order and the other the absence of it, but this is exactly what you get when you organize knowledge-work using principles and practices that originated in factories, when work was mechanical. By preventing knowledge workers from organizing effectively, standard management practices are a primary source of *dis*organization, contributing to both kinds of breakdowns. But, they are also ubiquitous, hence the expression "systematic disorganization".

Being saddled with practices that are wrong for the work you are doing is a bit like being on a manned mission to Mars that is heading in the wrong direction under a remote-guidance system that is malfunctioning. Everything seemed fine until the craft was on its way and someone discovered that the experts had programmed the coordinates of the craft's trajectory incorrectly. A sensible solution would be for the astronauts onboard to fly the craft; but ground control refuses to let them, claiming they have a better picture from the control room, they are sure it isn't a major problem, they have the tools to sort it out, and, besides, astronauts can't be relied on to make the right decisions. They haven't been trained for this. It is not their job.

How is this analogous to organizational breakdowns? It has to do with the high-control mindset: the idea that you leave everything to "the top" (to "mission control"), even though they aren't doing a good job and the people on hand are probably able to do a better one because they know what is happening. Management isn't all tools, like org charts or strategic plans, and titles, like "senior supervisor," "deputy assistant director," or—one of my favorites—"chief knowledge officer." These tools and titles, which seem to shout "control," are emblematic of a paradigm: a set of ideas and deeply held beliefs, attitudes, and values about how to run organizations, plus a language, which I'll call "management-speak." Together, these shape what people say and do at work.[13] The paradigm is to blame for the kinds of breakdowns I've described and, unfortunately, is much harder to change than tools and titles.

Pioneers in management include Frederick Taylor, who launched data-driven "scientific management," and Henri Fayol, who argued for an unambiguous chain of command along with well-defined roles and responsibilities. They didn't invent the management paradigm but simply took ideas about science, knowledge, and the way the world works (now known, collectively, as "modernism"), widely shared by intellectuals of the time, and built these into their prescriptions for organizing factory-work.[14] The ideas had been around for centuries. They coalesced in the Enlightenment, when scholars started shifting allegiances, placing their faith in empirical (i.e. data-based) science, rather than scripture, as the means to unlock the mysteries of the universe.[15] We are a hundred years beyond the contributions of Taylor and his early disciples, yet the pillars of Enlightenment thinking are still propping up our work places; only now, when most of us are knowledge workers, those ideas are dead wrong. For, as Tim Hindle puts it, "the way people work has changed dramatically, but the way their companies are organised lags far behind."[16]

Looking the wrong way, at the wrong things

To the Enlightened mind the universe is a giant clockwork mechanism, with the earth and everything in and on it governed by universal laws like the Law of Gravity, the First and Second Law of Thermodynamics, and the Newtonian Laws of Motion. The machine world isn't perfect but, fortunately, is inhabited by "rational man." A tiny subgroup of the species *homo sapiens* (literally, "wise man" or "knowing man") is trained in the methods of science. The duty of experts of every persuasion, from accountants to zoologists, is to make the world a better place by applying data produced by scientific analysis and discovering more laws (economists, for example, claim to have found some new ones, like the law of supply and demand, in the last century or so). In the process of practicing their craft, when gathering and using data, experts must obey one cardinal rule: never bring your own feelings, beliefs, values, or personal relationships into your work. Subjective feelings, beliefs, values, and relationships have no place in objective science.[17]

Rolling these and a few other principles together, into a theory and practice for organizing work, what you get is management science as we know it: a picture of organizations and work from the "outside," framed by a view from the top. The top in this instance isn't a place or position. The view from the top is a mindset born of a belief in empiricism and the idea that numerical data is king. To understand the mindset, just pick up a management book. There is very little that is not written from this standpoint. Now, coming back to the reasons for breakdowns and systematic disorganization at work, things fall apart because, with a view from the top, you can't see what knowledge workers are doing and you can't tell what it takes to do knowledge-work well. Relationships and meaning-making as well as attitudes and beliefs are just a few of the important ingredients of knowledge-work, but the combination of objectivity and empiricism hides these. What is the result? The view from the top has everyone thinking about the wrong things and looking the wrong way: at rules, structures, and data, rather than what matters to people when they're organizing (or how they see things) and how they share knowledge. With the substance of knowledge-work hidden or invisible, it is impossible to see that standard management practices prevent knowledge workers from doing their work properly and to tell why the practices do this. As you can't see the limits of your paradigm when you are embedded in it, when you are thinking and practicing management you don't know what you don't know about work or organizing it.

Going "inside" work

Looking at work through a management lens today, what you see are the six Ds: documentation, data, deliverables, directives, deadlines, and dollars. The fact that this is an "outside" view of work, which tells you nothing about what, how, or why people are doing it, matters much more with knowledge-work than it does with old style factory-work. Data can reveal a lot about production-line work, including its quality; for example, by measuring how much was produced and what percentage failed to meet your quality control standards. On the other hand, to see the quality of knowledge-work and to appreciate, for instance, that it is highly social and people's relationships and attitudes to one another affect the quality of their work, you have to be "inside" work. As knowledge-work is what I'm interested in, it is time to go "inside":

- To find out more about what knowledge workers do and how they do it;
- To shed light on both the problems I've lumped together as "breakdowns" and the management practices responsible for them.

In later chapters I'll look inside work for the seeds of organizing practices that enable people to do better work. By then, you will understand why, even though management methods are obsolete, it isn't going to be easy to discard them.

Getting into a building or an office is one thing, but how do you get inside work? For some reason this question brings to mind the film *Fantastic Voyage*. Its premise—and this was before anyone had heard of nanotechnology—is that scientists have the means to miniaturize machines and humans for short periods. They inject a submarine, complete with crew, into the body of one of their own, to navigate through his arteries and remove a brain clot.[18] On the upside, getting inside work only takes imagination, to see from a different angle what you already know. You'll quickly discover that this means looking below the surface of work as we normally see it (those six Ds, etc.), which may be why I think of submarines. But, when you work with new ideas, new possibilities for action often come to light and, as this is what we'll be doing beneath the surface, among the things we can expect to find are clues to new work practices.

"Inside" or "outside" is a matter of involvement

Being inside or outside work is a figure of speech; a metaphor that has to do with how involved you are in the work and of how much the work itself means to you. As knowledge workers interact and cooperate to do their work, being inside or outside is really a matter of how intimately engaged you are with others when you are doing something. Unlike factory-work, knowledge-work isn't limited to a particular workplace, like a workshop or the factory floor. You are just as likely to find knowledge workers, even the same ones at different times, in a room the size of a football field that is separated into a rabbit warren of small, identical-looking cubicles, or sitting together round a table in a conference room that is a dozen feet long, or, singly, in an airport departure lounge, checking emails on their smart phones, while waiting for a connecting flight.

If you are working *with* them, anywhere, especially if you are *participating in their conversations*—you could even be miles away, but on the phone or responding to an email—you are part of the work and on the inside. If you aren't directly involved, however, even if you happen to be nearby, in the same room, you're on the outside. The same applies, of course, if you are in another building, or on a different continent, where all you know about what they're doing is from updates like performance reports, which could be second-, third-, or fourth-hand.

Looking over the tops of cubicles you see people on computers while others are on their phones or are busy writing. Through the glass panels of a conference room you notice a bunch of people inside. Someone is writing on a flipchart and a few are obviously talking, though you can't hear what they're saying. In both cases your view of work would be limited and very different to what you'd know, hear, and feel on the inside, if you were working *with* those people, engaged with them in the work. With factory-work, the difference isn't that significant. You can get a good sense of what people are doing by watching them, which is what supervisors do. With knowledge-work, however, the difference between being inside or outside is crucial. Their work depends on them sharing knowledge by talking to each other. So, to understand what they are doing as well as why and how they're doing it, you need to be on the inside.[19]

In management-speak, work is about "requirements," "outcomes," "progress reports," and so on. This is an outside view and, normally, feelings don't enter the picture, but on the inside they do. You're aware of them all the time—your own and others'—as you are of relationships. Both have a bearing on your work. Intimately involved in one another's work, knowledge workers are also personally connected and think about the people they work with in the same way they do about their work: it is "*my* work" (even though others contribute to it) and they are "*my* colleagues, clients, or contacts." Feeling that what they're doing isn't right yet and that they've got some way to go, they'll wonder whether their colleagues will be satisfied and worry that the others won't appreciate how much effort they've put into it. When organizing—assigning tasks or trying to pinpoint the source of a problem—your *collective* experience is invaluable in getting things done and you share knowledge with associates or clients that you don't share with others. In fact, you use that collective experience and shared knowledge all the time: when reminding one another about your commitments; when looking for examples of how to handle a particular problem and of what worked and what didn't; or when you are "catching up," telling one another about what has been happening.[20]

Being on the outside of work is such a contrast that it is almost like being in a different universe. You won't, for example, have an insider's knowledge of how and how well things are going. No matter that you are keen to know everything that is going on, you can't. You never see things the way insiders do, because you don't have their intimacy with issues, or their feelings about the people they are working with and what is happening. Ask people what they're doing, why, or how, and you get a second-hand perspective, which means an outsider will surely come to a different conclusion, have a different opinion, or make a different decision. This might be okay. It is a matter of whether an insider or outsider's perspective is called for. Organizing work, when deciding what to do next, more often than not an insider's intimacy with people and problems is what is needed.

As an outsider, if there is a problem, it isn't *your* problem. You don't have the same motivation and aren't under the same obligation to deal with it as a participant in the work, on the inside; and you may not know how to. If the problem concerns a client, it is *their* client, someone with expectations of them, to whom they have commitments (expectations and commitments imply a relationship). If the problem has to do, say, with the integration of computer systems, an insider will probably know whether it is the people he or she is working with—who are so attached to their legacy systems that they don't want to give them up—or whether it is a technical matter involving incompatible datasets. And, if it happens to be the former, it is quite possible that he or she will have a sense of who, or what, is behind it and, perhaps, of whether or not it is going to be hard to get their buy-in. Call this instinct, intuition, insight, or experience; it is the kind of knowing-about-work that comes from being *in* the work and part of it—when you have relationships of some sort with those with whom you work *and* with the work itself—which plays a big part in organizing work.[21]

Work from the top

Only on the inside, with a view from practice, do you realize that knowledge workers spend most of their work time organizing. To explain why, I want to contrast the two views of work. I'll start with an outside view, and this is where I want to change metaphors. Because I want to emphasize that this is the way you look at work when wearing a management hat, from now on I'll refer to the "outside" view as the "view from the top."[22]

As far as a project team is concerned, their project manager, whose main responsibilities are to schedule, assign, and supervise their work, is an outsider unless he also happens to work on the projects, participating with them in their work. (In the *work of managing*, or organizing, however, he is an insider, when working with others on scheduling, assigning, supervising, and advising). As their manager, except for what they tell him, he probably knows little and doesn't want to know about their individual circumstances and day-to-day interactions with one another and their client. In managing projects he is interested mainly in their reports and in what he gleans from various metrics, in spreadsheets and databases, about their progress and performance.

His work talk, which has an industrial-era ring to it, is of action items, benchmarks, budgets, communications, core competencies, deliverables, efficiency, data, financials, goals, job descriptions, metrics, productivity, incentives, procedures, requirements, results, regulations, schedules, standards, and work flows. This is what work looks like, and sounds like, from the top. It appears to be comprised largely of object-like things (lists of requirements, budgets, and so on), so getting work done is a bit like assembling a box of furniture from IKEA; making sure all the pieces are there and that they go in the right places. Workers have clearly identifiable tasks and do defined activities, like the ones you might see in a job description, such as "analyzing problems" or "writing reports." Each task has a deadline, which means a team is going to achieve specific, clearly defined outcomes by a certain date and, while busy with a task, will make continual progress toward a definite goal. Teams need resources and tools (data, consultants, surveys, and perhaps travel and training) to do the work, and they need to know what to do. To function efficiently they need managers, at various levels, to plan, coordinate, and control their activities.

Managers see their teams as bunches of individuals, possibly pulled together from various places on their org chart, whose experience and qualifications vary (they've seen their profiles in a personnel database). They have a contract, plans, deliverables, a budget, and deadlines and, through the managers' lenses, are engaged in a "process," which has a starting and finishing point, with an outcome, and various activities in between. Managers are mainly concerned about whether they are within their budget and on schedule, fully utilized from day-to-day, and at the end, whether they've made the deadline and delivered on the contract.[23]

With your view from the top, it's unlikely that you'd be able to just step in and take over a team member's work, or, if you did, that you'd be able to do it well. What you don't have, in particular, is the wealth of tacit knowledge of people and circumstances, including knowledge of the client and his or her expectations and of anyone who has been working on a project, which gives a context to their work and the problems they have to deal with. Nor do you have the shared experiences of people who've been working together and their *collective* knowledge that helps them to connect more easily to get things done together.

Work in practice

Work even *sounds* different when viewed from practice. Participants don't use much management jargon (e.g. "deadlines," "deliverables"). They tend to have rather ordinary-sounding conversations: "What do you think is going on? I'm concerned about Jay's response. Do you think we can get her onboard? Do we need to? We seem to agree on priorities, so what is the next step? I see two or three different ways that we could deal with this." The differences in what they talk about and how they say it have to do with what people see as their work. From the top, when you are directing, coordinating, and supervising, you are thinking about those six Ds—documentation, data, directives, deliverables, deadlines, and dollars—and your job is to have everyone's attention on these. In practice, the language you usually use to talk to other people is fine for working with colleagues—because you work, organize, by talking together (talk is your work). It's not about things like deadlines and deliverables, but about finding out where people stand and getting their agreement.

To see what people do in practice, we'll look in on a meeting where software developers are discussing a client's complaints that were relayed to them by their manager. They set up this meeting at the last moment after a flurry of emails in which some team members said they wanted to hear from their client as well. All knew a problem was brewing. Now they have to deal with it and the question is how. Deciding what to do is typical of the work that knowledge workers do. They have to work out what the problem is and how big it is (i.e. *frame* the problem) and decide what to do about it. When they're doing this, they are organizing. What is their work? A few of them who spoke to the client feel their discussion wasn't very helpful, especially since he has changed his position on several occasions in the past. They are going to have to explain this to the others, then, together, make sense of it and their problem.[24] What does he actually want? How important are his concerns? Should they acknowledge that there is a problem and move on? Or is it time to do a fundamental review of the requirements against their original brief?

Most of the meeting is taken up with participants putting out ideas, asking questions, giving responses, and making suggestions. To a fly on the wall it might seem as if there is too much talk and that it isn't going anywhere, except round and round. But, notice what the team members are doing. *They are making meaning of a situation that doesn't make much sense.* They've come to deal with a problem but, in truth, don't know what the problem is, or, indeed, whether they really have one. So, first, they have to try to clarify and resolve this. Is the client being difficult? Have they strayed from the original requirements? Was the initial conception of what they would build accurate? Is it some combination of these? Once they have their interpretation of the problem, provided there is a degree of consensus—which isn't always the case—they can move on to deciding what they can and should do about it.

Knowledge workers aren't handed their work. From the inside, work isn't a box of furniture from IKEA, with a set of instructions to follow. Nothing is ready-made. They make it themselves. When they're assigned a task, it is like getting an empty container. Their job is to give it content, adding substance by negotiating with their client and framing how they are going to approach the work: deciding what the main issues are, which ones will have a lower priority, and so on. This is all part of the work of organizing, which they have to do, and do well, to get good results.

It is the team's meaning-making, in order to organize, so they can sort out the problem, that leads to decisions—about what to do, when, and with whom—and to more work. They are designing and creating their work in their conversations. So, it is no wonder they have a lot to talk about and that, at times, it may seem as if they aren't getting anywhere. Making meaning is a discursive and roundabout process, not a linear one. It's a process of reflecting, exploring, inquiring, clarifying, and resolving. People ask questions, respond, and make comments as they try to make sense of whatever has a bearing on the situation as they see it, including what they might have overlooked. "What are we missing" or "what aren't we seeing," they might ask.

Talking and listening to each other, while they probe and question or offer suggestions and register their objections, is the only practical way for them to organize: to frame problems so most or all agree on what is at stake; to lay out options for how to respond; and to take a decision about what to do. This work doesn't lend itself to shortcuts. They have to talk things through until they're clearer about what they are dealing with and pretty much agreed on what to do; or until they're *aligned*. The work of organizing isn't over until they've done this satisfactorily, conversation by conversation. And, while they're doing this, they're aware of one another's presence and attitudes; of what others are saying and how they are behaving. They're also aware of their feelings towards each other and their work—here, in the moment, in the context of "problems with the client." There is a certain amount of acrimony in their conversation, some animosity toward the client who "wasn't clear about what he wanted," and some bickering about what went wrong. If you asked them, they'd make no bones about these feelings. It is obvious to them that their attitudes have a bearing on what they say and do, hence how they work things out. The state of their relationships with one another, including their client, is integral to what goes on and to how long it takes them to align themselves for action and whether they are able to do so.

Behind the breakdowns

Organizing, while sharing knowledge and making meaning together, is the real work of knowledge workers. Unfortunately, however, none of what I've just described registers with anyone who has a view from the top. At the top, there is one way to run organizations. To do it efficiently, you do it the MBA way, just as the management books tell you, with one group, the managers, organizing and the other group working. From the top, "work" means completing that list of deliverables while meeting deadlines and following directives. What knowledge workers actually do, in practice, to deliver on time, is completely out of sight, so a manager has no reason to question whether, or how, his or her own actions—management practices—influence the way knowledge workers work, although clearly they do and are a prime reason for systematic disorganization.

Management practices discourage talk, which is seen as "a waste of time." Competition is the norm. Collaboration is not. Rewards go to individuals, not to teams. While their work evolves, rules and regulations limit people's flexibility, and hierarchy and bureaucracy create divisions and boundaries that make it difficult for knowledge workers to interact and share knowledge in order that they can identify and frame problems and get to workable solutions. Perhaps, the biggest obstacle of all is the old management–worker dichotomy, and the assumption that, with management in charge and doing all the planning, there is no need for workers to be doing anything other than "getting on with the job."

Systematic disorganization stems from a mindset. You can't eliminate part of a mindset. We need to put all organizations beyond management, by finding new practices: practices for organizing knowledge-work that are good for knowledge-work. To get there we need to know more about knowledge-work, about what knowledge workers do to organize, and how they do it. In particular, we need to know about "good organizing." How do people do it and how can you tell when they are organizing well? Would you recognize it when you see it? For that matter, are you able to see good organizing at all, and can you measure it?

CHAPTER 3

Organizing: getting the beat

Organizing is full of life

Organizing, as Stephen Fineman et al. describe it, is an intensely and probably uniquely *human* phenomenon and full of life:

> While [we are] ... "doing ... [our jobs]," listening to someone talking, tapping keyboards, talking into telephones, or soldering electronic components, we are also making and exchanging meanings—a fundamental human/social process ... As we interact with others at work, we bring our personal histories and our past experiences with us—finding common ground, compromising, disagreeing, negotiating, coercing.[1]

While our images of work ought to resonate with the collective energy of people doing things together (not always in harmony and not always successfully), books on management invariably make it seem inert, mechanical, and, frankly, dull. There is hardly a hint at how people depend on one another and what happens when cooperation is lacking, or of their shared satisfaction when they do a job well and their mutual disappointment, say, at failing to win a contract.

Wanting to remedy this situation, my object over the next few chapters is to breathe some life into the work of organizing, explaining how knowledge workers do it and why there are breakdowns, so that, in the end, knowing the difference between good and bad practices, we have a better sense of what it takes to organize knowledge-work properly. Making the work of organizing come alive, however, is much more difficult than it might seem, for two reasons. One is that what matters most about organizing is invisible. The other is a fundamental difference between describing "organizing" and experiencing it. I'll begin with the fact that organizing "lives" in the experience of doing it.

Writing about organizing is a bit like talking about music. Describing your favorite piece of rock music to a friend, you might say something about lyrics, the drumming, or guitar riffs. You can conjure up all sorts of images with phrases like "thumping, driving rhythm" and "mind-blowing tremolo," but a description, no matter how colorful, can never match the experience of listening to music. You get the beat only when you are immersed in music and feeling it, for playing or listening is a sensuous, full-body experience. Whether it is classical or hip-hop, and whether you love or hate what you hear, music affects your breathing, your heartbeat, and your mood.

You can say the same about being involved in organizing. There is this intimate connection between you, the work, and others who are part of it too. Each sees it both as "my work" and "our work" and, as it is unmistakably social, your relationships with one another, along with your moods and attitudes, good, bad, or indifferent, are part of the experience of organizing. This is where the view from the top is so different. Through a management lens, work is merely "activities" or a "process" that is neither human nor social. But, because it is a human, social phenomenon, a lot of what goes on is invisible and a good deal of what matters most is intangible, which is why business books steer clear of the whole subject and why you may not yet be comfortable associating organizing with work. Management deals with what scientists call "empirical phenomena" and very little about organizers and organizing fits this description.

Organizing is one of many phenomena that we know without being able to see, hear, touch, taste, or smell it. There are scores of these, like love, trust, responsibility, commitment, and integrity. Love describes one person's feelings for another. When you're "in love" you know it "inside" and you really only know what it means to be in love when you've experienced it and had those feelings. Max Weber, the father of sociology, who had a major hand in explaining that humans make meaning of whatever is going on in their lives, describes the role that dispositions, feelings, attitudes, and values, as well as relationships with others, play in the process. We, ourselves, experience feelings, express emotions, and have relationships. We're social beings with a capacity for "empathetic understanding" (he uses the German word *Verstehen*), who possess the power of language and, when we see and hear others in action, we interpret what they're doing in terms of dispositions ("she is utterly selfless"), motives ("it serves his ambition"), feelings, attitudes, values, beliefs, and relationships ("she cares about them" or "his commitment to the group and the task is extraordinary"); and we talk to one another, discussing and describing what we see and hear.[2]

You don't and can't actually observe people organizing or working. You hear them chatting in the corridor and infer that they're planning something. Or, sent a document headed "Strategic Plan," you recognize, as "work," the effort that went into producing it. Work and organizing are "meaning constructions." We use these to make sense of people's actions. Each "holds" other meaning constructions such as motives (ambition), relationships (trust), and values (integrity).[3] Humans live meaning-full social lives, continually making meaning, individually and together, and these constructs, which have to do with human life and human action, are integral to our meaning-making and our lives. We use them to figure out and discuss with others what is going on, especially what people are doing. So, although they're not things we can see or touch, feelings, values, relationships, and organizing are as much a part of our world—how we think and what we talk about—as the weather, traffic jams, our families, and objects and people around us.

The two challenges

As I see it, then, there are two challenges in writing about organizing. One is putting you "into" the work of organizing. This problem was resolved in a surprising but satisfactory way when I read Jeff Bennie's first-person account of his work as a project manager. I'll explain shortly what I mean. The second is that most of what happens and what people do when they're organizing—gauging motives, assessing relationships, cooperating, sharing knowledge, aligning—happens beneath the surface of what we see and hear and has to do with the meanings they make. Here, it appears I have two options. One is to explain as best I can what these are and why they matter, paying attention to things that are intangible and abstract. Or, as other business books do, try to skirt the awkwardness of having to deal with motives, values, relationships, feelings, and anything else that isn't empirical in the conventional sense of the word.

Networks provide one example of how those business books fudge the intangible aspects of human action and typically mishandle them. Nowadays, the words "networks" and "networking" refer to the interactions of people organizing. Of course, social networks are not objects. They're neither visible nor tangible. "Network" is a figure of speech and another meaning construction.[4] The terms "networks" and "networking" are borrowed from IT, where they're applied to computers, peripherals, and users connected by a combination of wires, fibers, radio waves, or in some other physical way. More often than not writers describing organizational networks, skirting the differences between social networks (comprised of people doing things together) and computer networks, leave us with the sense that they're entities made up of similar kinds of connections. How we understand the "connections" makes all the difference. If you use the expression, you might say that people being introduced to one another at an embassy party are "loosely" connected, but long-time friends or associates are "closely" connected. Besides conversations, what connects a group and distinguishes a loose network, say, from a tightly connected one, is how participants interact: what they say to each other and what meanings they make and share, along with their intentions, attitudes, and relationships, which you can't see and wouldn't know about unless you were part of the group. It is while participating, listening to what they say ("we ought to be helping one another instead of arguing" or "you need to decide what to do next"), and perhaps "reading" someone's tone of voice or interpreting their body language, as you make meaning of what others are doing, gathering something about their attitudes and relationships, that you have a sense of how a social network functions.

Whether they are colleagues, friends, casual acquaintances, or, to start with, perhaps, complete strangers, at some level relationships are *always* in the picture when people interact to organize. Do they have confidence in one another? How interested are they in what their team members are doing? These are questions about their relationships, and the answers may make all the difference as to whether they are careful and do the work of organizing well, or are careless and do it badly. You can say the same about their intentions, attitudes (for example, whether they are open to others' ideas), and their commitment to what they're doing. When the caliber of members of both a "great team" and a "mediocre one" is similar on paper, the difference is usually a matter of how they *combine*. Words like "team spirit," "commitment," and "synergy" each say something we know to be true but find it difficult to analyze and describe. A great team functions as a whole and, much like music, the whole is both different from and more than the sum of its parts. The talented individuals in it achieve heights with the team that they can't reach alone and the holistic spirit that allows them to do so isn't the result of rules or tools. It isn't something you can design, mandate, or "manage." More than training, it comes from inside the team: from the attitudes and relationships of the players, meaning their enthusiasm for and sense of commitment to playing with one another and for the game.

It turns out that, in writing about organizing, skirting invisible and intangible considerations is not an option. If I were to write about organizing and stick only to what you can see I'd be limited to describing people typing and writing, talking on the phone, watching a slide presentation, or chatting in the elevator, and this wouldn't get us very far. We'd miss what is most important in knowledge-work: the organizing that people do. There is no data about organizing. We see plans, not people planning. We see and hear them talking and taking notes, then we *interpret* what they are doing as planning, or, more generally, as working and organizing—conferring, deliberating, planning, negotiating, assessing, or confirming. *Making meaning (individually and collectively) is the real work of organizing.* This means you can't tell how people are doing and whether it's going well or badly unless you're inside with them.

Management, unfortunately, is impervious to this message. It is imbued with the spirit of the Enlightenment, when Western scholars, embracing the idea that empirical facts are the foundation of true knowledge, turned their backs on beliefs, feelings, values, and interpersonal relationships as sources of knowledge.[5] You may not know why you do it except that it is "good management," but, as a manager, you probably insist on sticking to what you can see, and above all measure, in the form of financial reports, performance assessments, and productivity charts (i.e. "the data"). If you do, you have the view from the top. Organizations are machines, organizers are mechanics, and most of what goes into doing good knowledge-work is an unfathomable mystery. Is it any wonder if management tools and techniques aren't doing much good?

To differentiate good, or productive, organizing practices from ones that produce breakdowns, we have to find out all we can about the socialness of networks and teams and the work that participants do in making meaning of what is going on. The journey starts by acknowledging that you won't find out much about teams, organizing, or meaning-making if you try to examine them empirically, as you would a car's engine (a physical phenomenon). If we want to know about organizing, then it is crucial to understand how people influence one another, to appreciate what shapes their attitudes, relationships, and interests, and to see what bearing these have on their actions and practices. One difficulty, however, is language. We don't have one to describe the work of organizing. Our workplace talk (management-speak) is about organizations and the things you find in them. Digging into the work of organizing means we go beneath organizations and behind spreadsheets, schedules, charts, surveys, agendas, budgets, and emails and, because the language of management doesn't cover this, we'll need new language to talk about whatever we find there. In the chapters that follow, some of the territory and terms may be unfamiliar. I'll invent new words and phrases when necessary and, if, at times, I'm heading in a philosophical direction you'll understand why. It is a necessary and worthwhile price to pay for a deeper understanding of what we are dealing with and, ultimately, for better work practices and better—more satisfactory and more rewarding—work lives.

A first-hand account

Even though organizing is as much a part of our day-to-day lives as talking or eating, explaining organizing is a challenge, because it is so closely tied to the experience of organizing. I had been struggling with this when talking to Jeff Bennie, a long-time friend and colleague who has worked for some large organizations, both corporate and government. Jeff is genuinely curious about work and I don't mean the politics or social gossip. He wants to understand what happens beneath the surface, or to "get the beat of the system," as he put it.[6] Life in organizations is complex and demanding, and Jeff has said that, to do their jobs well, everyone, especially if they have managerial responsibilities, ought to be asking "what is actually going on"; though they rarely do.

With shared interests in organizations, management, and work, Jeff and I talk when we can. I once encouraged him to keep a journal, saying that "the deepest learning comes from reflecting on our own experiences and trying to answer questions we have inside." It probably sounded patronizing but the idea must have caught his imagination because Jeff keeps a journal conscientiously.

He told me that he'd been trying to make sense of a situation that didn't make a lot of sense. "Project managers don't get enough leeway. People don't see what others are doing and, perhaps, they don't trust one another to do the right thing." "It boils down to way too much top-down control," he said, explaining that one of his teams was in the middle of a project (he is a senior program manager, responsible for a number of project teams) and he'd been told that key members were being reassigned to another project, which, as everyone knew, was well behind schedule. He'd been thinking about this decision, believing it would demoralize his team and undermine their work and that, quite soon, he'd again have to extricate himself and them from a mess in order to rescue the project and deliver what they had committed to doing.

What was going on and what would the consequences be? What is the mindset that makes disruptions like these common? And, what should or could he do about it? He said he'd achieved something of a breakthrough in understanding the whats and whys and offered to send me what he'd written. Reading the journal I realized that a first-person, first-hand account is a great way of responding to one of the challenges of writing about organizing. It is a way of going inside, to see what goes on. It is also a good way of helping us to understand our own work. Whether you manage a business or you work in local government, you are an organizer and can relate to the story. It will help you to "get the beat." Having asked Jeff if I could "borrow" his journal for my book, it was soon clear that it had to be the centerpiece. After you've read the next chapter you'll see that my story unfolds around his experience and insights, with lots of references to Jeff and his journal.

CHAPTER 4

Jeff's journal: project work on the inside

While the journal is almost exactly as Jeff wrote it, in addition to naming it "Jeff's journal" (which didn't require much imagination and is alliterative), and giving it the subtitle "project work on the inside" to fit my theme of going inside work, I've changed the names of the organizations he writes about. I've also organized his material into sections, with headings, and numbered his diagrams, so it is easier to find them when I refer to them later. In one or two places, I've inserted words or phrases that I use, which have the same meaning as his. My additions are in square brackets. One example is Jeff's "management view" and "project team view," which I call the "view from the top" and the "view from practice." I've used the same convention for notes. As you might expect, Jeff had no references, except for a definition or two or an idea that he looked up online. As his journal now has both a different purpose and audience, I've turned these into endnotes and have included additional references where it seemed appropriate to do so.

Part 1: questions that keep coming up

What's your problem, Jeffrey?

Melvin in government contracts emailed me today saying that three people on the Assurance Bank project are going to be reassigned to the ERP [enterprise resource planning] project being run out of the Herndon office. Actually, he said they would be "pulled from the project for five to eight weeks at the most." I don't like the word "pulled." It reminds me of a tooth being yanked out, whether it wants to come or not! My first reaction was, this is bad news for the AB team. One minute they're doing a great job, then the next minute . . . it's *kapow*! I began to think about all the knock-on effects.

I know what is behind this, but it doesn't make sense. It is common knowledge at TDM that the ERP project is in serious trouble. A contract with a federal security agency, it is worth millions to us and our subcontractors. They are approaching first phase deadlines but are way behind on deliverables.[1] Penalties kick in once they pass the completion date and no doubt divisional management wants to move things along by putting more people on the contract. Presumably, they're also thinking about the contract for the second phase. We're by no means assured of getting it. Melvin said he reviewed the AB team's time sheets and no one is maxed-out so he's expecting everyone to put in at least one day a week on the ERP project. Sally, Andre, and Lexi will be reassigned until the ERP project is back on track: Sally for her ability to work with customers and "turn them around," Andre for his team leadership, and Lexi for her extensive ERP experience.

Taking away the three and cutting into the others' time is going to leave a big hole in the AB project at a critical point. You can't build a stable, usable, quality product around a fixed number of hours. It is always a major challenge to deliver against contract specs, yet we consistently ignore the complexity of the work and manage contracts as if numbers are all that count. I'm sure that's why the ERP contract is behind schedule; it's a huge undertaking and there are lots of ways for things to go wrong. Melvin seems to have forgotten that everyone on the AB project is more stretched than it appears on paper. All have secondary assignments and you ballpark the hours you allocate to jobs when you're working for different clients. When we invoice, our rule-of-thumb is to reduce the hours by 20 percent. This is what Melvin is seeing.

A management malfunction

I'm sure Melvin didn't make the decision to reassign. My bet is it came from his boss at the Federal Projects division. No doubt she's doing what she believes is best for TDM. But, what was she thinking? If you treat people like chess pieces when you are trying to sort out one project, you play havoc with another. Management is supposed to keep the work on track. Doesn't she see this will derail us? I'm trying hard to understand why you'd make a decision like this, but I'm having a hard time doing so. It isn't logical and this isn't the first time it's happened.

Sometimes, if I sketch what I'm thinking it helps me to make connections. I'll have to start with management. To me, management is about getting and keeping organizations in order, so they operate efficiently. I learned at b-school (I remember it started with [Frederick] Taylor and the others who founded the science of management) that operational efficiency means a good set of plans, an inclusive pyramid structure, a comprehensive system of rules, plus data to monitor performance. Management's function is to provide these. Without them, and incentives and penalties, organizations would be in a state of random molecular motion—disorganized [as illustrated in Figure 4.1].

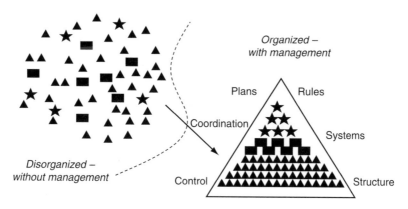

Figure 4.1 Management

I also learned one golden rule at b-school: "the customer comes first." It is supposed to guide management. Almost from day one we were told that organizations exist to serve customers. One professor said "when you are faced with a difficult decision, start by looking at what is best for your customer(s)."

Surely, breaking up this project team violates the golden rule. And what is efficiency if you don't follow it? We produce complex software. Our customers are government departments and agencies as well as corporate businesses, with a few large non-profits thrown into the mix. Our mission statement says "TDM produces the best customized software we can for our customers." It is simple and direct. Our goal is to deliver software tools that enable them to be more efficient and effective. The customer is integral to our mission: *customized* software. We also operate according to standard management principles. We're a typical top-down organization. TDM has hundreds of employees doing different types of work and management provides a system and a structure to make it work efficiently. That includes budgets and benchmarks, rules and regulations, and deadlines and deliverables.

Here is a paradox for me: we have all the pieces that management experts say we should have—like a structure, the tools, and good data—and we push the goal of customer satisfaction, but the organization is quite dysfunctional (the ERP project is a good example) and we don't always deliver what customers want. Quite often I hear myself say "we're in a mess." The AB project looks like another mess waiting to happen. If there was a funny side to this, I'd put it down to Murphy's Law, aka Sod's Law: "whatever can go wrong will go wrong."[2] But it is more than a random act of fickle fate. Reassignments are deliberate. Someone made the decision and, presumably, thinks this isn't just a good idea but is the right thing to do. I'm having difficulty seeing how it could be either.

The way I see it, TDM is a changing assortment of projects. We have to deliver a quality product each time, on each project, and the question I've been asking myself is would we manage projects this way, making decisions like reassigning team members, if the customer matters like we say he does. I believe the customer's interests are being sacrificed for something else and I'm realizing that there is more than one set of perspectives, priorities, and interests on what is the right course of action. Project teams' priorities, it seems to me, are clearly different from management's priorities and I'm in the middle, dealing with the fallout, and trying to work out why and what is right.

The "client" view of project work

In my experience the work of project teams revolves around the client even when they're dealing with a tight budget or there is dissention in a team. That is what I see when I'm wearing a project-team member's hat and it is quite easy to understand why they see things this way. You're on a team because of your expertise and experience. Your work is your craft and you want to do it to the best of your ability and, while you are doing it, the client is right there, in front of you.

Each project is a network of the people working together on something, like a proposal or lines of code. The network expands as the project moves from ideas to initial proposal to a product that is tailored to the client's needs. Every inch of the way is a learning process, with people figuring out with one another what is going on, what has to be done, what others are doing, and whether they are on track. Learning-as-you-go is vital to a project's success, more important even than solving the technical problems and people spend a lot of time sharing knowledge: exchanging ideas and figuring out what is going on.[3]

There is so much going on in a network, so many groups are working on different things, it is quite easy to lose sight of how important the client is; and I don't mean just at the end, when it is time to deliver. All along the way the client is central. You have to engage him continuously to find out what he wants. Quite often he doesn't know what he wants until he sees it—sees what you're doing or what you've done—so you go back and forth, getting to know him, sorting out his requirements, offering advice, making changes, and working to get through roadblocks together.

Over time, because of these interactions, there is a rich tapestry of information in a project network. It is made up of shared knowledge, ideas about what has to be done, views about what the customer requires, and so on. Most of this is tacit knowledge: the sort that is in people's heads and hearts, not written into documents or stored in computer files; the sort you probably don't know you have until you draw on your experience to explain something to someone.[4] When you reassign team members in the middle of a project you rip apart the fabric of the network. That puts severe strain on the whole project and has a big impact on a team's morale and their performance. For one thing, it drains the project of this tacit knowledge. Another part of the story is the client who gets the short straw because an under-resourced team has to scramble to complete the project at the last minute and perhaps features he wanted are missing or haven't been properly developed. A colleague, Dawn, put it this way: When word comes down from head office, "we take shortcuts and turn cartwheels trying to complete the contract on time and on target. In the process we short-change our clients and ourselves."

Where is the customer?

Figure 4.1 shows that reassigning members of a project group means something completely different when you wear a management hat. There are no customers in that drawing, because top management is responsible for the organization, which is everything *inside* the triangle and doesn't include customers. (Interestingly, TDM management prefers "customer" but the project teams usually talk about "our client.") Managing a contract means keeping your eye on dates, deliverables, and dollars, though not necessarily in that order. If someone asks where the customer fits into the picture, I'd have to say "under the base of the pyramid." Management is at the top, work at the bottom, and the customer must be close to the work. At any rate, he is outside the triangle and outside the view and responsibilities of management.

I think this is a fair assessment of how head office approaches the contractual obligations of a project. Customers don't feature prominently in top management decisions. It is the project teams that connect an organization to its customers, but to show this I'd have to include networks of relationships that are crucial to serving customers. They aren't in the picture because they aren't on management's agenda either. The organization—strategy, mission, and bottom-line—is much more real than the customer and, because these matter to management, they take priority. Customers matter, but only in the way the contract matters: in terms of costs, completion deadlines, a list of deliverables, and their bottom-line impact. It is different with project teams. They build relationships with their clients. You might say they are attached to them. It's an emotional bond. They want their clients to be satisfied with the work they do, both to show they are good at what they do and because they don't want to let them down.

Managing a contract and providing your client with a good product are different mindsets. I'm starting to realize that there is a deep tension between the contract-is-all approach, which is how organizations are managed at the top, and the people-and-client-centered attitude of project teams [the "view from practice"].[5] Putting the contract first explains why people get pulled from functioning teams and why their customers get short-changed and, because they come from different mindsets, perhaps there are irreconcilable differences between these two positions.

I'm sure there really is tension between management and project teams [see Figure 4.2]. I put it down to their different interests and values but I think this is only part of the story. Management values organizational performance, while project teams value the quality of

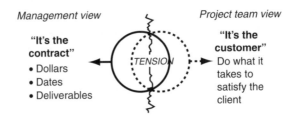

Figure 4.2 Teams' and management's views

their work and these don't mean the same thing. You can see the contract mindset in management directives and processes, which revolve around dollars and data (e.g. time-sheets). The management mindset is the one that prevails because it belongs to the people on top, in charge. Yet, to me, the idea of someone in charge and in control is really a sham. We say this is so, but it is all a pretense. We're supposed to follow directives (like the one to pull people from the contract), as if work gets done because management directs, authorizes, or approves it. Meanwhile, we aren't thinking about the crucial role of the project team and the whole network that surrounds and serves them. There is another side to how work gets done that is hidden. I believe the rest of the story about the tension between contract and customer is this: not seeing what it takes to deliver a quality product, we manage projects as if the other side doesn't matter; this is why team members get reassigned, putting a whole project at risk.

What is the right way to manage projects? I'm talking about the difference between how we *do* manage and how we *could* and *should* manage them, because customers and the work of project teams matters. TDM produces customized software, not standardized products. Our business is tailoring. We have to make sure that what we produce fits the customer properly. The devil is in knowing what the customer wants and being able to deliver it and the only way I know to do that well is through well-functioning project teams. How do we make sure project teams can do their work properly and produce good quality work?

Where to from here?

Is there a different way of managing projects that won't get us into the kind of trouble the AB team will surely soon be staring at? Or, is there only one way to manage? It seems to me that a good place to start is to look at what a project team does and how they handle their work. Standard practice puts management in the role of scheduler, controller, and regulator of work, but I don't believe the work we do is amenable to this kind of top-down control and it's not clear to me that the kind of structure we get from management—reporting lines, regulations, systems, and standards, all symptoms of a culture of compliance—is right for the work we do.

When I heard somewhere about "loose coupling," the idea resonated with me. We don't live in a clockwork world. "Loose coupling" seems to describe our work environment, so I Googled it. I found this on Wikipedia. "Loose coupling . . . is found in computer systems, and was introduced into organizational studies by Karl Weick. Loosely coupled systems are considered useful when either the source or the destination . . . systems are subject to frequent changes."[6] That last bit nails it for me. A lot of the work we do at TDM is subject to frequent changes. Not only that; project requirements are open-ended and ambiguous.

Suppose that you are a manager and you see it as your job to create a system of tight controls, including rigid rules and complex reporting requirements, because it is what you believe managers do. But, if work is and has to be loosely coupled, the system you've put in place doesn't fit and shouldn't be there. It becomes dysfunctional. You end up obstructing people's efforts (mine in this case), then they get confused and disheartened. That sounds to me like a fair description of what goes on at TDM a lot of the time.

We try to do everything by numbers nowadays, even thinking you can manage projects based on time-sheet data. Turn a contract into numbers (dates, deliverables, and dollars) and you end up treating it as a play-book; but it isn't.[7] A contract is a broad statement of work and you have to go from there to concrete action and a specific, satisfactory result. That is usually a tricky, subtle, and, also, mysterious process. Organizing the development and delivery of an elaborate piece of software reminds me of clouds forming (and reforming) it is so loosely-defined. You can't control clouds and you certainly can't do it by numbers. When I look at the work we do, I sometimes wish we had a play-book, but we don't. Sometimes I think we don't even know what the game is. We are constantly discovering this as we go and, to top it all off, we invent and reinvent the rules at the same time, which sets me thinking . . .

Part 2: how things actually work

Jeff's cloud theory

A project begins with a little cloud—the initial idea. It probably isn't possible to say exactly where and when it starts but it isn't a directive from the top, a well-developed plan, or a request to solve a specific problem.

A highly sophisticated piece of software and the incredibly complex process of creating and delivering it begin with somebody's "good idea." People get together and talk (perhaps it is a potential customer meeting someone from new product development). Sometimes those talks go nowhere but, if they have traction, there is more talk and sharing ideas. It isn't clear why some ideas go forward while others don't or why a project eventually lands in our laps. So much is going on behind the scenes that what happens is more art and luck than science. Was it our marketing? What about business relationships? How did people's motives play a role? What would have happened if our bid had been different?

When things do get moving, one little conversation becomes the seed of all the work people eventually do on a project. In the end hundreds might be involved and it all begins with a few conversations—the little cloud! Based on those conversations there are more conversations. People write proposals and prepare budgets—more conversations—and they move forward. Then they do more talking (and negotiating and bargaining). Now there are lawyers, HR and contracts specialists, and consultants involved. They talk, but not necessarily to each other, and things move forward a bit more. New people become part of the process and things move forward a bit more. They write specifications, set deadlines for the different phases, do more talking and bring more people into the process, and so on.

The idea that things are always moving forward is a stretch. Sometimes they stand still and nothing happens for quite a while as people deal with a setback or wait for approval. Usually there is a lot of groping around as well as moving and sometimes it seems we are actually in reverse. But with a bit of luck and because people work hard and put in long hours the cloud becomes a bigger cloud; then that bigger cloud becomes a bigger one, until the project is complete [as illustrated by Figure 4.3].

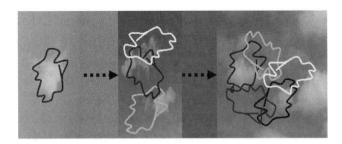

Figure 4.3 Clouds make a project

Listening to people talk about work, in terms of "efficiency," "feedback," "cycle time," "structures," "performance," and so on, you'd think they were all engineers, immersed in some or other technology. Clouds give us a totally different picture. Clouds don't have substance; you never take in the whole because there is always the sense that there is more than you see; and their boundaries are fuzzy and ambiguous. As a picture of organizations I like this one much better. Inside an organization everything depends on where you are. The organization you see at the top—say you are a board member—isn't like the one people see from inside the mail room, at the bottom. For the little their work has in common and the little they know about each other's work, the board room and mail room might as well be different organizations—or different planets.

The cloud metaphor helps to shake off the silly idea that an organization is a whole "thing." Why do we waste time and money trying to get people to buy into the mission and vision statements we pay consultants to produce for us?[8] There are five divisions, more than 30 departments, and who knows how many project teams at TDM. All are doing their own thing. Does the mission statement on our website, the lobby, and other public places keep these parts together and people on track, working like a closely knit family? If the mission statement isn't there when we get to work tomorrow, will it matter? Of course not! It may actually be an improvement, particularly if it forces us to talk about what our *different* parts (groups and units) do and whether they support each another as needed (Melvin's bunch aren't supporting me or the AB team). The idea that organizations are whole is just another pretense and it prevents us from seeing what is actually going on. People and groups work by making connections. We call the connections "networks," perhaps for good reason. There is a "net" of connections and this is where work happens (net-work–get it?). Things get done *when* people interact, *because* they interact, and *while* they interact.

The connections matter

[As illustrated in Figure 4.4] organizations are like ecosystems. We don't know what the whole looks like, but this doesn't matter. What counts is relationships – *interconnections among parts*, not the parts. Of course you can't see these interconnections (just as you can't tell why clouds are breaking, moving, or joining), but this doesn't matter either. Everyone knows about them and knows how crucial they are. Jose contacts Marina. She talks to Melita who speaks to Sandile. Once they connect and talk, they are off, working; discussing a deadline, reviewing an

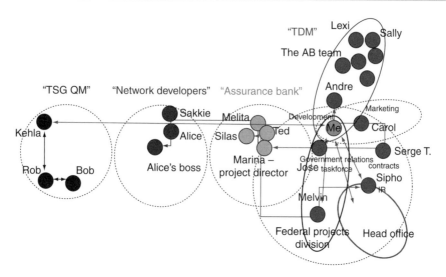

Figure 4.4 Connections make a project

agenda, or trying to resolve differences. Some interactions are momentary (you call someone for advice), others could continue on and off for a few days, or possibly weeks (colleagues who create a new training program together), and some go on for months and even years (those long-term projects, or work-relationships in a stable department).

[In Figure 4.4], I've shown some of the connections related to the AB project. If I had to describe in organizational terms what the AB project is about and how things get done, I'd talk about these, plus ones I haven't shown. We've got four organizations—ourselves, AB (the client), Network Developers, and TSG QM—and people in those organizations who are working on the project. It's their connections, as they network, that shape how the project gets done. As their manager, this is what I want to know about. Every interaction in every connection is a working relationship that influences how people work together, what they do, and what they accomplish. These are what I must keep my eye on, to see whether things are going well or badly [i.e. when there are "breakdowns"].

Our work is truly group work. No one works alone. But, the groups I'm talking about aren't nice, neat clusters of people, with clear boundaries, who get along well because they know and respect each other's strengths and weaknesses. Groups are made up of people from different departments, different divisions, and even different organizations. They might be working with colleagues they hardly know. This means relationships on a project are complex and potentially fragile. [As you see here] co-workers belong to separate units or organizations; they have different allegiances; and could be competing with one another for performance bonuses. People join and leave groups all the time, so boundaries are loose and flexible—talk about loose coupling!

I understand why it's hard to make group-work "work." People have to pool their knowledge, share ideas, and learn from one another. It's no good if they don't interact well or won't communicate. If they don't or can't cooperate, there are all sorts of problems. It is hard to find a cohesive core group like the AB team but, when you do and they keep the project together there is no holding back. Moving people from a project is like a sudden change of pressure that blows clouds away. It breaks the structure they've created by fracturing relationships and/or making it difficult for new ones to form. You can't just take a team apart and expect to put it back together again, later, like clockwork. This isn't how creative teams function.

Part 3: structure in organizing

Organizing = effort + magic

People do many different things on any project. Not forgetting that there are crises and crunches, the way a project comes together is actually extraordinary. So, how does it happen? In order to support project teams, it is crucial to have answers. Watching project teams at work, I've thought a lot about this and asked people what they do to bring it all together and keep it together as they go. What is interesting is that most can't tell me exactly what they have done or are doing. They can generally say why they're doing something, but a lot of what they do is intuitive. The way I see it, organizing a project is about equal parts effort—it is hard work and takes everyone's time and energy—and magic. The work I'm talking about gives projects structure; but there is another part that's difficult to explain yet is as important for success. It's there, it happens, but you can't reduce it to a formula or even explain it fully. That is why I think of it as magic.[9]

We recognize effort and want people to do more and give more, but you'd never know about the magic if you heard a group of HR managers talking about a pay-for-performance system. They'd be talking about incentives, outcomes, data, equity, buy-in, etc., as if this is all there is to the story. It isn't; there is magic in every project and if we don't see it, admit it, and try to support it (is it possible to cultivate it?) we're likely to kill the proverbial golden goose (like pulling people off the AB team?).

Work emerges

To me, it's magic how things get done without overall coordination and detailed plans, when there isn't anyone in charge. AB is quite a small project but it is mindboggling to think of what goes on. It reminds me of the old story of the three blind men and the elephant.[10] You have lots of people doing all kinds of work: like marketing work, financial work, and technical work. It takes their combined contributions to build the product or provide the service a client wants, but they're working at different ends of the elephant, on different parts. They have varied interests and responsibilities, each has his or her own perspectives, and no one knows how someone's work fits with everyone else's. Sometimes being inside a project team is really rough. When ideas or personalities clash there are arguments and bad feelings. But they are mature professionals and manage to organize themselves, by themselves, bit-by-bit.

Another part of the magic is that, for most of the time they are working on a project, team members don't actually know what they're doing or where they're going! Today's work *emerges* from what has already been done and from ideas about what to do next.[11] This happens from the very beginning. Remember the little cloud? A project is born before anyone makes plans. It's in someone's imagination: "we could really do with a software tool to aggregate and analyze our data." Lots of conversations follow. Eventually a product is delivered. It is like this every step of the way. What do project teams have to guide them? Usually, little more than a proposal that might have been revised and restated many times, plus their emerging ideas. All the while, they're planning, negotiating, writing, drawing, coding, and organizing to accomplish something that exists in their heads as varied and fragmented ideas. It is only late in the process, near the end, that they actually see what are working on. Until then they use their imaginations and improvise.[12]

Self-organizing

Organizing project work is a "just-in-time" phenomenon, with team members performing an intricate dance to keep things moving and get the work done.[13] The way they work is more like soccer, where play emerges in the moment as players assess and respond to what is happening, than American football, with a coach and his playbook. Team members juggle schedules so they can get to a client meeting on the

Beyond Management

West coast and be back to work on a new proposal. In the middle of the design process, software specialists hunt for someone to brainstorm with, who knows about financial software security issues. The process isn't seamless. It is a hoping-and-groping kind of dance. Things happen in fits and starts but it certainly isn't chaotic. Chaos means you have no idea what is happening, why it is happening, or what the consequences will be. That is very different from the kind of uncertainty you deal with on projects. Uncertainty means you are always feeling your way, improvising—that is the groping, and learning as you go. Without a playbook, you make guesstimates, while listening to your "inner voice," your colleagues' experiences, drawing on what they've learned from what worked and what didn't.

What Winston Churchill said about democracy applies to do-it-yourself organizing too. Imperfect it may be; but it is the only way to organize project work, so we should do it as well as we can, which brings me to the "effort" part of equation. Just as it does in soccer, practice helps. Participants who spend time working together build relationships and learn to function as a team. They come to know one another's skills, capabilities, and limitations. This is tacit knowledge that helps them read the state of play and take decisions. When a lot of what they do becomes second nature, their playing (or dancing) improves. It's by working together and learning together that they give structure to the work they're doing. "Structure" usually means an org chart, a strategic plan, or a requirements document. There is structure in project work too. It is a different kind of structure, but it is structure all the same, as it helps people organize—coordinate their activities and do their work. As I see it, the structure in project work comes from three things: talk, relationships, and something I call their "social spaces." As I put this all together I'm starting, at last, to understand what you damage when you break up a functioning team.

Networks of conversations

When the kind of work you do is complex and fluid, continual, person-to-person, in-the-moment *planning* is so much more important than having a plan.[14] Plans are out of date almost before the ink has dried, because someone has seen or done something that changes the plan. In our kind of project work, people coordinate their actions by talking: swapping stories, exchanging ideas, brainstorming, and strategizing. The heart and structure of project work is networks of conversations.

Whether it's by cell phone from the airport or email, people are always talking—planning, assessing, reviewing, and directing, giving and getting advice, encouraging one another, appealing for ideas, asking for more of a commitment than they are getting, or warning their colleagues about up-coming deadlines.

When I picture the conversations that keep a project moving [Figure 4.5] and I'm thinking of a network, I see the old type of telephone switchboard, with lots of lights, which you'd find in every office building or hotel before the digital age. When people are connected and talking a "busy" light turns on. When they finish their call, it goes off. The on–off flashing, which is all you see if you're watching a switchboard, tells you there is no underlying pattern. While they're on a project, working together, they may be in fairly regular contact; but people connect for all sorts of reasons and with lots of different folks, so what you'd see is random. You can't pin down networks either. If you wanted to find out who talks to whom, all you'd get is a snapshot of some conversations. It would be like trying to photograph

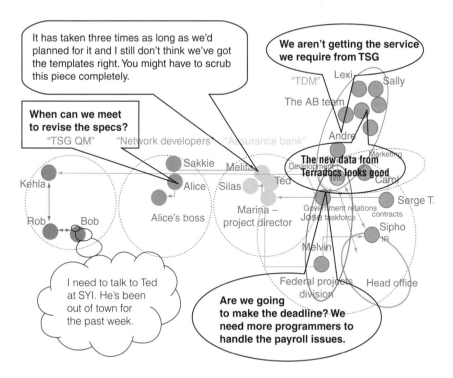

Figure 4.5 Conversations make a project

lightning. Networks are in continuous motion. Connections are unpredictable (the person you thought had the information you want doesn't, or won't let you have it) and the possibilities for new ones are endless. So, by the time you've got a handle on a few interactions, they are history. The whole process is self-organizing and has to be. Networks exist because people have to be in touch to get things done, but they're never sure with whom, why, when, where, or for how long.[15]

Relationships

There is another way of looking at what makes a project "go." Think of a molecule, made up of particles and forces. The particles are people. Their relationships fill the spaces between them. Relationships are the actual connectors. They are like attracting or repelling forces and are crucial. My team members contact me when they want support or approval or to report on what has been happening. They turn to each other for advice or call their colleagues when they are looking for a specialist to assist them. Their connections and interactions follow their relationships: who they report to; who they know; who they feel comfortable with; who they want to avoid; who they believe will get them what they are looking for; who they trust; and so on. The strength and quality of their relationships influences who they connect with and what they do when they connect. If the bonds are strong, because they are friends or there is mutual trust, they'll engage in one way; while, if the bonds are weak, because there is disinterest or, possibly, distrust, they'll engage in another way. In each situation, how they engage— "deeply" or "superficially"—has an impact on the way they work and the work they produce.

Organizing takes imagination, forethought, and ingenuity. You have to improvise and invent as you go, all of which explains why we work in teams. Team-work means collaboration and we know that when people collaborate extraordinary things can happen. There is always potential for creativity in planning a presentation, writing a proposal, or drafting a budget. Creativity doesn't necessarily mean artistry or innovation. Often it simply means finding a way of bringing in a project under budget while still doing good work, or using an appropriate image to get a point across to the audience. Project work is creative. The chemistry of collaboration is part of the structure that keeps people together and moving towards a successful outcome when they are working on projects. Groups appear to possess knowledge, wisdom, and capabilities beyond what any of them knows and can do individually. That is what I mean by "chemistry," although alchemy is probably a better word. Because collaboration is part magic, there is no obvious formula to ensuring extraordinary results.

When you are organizing and the magic happens, you might stop and say to yourself or to your partners, "we seem to have pulled an answer to this problem out of fresh air."[16] I have one particularly vivid memory of the chemistry of collaboration. We were planning a presentation, but were clearly bogged down and wondering where to go next. Then someone had an idea and we were off, creating a framework and giving it content. Playing off one another's suggestions, ideas lead to more ideas and we went from ideas and suggestions to creating the slides in no time. Seeing the completed presentation, I was struck by our resourcefulness, by how effortless it seemed, and I wondered where the ideas came from. I know I could not have created that presentation on my own. Somehow, a group's conversation taps into a hidden well of knowledge and draws from each of us something inspired that is relevant to what we are working on. As we talk I articulate ideas I didn't know I knew and adopt positions I didn't know I held. We engage one another and knowledge somehow gets "called forth" by the conversation we are in (it emerges, apparently from nowhere). The conversation itself generates ideas, or you might say "knowledge," relevant to the task: knowledge that could not and would not have come to light in a different conversation.

Each conversation generates its own possibilities for action. Opportunities that weren't there are created by the conversation, in the conversation, with each conversation generating a unique combination of ideas, perspectives, and possibilities. Every time people get together their interaction has its own personality. Another group, or even the same group at a different time or place, won't have the same conversation and they won't generate the same knowledge and possibilities for action. Now, this *is* magic.

Spaces for conversations

Using the AB project team as my case in point has brought home to me the different, conflicting perspectives, interests, and goals of management (the project, financial performance, and meeting contractual obligations) and project teams (their work, a good product, and satisfied client). This has given me a better understanding of why we are afflicted with bad decisions at the top. Trying to imagine how we'd do things differently and better, I've settled on how much project groups self-organize. Their conversations and relationships play a crucial part. In addition to these two, I see a third factor influencing how groups self-organize. But, I'm having a hard time explaining it to myself.

It doesn't seem to matter whether it is a large meeting, a private discussion in someone's office, or a farewell buffet, when people interact, they bring into whatever space they're in—both separately and together—a whole lot of unspoken assumptions and expectations about the situation and about others in the room. Those assumptions and expectations affect how they interact, how they speak to each other, what they say, and what they do. It's all a matter of how the group sees things—their personal perspectives and attitudes and ones they share, which have to do with the group's norms and the culture they're in.

Here is how their assumptions and expectations make a difference. The good, productive conversations, which can take you far in your work, are often one-on-one interactions or they happen in small groups. They are the kinds of discussions people have when no one is holding onto a formal role, like chairperson or boss, when the participants have a genuine interest in what the others have to say and, perhaps, in each other, so there is a sense of intimacy when they interact. Many of the bigger departmental and town hall meetings I go to are just the opposite and, generally, they're a waste of time, considering what the participants could accomplish together or when you think about what else they could be doing with their time. Not all meetings are like this. Team meetings, for example, can be very worthwhile. It all depends . . . But, on what?

Like a good meeting, organizing project work depends on people having good, productive conversations. Most of the time this doesn't happen by chance, so what is at work? I'm trying to put my finger on something that is part of our shared human experience. When meetings are unproductive, attitudes are partly to blame. Perhaps it is because people feel they have to be there even though they don't want to be, or because, when the top brass are there, they show up with agendas they want to promote, not to listen and engage one another. Relationships are also part of the story. I won't share my innermost thoughts about the projects we're working on with my boss, as I might do with a close colleague, telling her how she can improve things. My boss wants to know whether we're on target, on time, and on budget and, if we're not, that we soon will be. He's not interested in what I think. In other words, a lot depends on how people see and use their circumstances when they get together. I'm including the physical space. A big room, a podium, and a PowerPoint presentation aren't the way to share ideas. A good conversation requires some intimacy.

If we're going to pay attention to circumstances that are good for organizing, which we ought to do, it is important to have a name for the collective consisting of attitudes, interpersonal relations, expectations, norms, and culture, plus the physical work-spaces that, together, influence what people say and do. As far as I know there isn't an expression that packs them together, so I've invented one: "social space." How and how well people work together depends on their social space.

The way I see it, interactions happen in an interpersonal space—a social space—which people create whenever and wherever they get together. They don't do this consciously. Those spaces exist because humans are social creatures and every interaction, whether it's the briefest encounter or a long term relationship, is based on people's perceptions of the attitudes and actions of others and their relationships with them. No matter what the circumstances, whenever they interact, people "read" the others, trying to gauge their feelings, moods, emotions, or reactions (we interpret our circumstances more or less continuously). A social space reflects the feelings, attitudes, and assessments of those involved to what is going on, what others are like, and what is possible in the circumstances and it affects what views they share when they're working together.[17] There is one kind of social space if people know each other well; another if they've just met. It is the same if it's a boss and subordinates compared to, say, a gathering of friends, or colleagues who treat each other as peers. Board rooms and banquet rooms make different social spaces compared to workshops and cafeterias.

The sense you have of your group's or your team's cohesiveness, potential, and commitment is a feeling about your social space. It is one thing if they are enthusiastic and excited, or if they come together in a spirit of cooperation and optimism, but quite another if the prevailing mood is one of dissatisfaction, if they are irritated by their colleagues' attitudes, or are afraid of what others might do if they speak up to disagree. I've imagined the space of four of my colleagues [Figure 4.6] who are organizing a two-day offsite planned for later in the year as part of our next planning cycle. Just as their assessments of their circumstances have a bearing on the kinds of actions they'll consider, their outlooks, and attitudes to each another, either widen or narrow their horizons.

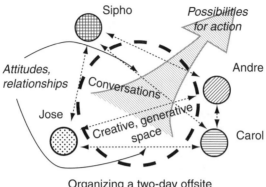

Organizing a two-day offsite

Figure 4.6 Picturing a social space

A space of anticipation and confidence affords possibilities for action that won't materialize when there is hostility and doubt.

Team members seem to grasp intuitively the importance of spaces that allow them to do good work, which is why they become frustrated, even angry, when colleagues don't play ball. Good spaces do a lot for the magic of organizing, although I'm certain that when we are focused on contracts and deadlines we don't see this at all. The AB project team has been a success because, being a bunch of committed and enthusiastic people who hit it off, they create good spaces for themselves when they work together. Whenever this happens the team's creative potential seems limitless, which may be exactly why Melvin or his boss wants to move some of them to the ERP project. If this is true, it is obvious (*if* you get the idea of social spaces) why the decision is a bad one. Without realizing it, they're fooling with the magic of organizing. This is unwise and possibly dangerous.

CHAPTER 5

Left-brain management and right-brain organizing

Parallel universes at work

Reading about taking team members off a project where everything seems to be going well, only to put them onto a failing one, did you have a sense of déjà vu? Your circumstances and experiences are probably different, but situations like these are quite common and, as it is highly likely a successful project will be derailed, the question is: why? Followed by: what do you do about it, or what can you do about it? Jeff's answer to the first is that, when they assess how a project is going, project teams and the managers who make these decisions aren't thinking about the same things. Their different ideas about what matters—actually different values—are a source of tension. "Tension" suggests a spring under pressure, or, as he sketched it, forces pulling in opposite directions (see Figure 4.2). What to do is more complicated. The immediate response depends a lot on the personalities involved, their motives, attitudes, and relationships. Can Jeff persuade someone (possibly Melvin, although he isn't sure who made the decision) to reverse it? The larger agenda, though, is to do something about eliminating the tension, so that people who aren't part of the team effort aren't inclined to mess with success.

How to approach this problem and what action to take depends on understanding what is going on "behind the scenes," which is where Jeff's look inside project teams, at how they think and operate, is tremendously valuable. He has opened the black box of knowledge-work. When I got his point about project teams' and managers' disparate views and values, the thought suddenly struck me that they occupy parallel universes, and that whether you can eliminate the tension between them depends on what you can do, at work, about these parallel work universes. Allow me to explain.

When managers say they want "results," they mean bringing the project in on time and under budget and fulfilling requirements. This is how they see a project. It's the view from the top. They don't really know, or care, how teams do it, provided they achieve a solid bottom-line performance. For project teams, on the other hand (with a view from practice), how they get there is as important as what they accomplish. "Results" are closely tied to whether they feel they've done a good job, individually and collectively. Their work, Jeff notes, is personal. Teams take pride in what they do and they haven't finished and haven't done the work properly unless their client is satisfied or they're agreed that this is the best they can do under the circumstances. Designing and building good software takes personal dedication and good cooperation, so how the team works together also has a bearing on what they feel about their work and results. In those situations—they do happen—when they realize it isn't practical to build features they'd agreed to include, it shouldn't be for want of having tried, and perhaps failed—together.

This, basically, is how I came to the idea that managers and project teams live and operate in different spheres, hence parallel universes; their views and attitudes to work are not only divergent but also disconnected. Now, it would be one thing if the worlds of managing and organizing were truly separate and they could function independently, but they aren't and can't. While they are working, as they interact and share knowledge, project team members and managers alike adopt typical work-organizing practices, which have their own rules or logic. At the same time, managers and team members wear other hats: either a managing hat (managers) or a being managed one (team members). This means, while working and organizing, both lots are following management-universe practices, which have entirely different rules or logic. The two universes are interconnected, but by sets of practices (one work-organizing, the other managing) that don't belong together and won't harmonize. This is what creates the tension Jeff describes, which leads to organizational breakdowns.

In one universe, where the view from the top rules the roost, the logic of machine efficiency dominates, with structures that have to be observed, systems you must conform to, and orders that should not be questioned. In the other, where you are involved in the work, the logic is quite different. This isn't a mechanical world. There are no permanent structures or universal laws associated with organizing. Things you initially thought were true sometimes turn out not to be and people, though generally consistent and reliable, at times, are not. You are on a perpetual journey into the unknown, uncertain about what is going to happen and in a state of permanent discovery, or learning. These are "truths" of knowledge-work. You learn to live and work with them and to muddle through: gauging when things aren't right and when it's time to drop this plan and, perhaps, come up with a new one; when to speak up; why you need to rely on your judgment; and when to go with your intuition.

The two universes represent different ways of being, meaning people have to behave differently in each. The gods of machine efficiency demand you comply with their laws, but you must serve the gods of uncertainty and learning with imagination and flexibility. It's not possible to dedicate yourself to one set of gods (e.g. obeying orders, sticking to the plan no matter what) without abandoning the others' imperatives (e.g. being open, agile, and creative). In fact, the only way I can imagine occupying both the organizing and management universes, as knowledge workers are expected to do, is to become schizophrenic, which is a sure sign that breakdowns will happen at work.

The two problems in coming to terms with this situation are, first, being able to see and agree that there *are*, indeed, two universes; and second knowing what to do. It takes some effort to see beyond the management universe, which is the one we know well because it's in your face at work. When we think and talk about work we use management-speak. "Performance," "outcomes," "efficiency," and "results" are what count. "Work" has to do with making lists of requirements, producing work schedules, devising charts—like activity and Gantt charts—creating benchmarks, racking up billable hours, and meeting performance targets. Work also consists of activities on the calendar, like scheduled appointments, meetings, and presentations, with talking points, agendas, and PowerPoint slides. Everything revolves around the six Ds of documentation, data, directives, deliverables, deadlines, and dollars. Teams work toward "milestones," submit "status reports," and so on, and, whatever they are doing, people are reminded of their relative status in the hierarchy.

But, when they are working and organizing, they definitely don't follow this script. Life in the other universe is characterized by an entirely different mindset. Officially (in the management universe), there is no room for talk, but they spend a lot of time talking: calling one another for advice, to explain what they've been doing, or to complain that they haven't received the report they were promised. Much of their work consists of ordinary conversations. These begin with thoughts like "I need to contact Sandy" or "I promised Pete a draft before the weekend." Knowledge-work, prompted and shaped by what people have decided or promised one another in the past, is influenced by working relationships more than directives and schedules. While organizing—making plans and sorting out responsibilities—a lot of what knowledge workers do is ad hoc. It doesn't follow a master plan, they don't have a list of specific outcomes or deliverables, and they work person-to-person and peer-to-peer, without the trappings of hierarchy.

Because management is so in your face at work, I imagine the management universe as a brightly illuminated place, where everything is clearly visible. Not only does everyone acknowledge what goes on, but also there is a kind of reverence for what people do and how they do it, recognizable in the way we devote ourselves to the gods of management and give obeisance to "deliverables," "status reports," "performance measures," "incentive systems," and more. Or, perhaps I should say it *appears* that everything is clearly visible and that everyone knows what's going on. Action follows the view from the top. There is a system, a structure, and rules; but no one seems to appreciate either that knowledge workers must organize themselves or that their efforts to do so are constantly undermined by management's "best practices" and "efficient solutions."

The chances are that, if asked what you do, you'd mention your job or profession. "I build houses," you might say; or, "I help people find jobs"; or "I'm a ____" (and you can fill in the blank with plumber, teacher, executive vice president of marketing, financial advisor, management consultant, social worker or any name or title from a more or less endless list). It surely never occurs to you to say "I'm an organizer." I'd bet, too, that your job description says nothing about organizing. Titles are given out on the basis of what is visible, or what matters to management. "Organizing" is not visible and does not matter to management. With the work of organizing shrouded in mystery, it's easy to think of this universe as dimly illuminated, dark, and shadowy, but it's quite bizarre and unfortunate that it is. It is bizarre because everybody organizes. It is unfortunate, because the fact that the work they do to get organized is invisible to just about everyone spells big trouble for knowledge workers.

Left-brain management and right-brain organizing

To explain why, taking a leaf out of Jeff's book, I'll begin by illustrating the two universes. Comparing and contrasting management with organizing will help to highlight the differences between them and to bring the image of parallel universes to life. I've chosen the brain as a way of depicting the two universes, with the left hemisphere representing the management universe and the right one organizing. Figure 5.1 is the first of a two-part narrative of what's behind this picture.

Imagining the management universe was easy. Borrowing from management-speak, I simply created a word-picture of work, as viewed from the top. Then I put this word-picture of the management universe on the left for a reason. Management aims and claims to be linear, empirical, analytical, and certain: science rather than art. Describing organizations and work in technical engineering terms (e.g. "efficiency," "productivity," "data"), management-speak makes us think of these in a machine-like way, compatible with what we understand by left-brain dominance.[1]

Management   Organizing

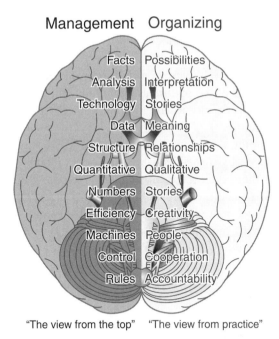

"The view from the top"   "The view from practice"

Figure 5.1   Parallel universes of management and organizing

It is more difficult to describe the organizing universe. Scholars and writers haven't paid enough attention to this common place occurrence to have produced a distinctive language of organizing, so I've used familiar words to do with people, their relationships, language, and meaning-making to describe the universally known phenomenon of people doing things together. Organizers spend a lot of time discussing what is going on or talking through their next steps, making meaning of what they're doing, and thinking about the people they work with (e.g. about their motives, expectations, attitudes, responses, and so on). Besides being cooperative work, organizing is creative and energetic, giving presence to the human spirit and psyche in addition to the intellect. In the management universe, where no one wants surprises, certainty is the prize and you are supposed to strive for it. Everything must be planned, structured, quantified, and justified. In contrast, when people are organizing, never knowing quite what to expect, they live and deal with the uncertainty. This composite picture of organizing corresponds with our ideas about right-brain capabilities, so the organizing universe is on the right.[2]

I wanted to make the distinction between managing and organizing as stark as possible because it is differences in how people think and, especially, in what they do in the two universes that are important both for

understanding knowledge work (and how people do it) and for appreciating why management practices spell trouble for knowledge workers.
To heighten the contrast I played with the words on each side, arranging
them in pairs across the halves, hoping this would make the differences
clearer. The message of the picture as a whole is that at any time there are
people managing work and organizing it. I hope the picture reveals how
different these are.

Aware of it or not, one group does things the MBA way, their thoughts
and actions shaped by a management play-book. Thinking "efficiency,"
managers have their eyes fixed on financial factors, contractual obligations, and performance measures. Data, delivery dates, deliverables, and
bringing the project in at or under budget count for more than what work
is being done, why, and how. (Unless he or she is part of the team, a
manager probably won't know much about these anyway.) Notice that a
manager's attention is on *things*, such as spreadsheets (financial data) and
work-flow charts. It is "tools" like these that are the mainstay of the work
of managing.

Organizing, on the other hand, is all action and interaction. People,
when organizing, engage one another. Thinking about their colleagues'
contributions, their clients' requirements, and their bosses' advice, and
their own responsibilities, they listen to and interpret what others have
said, gauging their attitudes and reactions, and frame their own responses.
Because they are doing something together, to do it successfully, they need
to *align*. Explaining alignment, Etienne Wenger says "participants become
connected through the coordination of their energies, actions, and practices . . . We become part of something big because we do what it takes to
play our part."[3] Notice how Wenger associates alignment with participation and coordination. You'll find each of these at the heart of the work of
organizing and I'll have a lot more to say about both in later chapters.

Tools and talk

Now that I've dissected and contrasted what goes on in organizations,
I can get to the other part of the picture, which is actually the crux of
my story. Managing and organizing are like parallel universes because,
for all the notice we take of the work of organizing and what it takes to
do it—the human spirit, creativity, relationships, cooperation, accountability, and meaning-making—I might as well have left the right-hand side of
my picture completely blank.[4] Managers can't do their work—the work
of managing—without also organizing, because all the action at work

has to do with people's interactions, so they manage and organize, or organize in order to manage. In fact, as we are all knowledge workers, managers included, we are all organizers, organizing. But, you wouldn't know this from the way we talk about work or from what we pay attention to. In Figure 5.2, the text over the right brain is almost invisible, as a reminder that the work of organizing doesn't count as work. "Work" means what is on the left.

Jeff puts the tension between management and project teams over what matters down to values. The bulleted lists on either side of Figure 5.2 highlight what is "necessary" (i.e. valued) in each universe. I've summarized the differences in two words: "tools" and "talk." In the management universe, tools matter. Organizing depends on talk. By "tools," I mean IT systems, org charts, financial data, and the like. "Talk" is just that: people engaging and making meaning together.

Because it is crucial to understanding why tool-oriented management practices are completely unsuited to organizing talk-oriented knowledge work, I want to explain how I boiled down the differences between management and organizing to tools and talk, what these mean, and what happens when we become too attached to one and we ignore the other. At the same time, I'll outline my case for new work practices, or for taking organizations "beyond management."

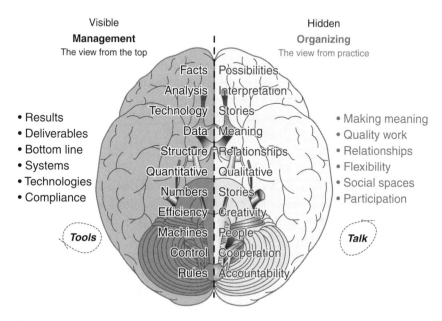

Figure 5.2 What we see and don't see

Organizing practices: talk and tools

Whether you are planning a social event, checking on a patient, asking a colleague to stand in for you at a conference, formulating strategy, or holding a meeting with clients, organizing begins with people talking. Although it's quite possible that you're not aware of them or the connections, earlier conversations, most probably with other people, led to these ones. So, you can think of every conversation as part of an enormous, but invisible, dynamic web of ephemeral conversations on all sorts of issues, which connect multitudes of people in a myriad of ways. As there is enormous variety in the web, the people who are connected now may well have entirely different purposes and be in different circumstances.[5]

This web is without bounds and, nowadays, many of the conversations are not face-to-face meetings in an office, or impromptu chats in the elevator, but happen when people connect "virtually," by phone, email or text message. In every instance the reason why they explain themselves and their problems, ask questions, tell stories, and make jokes is the same: they are "sharing knowledge" to get something accomplished. To give the web, or network, the knowledge-sharing, and the organizing a context, imagine what conversations lead to a group of German specialists in tropical diseases discussing with municipal health officials in Kenya their plans for clinical trials of a vaccine. And imagine how small the common ground is that the two groups now occupy.

So much for "talk," but what about "tools": what are they and how do they fit the picture? While they're sitting round a table talking, one of the participants takes notes and, later, distributes minutes of their meeting as a record of what was covered and what decisions were made. During that meeting, when there was disagreement over who would be eligible to take part in the clinical trials and how they'd be selected, one of the doctors handed out a protocol drawn up by the pharmaceutical company and they looked over the material together. Besides the minutes, documents with data, slides, spreadsheets summarizing costs, and notes they take while working together, they have access to online databases, survey forms, strategic plans, personnel manuals, organization charts, timesheets, and many, many other artifacts that help people do their work. As they work, they will move seamlessly between their talk and these tools. After they've looked at a draft budget (a tool plus talk), a committee member will update the spreadsheet (tool), circulate it, and wait for the others to comment (more talk). Eventually, when the committee meets again, they'll review the latest version (more talk around the tool), and the chair will sign off on appropriations they've approved (another tool).

Sometimes it is hard to tell the difference between tool and talk: for example, when an email (talk) is the means of verifying what commitments were made (tool). But, most conversations are ephemeral, though we carry snippets of them in memory and pass on to others what we've heard. Tools, however, like minutes of meetings and org charts, have the advantage of what Don Lavoie calls "returnability." You can circulate them, hence share them and come back to the contents in another context, at another place and time, with other people.[6]

The relationship between talk and tools is a symbiotic one. Though it would be much harder to organize without notes, lists, and plans, and perhaps impractical to run organizations without them, it is impossible to imagine organizing without conversations. Talk, after all, is how we make meaning. It is how I establish whether there is a problem or confirm whether my idea really is a good one. Tools may be indispensable, but they are useless without talk. Spreadsheets and databases have to be interpreted, analyzed, summarized, and reviewed, and so on. Whenever we use tools, from project schedules to driving directions, balance sheets, and lists of requirements, we make meaning of them, mostly by talking to one another.

The unmistakable message, when you learn to manage the MBA way, is that words don't matter—numbers do. You'll learn to create and handle tools: to read a balance sheet, formulate a competitive strategy, calculate the net present value of a stream of anticipated earnings, understand exchange rate movements, estimate the risk associated with different portfolios, map work flows, and measure performance. Perhaps you'll also practice negotiation skills, but, most likely, not with an emphasis on finding common ground, but on reading body language and using psychology to trump your opponents. This is an industrial era mindset and you can tell, just by looking at office work spaces designed for "maximum productivity" that the mindset still prevails at work. Spaces are arranged so that it is difficult for people working a few feet apart to have a conversation.

Few managers are open to the possibility that the substance of work—both theirs and their subordinates—is conversation. And, even if it is not a conscious decision to push talk to the periphery of work rather than have it at the center, the very ethos of management—control coupled with competition and compliance—undercuts people's ability to engage, to talk, and to align. Hierarchy and bureaucracy, both integral to the way management is practiced, keep people apart, while competition among employees discourages them from sharing their knowledge. If good conversations nourish knowledge-work, for all these reasons conventional management practices provide entirely the wrong diet for knowledge workers.

Taking on the work of organizing

There are hardly any production lines left in the West. We are nearly all knowledge workers now. And, with people everywhere looking for new organizing practices, the metaphor of parallel universes turns out to be a useful way of framing the options for the activists out there who are thinking about what they can do to change things, weighing up possibilities for new ways of managing or organizing work.

One option is to try to patch up and/or revitalize "old" management, which means improving existing tools and techniques and looking for new ones, in the hope of dealing with serious flaws in current practices while maintaining essential elements of the management philosophy we know and use and some even seem to love. Perhaps the solution lies in a new generation of IT tools which allow people to access and share information more easily. It is an idea management consultants like to peddle (remember, their livelihoods depend on maintaining the status quo) and, given encouragement, it's the option lots of people are drawn to because it is an evolutionary route to new practices. There is nothing radical here. "Use this new tool. You can keep doing what you know and keep doing it the way you've been doing it. Just make a few changes at the margins and everything will be fine." These are common threads in consulting-speak.

A much more revolutionary idea is to abandon management for organizing, so knowledge workers aren't waiting for instructions from above, which may never come, or, if they do, turn out to be misguided. Instead, regarding it as their responsibility to do so, they take it on themselves to organize and to do this well. The third option is to compromise, finding the middle ground, if it exists, between left-brain management practices and right-brain organizing ones, where top-down management coexists with people self-organizing. This would mean bringing the organizing everyone already does (i.e. the "informal organization") out of the closet and having it accepted as legitimate work, which is necessary and *at least* as important as managing.

Perhaps it is obvious why the third option isn't a practical one. In the middle ground, between management and organizing, managers would not only accept employees doing their own thing but also encourage them, allowing them to organize themselves and disregard any directives they felt were unnecessary. Employees would be equally comfortable organizing themselves and accepting directives from above. I can't imagine anyone being satisfied with this arrangement, can you? High-control management and low-control (self-) organizing rest on such fundamentally different values and beliefs, about people—e.g. whether they are dependable and capable of sound judgment—and work—the purpose and how to achieve this—that I don't believe there is a middle ground.[7] Which means only two options for going beyond the kind of management we all know: evolutionary change, or management-as-usual with minor adaptations; and radical change, with everyone organizing themselves, without a top or chain of command. In the chapters that follow, I begin by having a good look behind the scenes, at why knowledge workers organize themselves, how they do it, and at what works and what doesn't. Then, with the help of some case studies, I'll explain why nothing can be done to patch up management and cover its deficiencies. By this time it ought to be clear that the "radical" option, of abandoning management, is actually the sound and sensible one. If it has to be *either* management *or* organizing, which I believe it does, I'm for organizing, and I'll explain why we all ought to be.[8]

I'd like you to think of the rest of my story as a journey in search of effective organizing practices. Thinking of the left and right brains, the destination is the "other side" of management. En route, I'm going to explain why that is the right place for knowledge workers to be, that it is a practical option for organizing work, and where activists can start. I will also explain what they can do to take on organizing. On the next leg of the journey, the object is to understand what it is about knowledge-work that makes it necessary for knowledge workers to organize themselves.

CHAPTER 6

Knowledge-work in close-up

What is knowledge-work?

It may be one of the great paradoxes of work life that we spend so much time at work but have so little to say about the nature of work. In business books, hundreds of writers have had their say about organizations, management, and leadership, but haven't shown much interest in work.[1] When they do, they don't distinguish one kind of work from another. It is all just "work." As a result we are surrounded at work by talk, images, and practices of factory-work. These aren't helpful because this isn't what people are doing.[2]

If someone says "that was hard work" or "it took a lot of effort," doesn't it sound as if they've been doing something physical? What about words like "training" and "rewards"? What do these conjure up? Doesn't training sound like rote learning? We train sniffer dogs and performing seals, rewarding them with a pat or a treat when they repeat what we've taught them. You can train people to feed material through a cutting machine repeatedly or to pull a lever whenever a component reaches a particular step in the manufacturing process, but the learning that stands knowledge workers in good stead is something completely different. We're talking about being able to "read" people, to use one's imagination to "see" potential pitfalls, and to think laterally. Meanwhile, in IT companies, consulting firms, and government agencies, where work talk is about "efficiency," "productivity," "feedback," "optimization," "benchmarks," and "performance," you can be forgiven for thinking you are in a workshop, dealing with engineering problems; although, as a knowledge worker, you may actually be interpreting a report or facilitating a meeting of school administrators. "Supervision," "billable hours," "performance evaluations," and the obsession with metrics, are, like training, all vestiges of the shop floor; legacies of practices initiated by Fredrick Taylor for standardizing factory-work. He and his assistants stood by, stopwatch in one hand, clipboard in the other, instructing workers to repeat sets of motions while they determined which were the most efficient. He hoped to devise a performance benchmark for every kind of industrial activity, but it didn't take very long to see this couldn't be done. And, although the mindset lives on, if it can't be done for factory-work it is even more futile to apply these practices to knowledge workers and knowledge-work.

Little about knowledge-work can sensibly be measured, but this hardly discourages people from trying. One of the consequences of attempting to satisfy the promiscuous desire for "suitable numbers" is that knowledge workers spend their time doing things that are peripheral to their work, distracted by management's focus on performance measures. Almost everyone has examples. Here are a few from Jared Sandberg, writing for the *Wall Street Journal*.[3]

> David Fahl [who] worked for an energy reseller . . . noticed that getting things done right wasn't always as high a priority as making deadlines, meeting deliveries or being on budget.
>
> "You can get all those things done without doing any good work," he says . . . "*Managers create all sorts of surrogate measures that they can measure*, like PowerPoint slide counts and progress charts," says consultant Tim Horan . . . Jon Williams once worked in an auto-claims department where the number of new-claim calls . . . [was] tallied with the same weight as brief reminder calls to customers. . . . His greatest sense of accomplishment was transforming an initially angry and frustrated customer into someone who was satisfied and even laughing. "That wasn't measured at all."

A definition

To understand why the usual ideas about work are so wrong-headed, we should get to know knowledge-work and, to do this, I'm going to begin with a definition. "Knowledge-work" is what people do when they interact, talk to one another, and share knowledge, so they can accomplish something together. Sharing knowledge means posing questions and listening to the responses, offering and receiving advice, getting clarification, asking permission, telling others how you feel, or explaining what has been happening. People share knowledge by making meaning together, typically by talking and listening, but also with gestures, facial expressions, and other body language. They do it to decide what to do; to assign roles and responsibilities; to agree on places, dates, and times; and to check on what they are doing and whether they've done what they agreed to do; in other words, to organize.

Notice that my definition doesn't refer to categories of work or workers, but to *practices*. It is deliberately broad, covering anyone whose work involves organizing and who shares knowledge in the process, including anyone who serves others, whether as a secretary or a chief financial officer. Everyone does some knowledge-work and you are a knowledge worker because of what you do, not because of your position, job title, qualifications, or the industry you are in. The kind of "doing" that defines knowledge-work is human and social: negotiating meaning with others. Those who do the least knowledge-work work alone, without the benefit of others' knowledge (it is difficult to think of examples, perhaps a hermit or an artist who prefers his own company), or they're employed on an assembly line or do repetitive manual labor like digging trenches or dispensing espresso coffee. Being routine or mechanical and largely physical, their work doesn't require much sharing of knowledge. Here is an example of knowledge workers at work:

> After a few formalities, an Italian aide introduced her to . . . the embassy press spokesman. [They] . . . walked across the embassy's walled grounds and sat down for a cup of coffee in the cafeteria. [She] . . . told [him] . . . that she had some documents about Iraq and uranium shipments and needed help in confirming their authenticity and accuracy. [He] . . . interrupted her, realizing he needed help. He made a phone call summoning someone else from his staff as well as a political officer. [She] . . . recalled a third person being invited, possibly a U.S. military attaché. She didn't get their names.
> "Let's go to my office," [he] . . . said.[4]

This description of a man and a woman talking to each other and to at least one other person by phone, as they walk across a garden to a cafeteria, makes a rather charming picture, particularly if you ignore the fact that their work appears to be international espionage, to do with Iraq's nuclear capabilities. While walking and talking, they are working and, clearly, also, organizing.

To knowledge workers, "work" could mean phoning colleagues to ask for information, scheduling a meeting to plan the next steps, or circulating a draft proposal. To do it, people talk, telling one another what they think, listening to what they have to say, asking for their advice, or, more generally, sharing knowledge. Why? They are getting organized, so they can get their work done. Press officers and journalists, financial advisors, lawyers, consultants, and others, in almost every walk of life, do the same. Teachers prepare lessons, draw up schedules of classes, and devise exercises for students. Then, in the classroom, they'll divide them into groups for a particular activity, tell them about next week's project, and give them their homework. Work *is* organizing. For knowledge workers, work and organizing are indistinguishable.

Picturing knowledge-work

I want you to be able to picture knowledge-work, but this isn't easy to do. It is much easier to picture industrial work, which, to me, means machines and people: either people performing like robots and turning out hundreds of identical objects, or some sort of assembly line, or a forest of machinery interspersed with a few workers who attend to the machines that are a dominant presence. When I think of industrial work, two films in particular come to mind: Charles Chaplin's timeless almost-silent classic *Modern Times* and Fritz Lang's *Metropolis*, an even earlier dystopian vision of industrialization and the "tyranny of the machine."[5] To picture knowledge-work it probably helps to start with industrial work and contrast the two. The two images I have chosen, from the heyday of manufacturing, come from 'Behind the Scenes in the Machine Age,' a part educational, part propaganda film, about the importance of avoiding 'human waste' in industry, produced by the Women's Bureau of the Department of Labor in 1931 (Figure 6.1)[6].

Now, for my representative knowledge workers, I've settled on telecommuters, who could be doing anything from accounting to wedding planning. How you picture knowledge-work depends in part on how I contrast what they do with the kind of work you see in the pictures. I certainly want to emphasize that the differences boil down to much more than their computers and the technologies that make telecommuting possible.

One of the most important differences is talk. You'll notice that the factory workers aren't speaking to one another. In fact, they're not even paying attention to what the others are doing. They don't need to do either to do their work and the rules of the workplace probably forbid them from talking on the job. The combination of rules and the repetitive, practically mechanical work they're doing means each worker is both a robot and an island. A telecommuter, on the other hand, might well be in her own home, or in the car or train, at the airport, or in a client's office, but this doesn't mean she's isolated, or works alone. Her machines connect her into her networks of colleagues and customers and she's in constant contact with them, on the phone, or by email, or face to face if they've arranged a meeting or if she's on a service call. Why? Knowledge-work is collective

Figure 6.1   Two pictures of factory-work, ca. 1930

Source: "Behind the Scenes in the Machine Age," 1931, a film produced by the Women's Bureau of the United States Department of Labor.

and highly social. She, her colleagues, and clients are together in the work, doing it together, mainly by talking.

Another difference is that factory-work starts and finishes with each shift, whereas knowledge-work rolls on, more or less continuously. At the end of her work day a factory worker can say, "I've done my work. I met my production quota." To a knowledge worker, work doesn't have clear-cut beginnings, or nice, neat endings, which allow him or her to draw a line and say, "That work is finished. I will make a new start tomorrow."

We talk about "tasks," as if these are separate, but this is an industrial-work mindset reasserting itself. Knowledge-work is ongoing and more or less continuous. Before one task is complete it's highly likely her next is already being shaped by what she's doing. At the end of her work day she'll still have a list of people to contact and a proposal to review. She probably won't leave her work "at work" and, if she doesn't work into the night, she'll start early, before she actually has to be "at work."

Finally, here are two more differences to consider. Although you can't see any supervisors in these pictures, with factory-work it's a safe bet that they are close at hand, watching to see that workers are doing the work correctly and aren't slacking. Knowledge workers, however, organize most things, including their work schedules, for themselves, with little hands-on management. When industrial workers say they're off to work, it's a safe bet that they're headed for the organization that pays their wages. But, if our telecommuters are consultants or work for government contractors, in security or IT-related positions for example, they could spend all day, everyday, working for clients at their clients' sites, knowing almost nothing about what is going on in their own organizations, with their paychecks as the main reminder of who actual employs them!

Network maps are traps

With the popularity of Facebook, LinkedIn, and other social networking sites that have come and gone or stayed, it is hardly surprising that if one clear image comes to mind when people think of people sharing knowledge it is a social network.[7] And, with many professionals, from consultants to security analysts, taking an interest in networks, web-like maps of organizational networks, like Figure 6.2, are sprouting up all over, especially in the field of knowledge management.[8]

Based on the idea that information has to flow between them for people to be able to do their work, the purpose of a diagram like this is to show who is connected to whom, through whom, and to identify which individuals play leading roles in connecting people at work, as the main hubs or nodes through which information flows.

To be sure, pictures like these certainly have a place in understanding knowledge-work, but we need to be careful about how we interpret the word "network" and what we make of network maps. It is easy to misinterpret both. With this network map in hand, showing interactions among people, equating "network" with "organization," it could be a short misstep to thinking of networks as structures and networked organizations

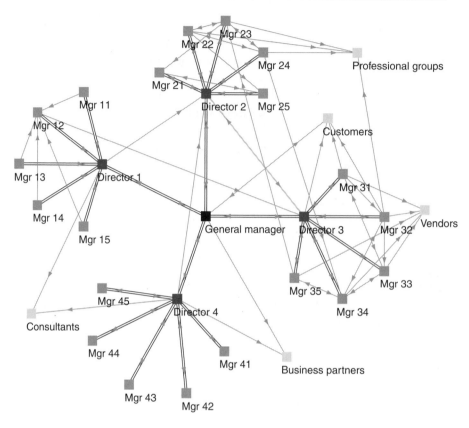

Figure 6.2   Diagram of an organizational network

Source: Valdis Krebs (www.orgnet.com/decisions.html). Reproduced with permission.

as real, updating your mental image of an organization from pyramid (the org chart) to network. Treating social networks as if they are hard-wired, like computer networks that have definite and (in the short term, at least) fixed structures, is a gross misinterpretation of what it means to "network" and of what people do when they organize. Pictures like Figure 6.2 actually tell us very little at all about social networks, knowledge-work, or organizing.

When it is used to describe knowledge workers, the word "network" is a metaphor for people engaging and talking. "Engaging" could mean brief, more or less accidental, unintended interactions. Or, it could mean intentional, long-lasting, ongoing, and possibly regular contact. A network covers all of these. Networks are comprised of invisible, often hard to describe person-to-person (i.e. social) interactions that cover a multitude of different relationships, such as those between friends, colleagues, superiors and subordinates, and individuals who trust each other implicitly, or business partners who, if they could help it, would prefer never to talk to one another again.

Networks are never complete

You may remember Jeff saying that trying to draw a network is rather like trying to photograph lightning. It is a warning that a network map is something of a trap; that all we ever really know about networks are a few interactions at the moment they occur; perhaps an exchange of business cards, snippets of conversation, and body language in the form of a handshake, a kiss, or a smile. A network map like *Figure 6.2*, however, seems to tell a very different story: that we are looking at a whole set of interactions and have a comprehensive picture of how knowledge-work gets done.

What is fishy about the picture? First, a knowledge network is never complete. As knowledge workers are always in the middle of doing something, like contemplating and planning their next moves, or waiting for responses to inquiries they've made, they are always in the process of ending some of their current work relationships, making new contacts, or renewing old ones. With old ties being severed and new connections being made, networks are in flux; never fixed for a moment. The other problem with network maps is that they don't show what is most important to the work of organizing. It's not possible to map factors like the depth of each person's interest in the project they're working on, or the qualities of their relationships with others in the network, hence their commitment to their work and each other.

A network map is actually a view-from-the-top perspective, from outside the network, not the view of someone involved in it, who is experiencing and making meaning of what is going on in practice. If we're not careful, we might end up treating network maps as managers do their project schedules or org charts. Believing we know more than we actually do about what is going on, lulled into a false sense of being able to "see (and know) it all," we might be tempted to intervene—to *manage* the network—intending to control and streamline it to make it more efficient. This would be a serious mistake. While it may be both desirable and practical to "improve" the way things work, this is the responsibility of participants, on the inside, who do it interaction-by-interaction and conversation-by-conversation. It is part of what they do when they're organizing.

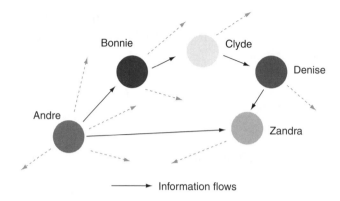

Figure 6.3 The standard view of what happens in networks

It's generally assumed that the function of a network is to get *infor-mation from one node (person) to another* or to others, as I've shown in Figure 6.3, with information flowing from Andre to Zandra and via Bonnie, Clyde, and Denise. There are two basic premises, here. One is that knowledge-work is done by *individuals*, just like factory-work; only, instead of being done at workbenches or on production lines, it is at the nodes on each end of a network connection, wherever those happen to be. The second assumption is that someone possesses information and must pass it on to others who need it, but don't have it. The connections, like electrical cables, are there to move work (information) between nodes. If you take this line and want to improve the way things work, you'd pay attention to the nodes (e.g. to who has the information and who needs it). Then, checking to see whether there are breaks in the cable, you would see to it there is enough bandwidth to allow the information to flow freely between nodes. All of which suggests that managing knowledge-work is straightforward; essentially "management as usual."

Knowledge-work is social and in "the spaces in-between"

At this point, I can state that I'm taking a radically different line on what knowledge-work is and on how people do it. What *individuals* think, believe, and do certainly matters: in fact, it matters a great deal. In terms of getting things done (i.e. making things happen or getting results), however, the real work is what knowledge workers do *together*. Without the work of organizing, which is truly *collective*, not individual work, nothing much would ever get done. *The work of organizing is in "connections,"* not at the nodes. Knowledge-work is social: participative and cooperative. The work of organizing is about people engaging, interacting, making meaning together, and *aligning* to decide what to do, when, for whom, and so on. The fact that the work of organizing happens *when people interact, in conversations among them,* is really what distinguishes knowledge-work from factory-work, sets the work of organizing apart from management, and explains why you can't manage – only organize—knowledge-work and networks.

Management practices rely on and reinforce an individualistic rather than a collective and social view of work. Work is what individuals do, by themselves. Each does his or her own piece of work at his or her place on the assembly line. Workers might need to "communicate"—perhaps one needs to tell the other to change places—but their work is their own and "communication" means passing on information, not sharing knowledge while making meaning together. Management practices and tools designed with individuals in mind, rather than people working together closely and collaboratively, focus on nodes, not connections. Managers are trained to encourage and incentivize individuals to compete, then to reward those who outperform the others.

Where is knowledge-work?

"*Where* is the work of knowledge-work?" might seem like an odd question, the kind you might expect to hear on a quiz show like *Do You Want to Be a Millionaire?*, but there are two good reasons why I'm going to dip into it. First, the ideas I'm outlining—what is the work, who does it, and how they do it—aren't standard ones and to really understand knowledge-work (i.e. the work of organizing), we need to know *where* it is. The other reason is that the answer is a crucial piece of the puzzle in terms of showing us the way to the kinds of organizing practices that enable people to do better work.

Suppose a group of department heads is puzzling over a directive about internal changes, asking "What does this mean?" and "What are we expected to do?" As they talk together they're organizing together. Their conversation is their work. They are framing their problem and crafting a way of dealing with it. This is what they do at work. And, as the conversation moves back-and-forth among these managers, ideas start to crystallize. At first theirs are probably rather pale and possibly inconsistent views, but they become more coherent and colorful as the participants respond to one another's ideas, questions, suggestions, and comments and

Figure 6.4   Some knowledge workers at work

clarify what they are talking about. Talking together, they get ideas about what is going on or what they are dealing with, which is when they begin to "see" the problems: "so, these are the issues"; "now I'm starting to realize what is behind it"; "how is this different from what we're doing now?"; "his requirements aren't consistent"; and so on. With luck, as they talk, they'll settle on what to do. This is how they *make* their own work. I've shown them at work in Figure 6.4. (Try to keep this image of knowledge workers at work in mind. I'm going to return to it from time to time.)

The department heads are grappling with a series of problems. Now, when you hear the word "problem," what comes to mind? Is it something someone has to fix? Perhaps there is a lock that won't turn, or you remember how you struggled to use your mobile phone to send a text message. If so, you'll appreciate that this group's problems (or, for that matter, any group saying "What does this mean?" and asking "What should we do?") are different. You'll also appreciate why I want to emphasize that they are working on and working out *their* problems.

No one has handed them a ready-made problem, saying "Here it is, get on with it." Instead, in groups, like this one, or in pairs or project teams, they will define or frame their own problems as they make meaning together. Both the problem(s) and solution(s) they come up with will *emerge* in—or out of—their discussion; so you can see that *these are not individuals' problems* (or solutions). The problems actually *belong* to the group (although, when they work on them, particular individuals may ultimately be responsible for specific aspects of the work). The problems are defined, or constructed, by the group, as they work together, in and through their conversations. *The problems reflect the way they come to see things as they engage and talk together.*

What these department heads are doing provides the clues we're looking for to what might seem an arcane question but, actually, is a very practical one. If this were a TV quiz show, with a big prize for the correct answer, there would be a drum role or trumpet fanfare, now, as an announcer gestures flamboyantly toward a large screen: "The answer to 'where is the work of knowledge-work, the work of organizing?' is [pause for effect] . . . in the space between," which happens to be the title of a song by the Dave Matthews Band [Ta-da!].

What does this mean? "The space between" is created by conversations, grows out of conversations, and *"exists" in the "middle" of conversations.* To organize their work, people talk. They might do this in person, or on the phone, or in a variety of other ways, even by email. *Their conversations and what happens between them is their work.*[9] While talking, they frame the problem, identify the issues they are dealing with, set priorities, and discuss what to do, and so on. Their work comes from their *interaction*; not from the participants themselves. As they talk—asking questions, testing one another's reactions to ideas, giving their views, and arguing about what other people expect from them—they make meaning together. The problems they'll deal with, as well as the options and possibilities for dealing with them, which lead to action, *emerge from their conversations, in the space between them.*[10]

Social spaces

So, now, we have another image of knowledge-work besides networks. The new image is the "space between" people. Actually, I prefer Jeff's term "social space." It means the same as "space between" but it hints at people (possibly many) being linked together by a kind of force-field that embraces everyone involved, influencing their behavior. I've drawn a circle around the group in Figure 6.4 to symbolize their social space. Even though the idea seems abstract and disconnected from practice, it is easy to find examples to illustrate social spaces. In a business meeting participants are supposed to be polite and respectful and not behave as if they're at a political rally. It is possible that if the same people were present at each they'd behave entirely differently and it is the spaces—of business meetings and political rallies—that make the difference. Social spaces are so much a part of the work of organizing; and there are both good and bad spaces for organizing that, as we're interested in organizing practices, we need to know what makes "good spaces" good and whether and how knowledge workers can influence their spaces, turning "bad spaces" into good ones.

Sacred places

We can learn something about social spaces from the qualities of places held sacred by indigenous communities; places like *Ayers Rock*, in Australia's Northern Territory, known by its official Aboriginal name, *Uluru*.[11] These places may have unique physical characteristics but their special powers have to do with relationships. For animists, as many indigenous peoples are, the world is alive. Humans have a caretaking role in the world and their relationships with what David Abram calls their "animate, expressive world" are as important as their social ties. Everyone and everything is joined together, people with people and people with places, in "complexly interwoven relationships."[12] In sacred places people experience those relationships most powerfully. So, when there are important matters for the community to deal with and decisions to be made, or there is something to celebrate, when it is time to organize, to worship, or to honor the living or the dead, they gather in their sacred places, where they talk to their ancestors and hear the voices of ancestral spirits most clearly. Through them and in their rituals they participate in their sensuous world, their communication, community, and communion enabled by this sacred place.

Each of us has experiences of places that have the power to bring out particular types of behavior. If you are a practicing Catholic, perhaps it is the confessional. The combination of your wishing to confess and the place itself makes confession possible. The place, which includes the trust you place in a priest to keep whatever he hears to himself, is integral to your actions and, whether it is confessing sins, telling the truth in a court of law, or telling your secrets to your closest school friends in your "den," places have the ability to "hold" or call forth different kinds of action. Although artists' studios and workshops might qualify, it is difficult to think of workplaces as sacred spaces, probably because organizations can be impersonal, even anti-social, and work is no longer place-bound. Among the tribal elders—typically, executives and senior administrators—who hang out there, however, board rooms and clubs enjoy a particular mystique that other places, such as cafeterias, don't; and different organizational rituals, like the annual performance evaluation, or ones where people dress up (award ceremonies) or down (casual Fridays), have some of the characteristics of sacred places and call forth particular behaviors and feelings.[13]

Whenever and wherever people get together, whether online or in person, as they must in order to organize, they create their own social spaces. Like the one I've added to Figure 6.4, these are completely invisible of course, but, whether they're organizing in person or by email, their spaces make their presence felt in a variety of ways, as participants read the mood of the group, observe the norms of the meeting place, or, because of their anonymity, feel free to "flame" others when they're online. No doubt you've seen how, when team members email one another, they tend to express themselves differently when their boss is party to the exchanges. His or her virtual presence on the "address" line influences their social space.

The qualities of social spaces

Social spaces, which hold the interactions and conversations of people organizing, shape their behavior, influencing what they say and do as they plan, schedule, make assessments of problems, or take decisions together. Some spaces—think of them as *open* spaces—allow participants to tackle contentious issues because they feel free to speak their minds without recrimination. But, in other, closed spaces, where they feel they have to be guarded to avoid others' scrutiny and, possibly, hostility, they'll steer clear of matters they consider controversial. My point is that social spaces have different qualities, and those qualities, which affect what people say and don't say and how they behave, have an important bearing on how far they're *aligned* as they organize, hence on how well they work together.

Like the sacred places I mentioned, the qualities of social spaces have everything to do with participants' emotions, beliefs, feelings, and their relationships and attitudes to one another. Some—"open spaces"—make people feel welcome and eager to participate. Others are the opposite. Participants, feeling cut off from each other, hold back, possibly because of earlier experiences with some of the people involved. They're meant to be assessing their options and making plans together, but the circumstances aren't conducive to a frank conversation and there may be a general mood of apathy among them. Behaving as if there are actual boundaries—barriers—that prevent them from engaging productively, they don't get into the kinds of conversations that are necessary for them to align and move forward.

Where do these arguments lead? There are good and bad social spaces for organizing; or spaces which facilitate people's efforts to organize—which are good for organizing—and ones which don't. Good spaces support cooperation, creativity, participation and collaboration, knowledge sharing, and aligning. Creative energy—*synergy*—happens when people are aligned, collaborating, and pooling ideas. When this happens, they become *co-creators* of whatever they are doing. The whole is greater than the sum of the parts and they experience what Jeff calls the "magic of organizing."[14]

John Seely Brown and Paul Duguid say knowledge can be "leaky" or "sticky." It is leaky when it moves around easily (when people readily share knowledge) and sticky when it doesn't. One of the characteristics of a good social space is that, when you are in it, knowledge is leaky. We know this happens among trusted associates or close friends with common interests. There are few boundaries between them.[15] Conventional management practices, on the other hand, make knowledge sticky.

The combination of competition, hierarchy, and bureaucracy is lethal for organizing. When every department is a boundary that is difficult to cross (those "silos" and "stovepipes" everyone talks about), every rung on the org chart is a potential barrier between a superior and a subordinate, and skills and job categories become obstacles that are tricky to negotiate (like the boundaries between hospital administrators and medical personnel), people won't and don't share knowledge, even from top to bottom, down the chain of command. Although we blame the individuals when they fail to tell us something important, saying they are "hoarding information," we also acknowledge that there is a "power game going on out there." All this plays out, daily, in the social spaces you find in high-control cultures. There are few opportunities or reasons for people to engage, build trust, and encourage cooperation, so there is little aligning. Simply put, the social spaces people create when they're following standard management practice are bad for knowledge-work.

CHAPTER 7

The work of organizing with giant hairballs and wicked problems

What is the work of organizing?

Conventional thinking about work is hopelessly out of date and completely wrong, but, somehow, survives. In personnel procedures, training programs, job descriptions, and management practices in general, work consists of specific, separate, named activities, like "writing reports," "archiving material," "drawing up contracts," "designing customer surveys," "developing training courses," and more. Work is measurable—both the effort and the results. Many business organizations bill their clients by the hour and managers expect "measurable outcomes" for each bit of work. Work is also what individuals do, alone. Who knows of an organization that pays its teams or work groups for their collective efforts? It is easy to see that these practices are hand-me-downs from the days of factory-work on production lines.

Now, take a look at what knowledge workers do. In an investment bank, two are briefing colleagues on why new legislation has created gaps in their training on mergers and acquisitions; others are wrestling with the question of what material is worth archiving and for how long; and some are busy cultivating the relationships they hope will pave the way for an add-on to their contract. In each case their only identifiable activity is talk. What they're doing is not measurable in any practical or useful way; they're doing it collectively, not individually; and it is hard to imagine how you'd value it in order to bill it by the hour or day.

Although it defies conventional thinking, what they're doing, most definitely, is work, and it is necessary work. It is the work of organizing. If, in managing work, we keep looking the wrong way, at the wrong things, emphasizing and encouraging the wrong practices, is it any wonder if knowledge workers find it difficult to do their work properly and there are breakdowns at work? To move beyond old and dysfunctional ways of thinking and onto new and better organizing practices, we need to pay attention to the work of organizing. First, we need to understand it, by examining it bit by bit. The problem is we are dealing with social practices, and social practices are not wooden puzzles. They are difficult to take apart.

I've identified four facets to the work of organizing, which I'll call "threads." They are:

1. Negotiating meaning
2. Creating work
3. Building networks and negotiating boundaries
4. Aligning[1]

These aren't separate parts. Looking for an analogy, I'd say they are like images from different cameras following the players at a football game. You have a good sense of the action (in this case, what people do to organize) only when you've seen them all. Just as important, these aren't a sequence. I've numbered them for convenience, because I'm going to discuss them one by one. But, there is no right way to disassemble knowledge-work. In practice, these are threads running through a seamless cloth: the work of organizing.

The case study

To explain each of them, I need a case study of knowledge workers at work, organizing. In the one I'm going to use I came into the picture shortly after employees across quite a large nonprofit organization received new job descriptions. A few weeks earlier, on a conference call, a senior executive had announced a reorganization (reorg), explaining that management wanted to improve the organization's overall performance to shore up his firm's funding and that employees would shortly have new roles and goals. Sure enough, within the week they received new job descriptions via email, but when they got them they didn't know what to make of them and, before they could respond, had to organize themselves both to make sense of the information and to decide what to do.

I soon discovered what lay behind the reorg. Wanting to strengthen the organization's finances, the CEO was adopting a formula that matched Fredrick Taylor's prescription for making industrial firms more profitable: get workers to deliver more. It is based on the idea that there is a straight line from additional revenue (or income or receipts) to improved productivity, which ends with job descriptions and performance measures and standards: except that it runs the other way. This nonprofit's income, a combination of donations, grants, and appropriations, depends on the generosity of funders. Most either run a corporate business or are advocates for corporate management practices. Their idea of efficiency is the standard management rhetoric about "doing more with less" and the reorg, designed to produce a measurable improvement in overall performance, was intended to persuade them to give more. How do you show demonstrable gains in performance? You set new performance goals for the organization then change the way your employees work (what they do and how they do it), starting with new job descriptions that orient them to the new goals.

The middle managers closest to the reorg had spent a lot of time framing a strategy for senior executives to sell to funders and had everything planned, right down to the level of work. They'd thought about the results they wanted in terms of measurably improved outcomes for and from the organizations' clients, then, with HR's help in assessing what it would take employees to achieve these, had crafted new job descriptions. Knowing that most employees get a lot of satisfaction from their work and are dedicated, they expected them to be enthusiastic about the initiative and "get on with it," but their response was disappointing. Instead of action, the managers got questions about what was going on and what to do. They didn't have answers, because it wasn't *their* work on the line.

According to one manager, it was field representatives, known as "field reps," who "pushed back hardest." This organization's mission is improving the well-being of people in poorer urban communities and everyone recognizes that the field reps are pivotal. They work directly with community leaders, the organization's clients, and act as a bridge. Together with their clients they plan neighborhood redevelopment projects and set goals for each project. When they're satisfied that a plan will meet their organization's funding criteria, the field reps liaise with colleagues back at their regional offices and, when funding is approved, monitor the project's progress while continually advising their clients. Seeing a project through to a successful conclusion is a matter of pride for them and they know they are judged on this. So, it was hardly surprising that one of their concerns and complaints was the stipulation in their new job descriptions that they take on more clients, working with six to eight at a time instead of three or four.

The field reps' frustration had to do with the fact that when they think about work it is about what they do and how they do it—their practices—and their new job descriptions didn't give them anything to go on. (Remember that job descriptions originated in factories.) How could they do what they do but do more of it and still do it well? Acquiring practices is actually an ongoing, life-long phenomenon. As you interact with bosses, clients, and colleagues, you learn what everyone expects in terms of "good work" and how to do it. This process never ends and practices aren't just about skills. They have to do with roles (yours and others'), responsibilities, and relationships. People's identities are wrapped up in their practices.[2] Although it was obvious to the field reps that they were expected—somehow—to change their practices, when you don't know what is involved or what to do it is natural to wait and see while you try to fathom this out individually and collectively; which is just what they did. In phone calls and emails back and forth, they tried to figure out what they should, could, and would do differently. At the same time they speculated about how this strategy would affect them and their clients and expressed anxiety about their futures. This wasn't what their managers expected or wanted to hear. They wanted action.

The work of negotiating meaning

People start to organize by talking about why they're there, what each is up to, what needs to be done, and so on. In other words, organizing starts with making meaning, so that's where I'll start; but remember that making meaning isn't just a phase in the work of organizing. Social philosophers tell us that making meaning of what someone said, what the weather will do later in the day, or why the neighbor's dog is barking, is a human quality, perhaps uniquely human. "Sensemaking," as Karl Weick calls it, is something all of us do, all the time. As long as people are conscious of their surroundings (including other people), themselves, their feelings, and their actions, they are making meaning of what is happening to them, around them, and to others.[3] You might say the work of organizing *is* negotiating meaning. But, equally, it is all the other threads too. Meaning making, creating work, building networks, and aligning are completely interwoven.

Whether they ran into each other unexpectedly at the bus station and are doing it face-to-face, or are sitting at computers, having a scheduled meeting in cyberspace—when they organize, people hold up their own perspectives and interpretations of what is happening, or what was said, for scrutiny and discussion by everyone involved. You say what you think or believe, or what you heard, or you offer a suggestion and expect a response. This is how we make meaning together, negotiating amongst ourselves about the nature or significance of what is going on and what we ought to do about it. What is this about? What am *I* supposed to do? How should *we* respond? These are just some of many questions field reps would have been asking themselves as they chewed over the emails which contained their new job descriptions. Very soon they were asking each other.

When the field reps started to organize, emailing and phoning their colleagues, it was because they genuinely didn't know what to do. They weren't trying to sabotage the reorg and weren't "resisting change."[4] What problem or problems were they dealing with and what kinds of responses were possible and desirable? Who were they responding to: their bosses; colleagues in other departments; clients; or those at the top? And, what did they want? What was behind the new job description? What were the immediate consequences likely to be and what would happen in the near future? To figure this out they had to do the work of making meaning of what others were doing. What were their managers (and others) thinking? What did they expect? What were the implications? What approach would be effective and acceptable? Until they had *some* answers, they couldn't take *any* action.

I've named this thread *negotiating* meaning because people have lots of ideas and, quite possibly, different perspectives and varied agendas.[5] They engage and talk and their ideas encounter others' ideas. They pit their beliefs against others' beliefs and learn that others' values either match or run counter to theirs. Initially, nothing is fixed or settled. Working out what to do and how to do it requires a good deal of give and take, to resolve differences and find a way forward. As it is important that participants are able to engage one another productively in these situations, their social spaces are crucial. If it is the kind of environment that shuts down discussion, or if people don't listen to each other, progress will be slow and it will be difficult for them to align.

The work of creating the work

Like the field reps working through the problems of what is going on and what to do, press officers, executive coaches, ambassadors, software developers, lobbyists, trainers, property developers, fashion designers, and journalists—in fact, all knowledge workers—are architects of their own work. Do you remember Jeff's "little cloud"? Conversations are the clouds of the collective work of organizing. Ideas seed other ideas, which eventually lead to action. "Creative," meaning "originative; productive; resulting from originality of thought, expression, etc.; imaginative," is exactly the right word for this work.[6] What is more creative than ideas building on ideas?[7]

Organizing in response to management's strategic reorg, the field reps are doing much more than framing their immediate actions. Their decisions and actions are almost certainly going to have a ripple effect. They'll bring other people and groups into their conversations, extending their network as they organize and, together, they will generate new conversations. Eventually, these will reshape their work and that of other employees, possibly well into the future, and in ways no one imagined or intended. This is why I think of knowledge-work—organizing—as open-ended or as filling an open future.

People come together to deal with a problem because they have a common interest in solving it, or because they've been asked by others to participate, or just out of curiosity. They expect to accomplish something.[8] But, early on, in their initial conversations, they may know little about what they're going to do, what they'll accomplish, or even why they are there; and they don't have a plan or place to begin. Instead, they extemporize when they start to organize. They put out ideas and offer suggestions about why they are there and what they can do. Then, the sense of what they'll do—their work—emerges, bit by bit, conversation by conversation. Usually, as this happens, a network grows along with their conversations. "I'll talk to my colleagues," someone says. Another feels their supervisor ought to be involved; and someone else has a contact who she thinks has worked on this sort of problem before. Now they're part of an evolving network, which, soon, takes on a life of its own. They may have initiated the process but, with ever-expanding connections, there are people in the network they don't know, doing things they aren't aware of.[9]

Isn't it an exaggeration to say knowledge workers "fill an open future"? After all, everyone has parameters and guidelines to work to and, as we work with and around others who have work to do, we have to fit in with them and can't go off in any direction we please. A combination of rules, plans, proposals, regulations, contracts, precedents, procedures, directives, and our own rules of thumb, derived from our experiences of what worked and what didn't work, give us direction and limit the scope of our actions. This is highly desirable because, when people are working together, organizing, they want to know where they stand. Another factor that places limits on what people can do is that knowledge-work is highly social and if they don't keep to their commitments and promises, fulfill their obligations, and meet their responsibilities little gets done.

Having guidelines and commitments isn't the same as having a script to follow. Just as job descriptions don't tell people what to do, neither do plans, schedules of activities, and the lists of requirements that software developers draw up at the start of a project. Each of these is a *tool*, which, by itself, is a hollow shell. Plans and directives as well as responsibilities and commitments *have to be* interpreted. People have to make meaning of them and this is where creativity begins.

To get to action, we need *talk* as well as tools (I explained in Chapter 5 that practices always consist of both). Think about the field reps. It is in conversation, *together*, that they begin to work out what the new job descriptions mean to them and how they're going to deal with them. Without conversations, plans and directives are words and ideas. Discussions, negotiations, and deliberations, with clients, bosses, suppliers, or colleagues in other departments, transform them from "empty rhetoric" and "abstract ideas" to something practical: instruments of action. It is in their conversations that people find their reasons for taking action. That is where they become aware of why and how specific problems or issues matter to them and of their level of interest in getting involved to deal with them. So, conversations produce the motives for doing the work, or at least help to shape them and, while they work out what they want to accomplish, what to do to accomplish it, and who is going to do it, they assign responsibilities and generate commitments. Without these it is difficult to move forward.[10]

Hairballs and orbiting

Having spent his entire working life at Hallmark, the greeting cards company, where he started as a very young artist and school dropout, Gordon MacKenzie understands creativity and writes about it as few others do: from the perspective of knowledge workers and their struggle to become and stay creatively engaged at work. You'd imagine that, in a company where creativity is a must, management would pull out all the stops to foster it. Not so, says MacKenzie. Hallmark was (and possibly still is) the antithesis of a creative place to work. He blames the corporate culture, which he calls, memorably, a "giant Hairball."[11]

Hallmark is certainly not an isolated hairball. "Corporate culture" is a nicely alliterative term for standard management practices. You'll find hairballs wherever organizations put conformity, consistency, and compliance (as well as competition) ahead of originality, imagination, resourcefulness, and cooperation; which means there are hairballs as far as the eye can see. Those "Cs" of corporate culture trump the "Cs" of creativity and cooperation. This is an objectionable combination for people whose work is creative, so the term "hairball" fits, although MacKenzie admits he wasn't comfortable with it at first. As he explains it, every hairball is a powerful center of gravitation, able to suck up anything and everyone in its path. When employees get pulled in, as, inevitably, they do, it is the end of creativity and cooperation. It is risky for them not to comply and it is hard to be creative under a regime of rules, regulations, and rigid routines.

MacKenzie's position is corroborated by every business that wants to spur innovation or is in a hurry to get products to market and sets up a "skunk works" or spins off a smaller, largely independent, operation to handle the task.[12] What makes these more successful than their much larger counterparts is that they are unencumbered by "bureaucratic red tape." For red tape you can read "lots of conventional management tools." As creativity thrives outside the box of rules, regulations, and requirements, the challenge is to get outside and stay there and it isn't just creative folks, like artists, who need to do so. "Thinking outside the box" has become the manager's mantra, for good reason. The human urge to create is so important to the work most people do, particularly the work of organizing, where they share ideas in order to frame and shape future action together. The desire to create—to accomplish something new or different—is also important as a motive, spurring people to move beyond ideas and words and into action.[13] So, while there is every reason to respect and encourage creativity, hairballs, which favor compliance and conformity, don't. Here is the paradox of management today in a nutshell. Managers complain that employees do not think outside the box, but it is the management system (i.e. practices) that keeps them firmly inside.

MacKenzie's way of describing what it means to escape a hairball is just as unique. He calls it "Orbiting"; a word that is perfect for understanding what is involved. To avoid the straightjacket of practices that were designed with compliance rather than creativity in mind, in the interests of doing good work it is the task of knowledge workers—actually, their obligation—to organize themselves to get into and stay in orbit above their hairballs. In orbit they can see and do things others can't, but are still tethered to them by invisible bonds—the force of gravity. They have work to do, which means responsibilities, commitments, obligations, and so on, which means they aren't free to go off on their own to do whatever they want to do.

The unmistakable meaning of orbiting, though, is that knowledge workers need—so have to make—their own (social) spaces that allow them to work creatively. The object of orbiting and the obligation of orbiters is not only to escape the pull of hierarchy (remote control, from the top) and bureaucracy (administrative procedures that emphasize rigid rules and fixed roles), but also to create different spaces. You can't be creative in social spaces that are wrong for organizing creatively. To *think* outside the box, people need to *be*—i.e. to *work*—outside the box. What kinds of social spaces do you want for orbiting? Ones where you have open conversations and can challenge one another's positions, not simply "do what you are told"; where you improvise together, not just follow rules; and you pay attention to each other and hold one another to account for what gets done and how it gets done.

The million dollar question is *how* to avoid practices that kill creativity, which is really a question about *new* practices. What practices facilitate creative work? MacKenzie says "get into orbit," but his answer reveals some blind spots. He fails to explain that the practices blocking the path into orbit are extremely difficult to circumvent. The pyramid structure and high-control ethos, both carry-overs from the era of industrial work, were intended to put decision-making firmly in the hands of those at the top. Employees weren't meant to think or organize for themselves and, as those practices still prevail, getting into orbit is a very tricky business.

The gravitational pull that keeps them from escaping their hairballs is a function of two factors: the power some have to make others conform to their rules, regulations, and procedures, plus the amount of effort that goes into seeing that they comply. Income differentials are a good clue as to how unequally power is distributed (very unequally), while layers of "oversight" tell you how much effort goes into ensuring compliance. In large organizations, even the "flattest," there are lots of these. It is a safe bet that top management is not interested in orbiting, because corporate culture serves the top well (it was designed to do this), but, equally, has no interest in others orbiting. There are two reasons why. The explicit one is that, in the view from the top, orbiting undermines management. Unless rules are enforced, senior executives say, there is potential for chaos. The other, tacit, therefore less obvious, consideration is that allowing orbiting would weaken the position of those at the top, undermining their identities and, eventually, their inflated earnings. Power, salary packages, and identity are all nominally tied to control; the idea that "someone, above, is in charge," which is why it is so difficult to orbit from below. How do you self-organize, successfully, for long, beyond the reach of rules, regulations, and requirements that get in your way, without being fired?

Organization development (OD) consultants have struggled for years to lay foundations that would give employees the latitude to orbit, advocating for open organizations with more decentralized authority. The OD profession doesn't have a great deal to show for its troubles, however, besides occasionally being seen as heretics.[14] It can't claim to have transformed organizations and work practices. If, as I suspect, the problem is that control and resourcefulness are a bad match, as long as the standard operating procedures of management are in place, encouraging people to orbit isn't the answer for greater creativity. In fact, encouraging them is likely to amplify tensions, making managers feel they are under siege from would-be orbiters. What is the alternative? First we need to be clear that management is not adequate for organizing knowledge-work and to know why it is broken. Then we need to pursue options that include getting the top to sign on to new organizing practices.[15] I'll deal with both sets of issues in the last few chapters.

The work of building networks and negotiating boundaries

Another of MacKenzie's blind spots leads me to the third thread in the work of organizing: the work of building networks, which, equally, is the work of negotiating boundaries. It is normal in the West to downplay the socialness of human life, not only to regard work as individual rather than collective effort, but also to treat creativity as a personal, individual trait. There is a basic premise that individuals either do or don't have creativity, though it can be fostered in those who don't have it. MacKenzie follows the standard line on this. But, knowledge-work is collective work. Knowledge workers network to organize and must orbit together to work creatively. To get a sense of what it takes to orbit together, I need to highlight how complex social networks are.

As they work and organize, people connect with others and networks grow, or, rather, mutate, because the process of building a network is certainly not a linear one. The connections that form new branches may cause existing ones to wither when people, who were working together in some fashion and were connected, aren't any longer. Originally a technical term, "network" is now such a familiar metaphor for person-to-person connections that I don't have to explain why "building networks" is a thread in the work of organizing. The other part, about "negotiating boundaries," however, is a different matter.[16]

Every connection in a network is an interpersonal relationship of some sort, where people's attitudes, values, beliefs, intentions, and interests come into play. This makes every relationship connection a *boundary*, which helps or hinders their work together. A standard management tool-box, containing tools like scorecards and balance sheets, relies on "hard data." Interpersonal relationships are "soft," so boundaries have escaped attention; but everyone ought to be conscious of them, as well as how to handle them and when to act, because the work of organizing—where participants negotiate meaning, ideas are generated, and decisions are taken—is always at the boundaries. Paying attention to and negotiating boundaries when they emerge is the way we align, so we can get things done together.

Boundaries as bridges and barriers

Relationships, always present in the work of organizing, are never neutral. Take superiors and subordinates as an example. Wherever they work together, their awareness of their relative positions is part of the mix that makes up their relationships. Whenever people from the same organization meet they are likely to be in one category or the other (either superiors or subordinates). This means there is a dynamic in play which contributes to the way they interact to create a social space together, influencing what they say to each other and what they do or don't do. But, as relationships are complex, it is difficult to say how these will play out in a particular situation or what impact boundaries will have as people organize.

Sometimes a boundary turns out to be a *bridge*. If a superior is a good person to turn to for advice, and is capable and caring or supportive, then it is more than likely a subordinate will ask that person for advice. On the other hand, if asking for advice means "showing your ignorance" or "admitting you don't have all the answers," this won't happen. Here, the boundary is a *barrier*. The same applies to delivering bad news. It is unlikely that subordinates will give their superiors their candid assessments of a project that is stalling if they think they will be blamed because they are the subordinates.

When peers work with peers there are boundaries between them too; but, their relationships being looser, they have more latitude than superiors and subordinates in what they say to each other, how they say it, and in how they behave towards one another. Given both the ups and downs of work life and the fact that knowledge-work is personal, where some situations call for humor, in others it is important for people to speak plainly. So, when someone believes another hasn't been pulling her weight, he may be very frank, speaking his mind in a way that makes a third party, who doesn't know them or their circumstances, feel awkward. At another time, however, knowing she is under a lot of strain, to avoid making things worse, instead of criticizing he will chide her gently: an approach the outsider may consider too tolerant. This kind of flexibility helps peers to avoid damaged relationships, hurt pride, or bruised feelings. It doesn't mean their boundaries won't lead to breakdowns, but it helps to minimize breakdowns and, when they occur, makes them easier to repair, so they are aligned and willing to work together.

Fragmentation contributes to boundaries

If you were looking for them, you would have noticed boundaries popping up all the time as field reps talked about their new job descriptions. This may be surprising. After all, they are "on the same team," working for the same organization and doing similar work. But, there are many reasons why boundaries emerge in the context of something as traumatic as a reorg. Diversity within a group has a lot to do with it. With widely different experiences and varied interests, attitudes, and perspectives, each makes meaning of the new situation in different ways. Then, when they network and make meaning *together*, their positions may turn out to be either bridges or barriers.

Another example of the production-line mentality that prevails at work is the unrealistic assumption that people with similar jobs ought to think and act alike. Seeing boundaries emerge among field reps as they talked, I was struck by how they had come to this job along so many different paths, bringing varied experience and histories to it, and how this factor, quite apart from personalities, attitudes, family circumstances, education, and, possibly, gender accounts for their different outlooks. At the time of the reorg, some had been with the organization for years, but had only recently been appointed as field reps. Others, calling themselves "survivors," had worked as field reps for a decade and more. Both groups had "seen it all before," but from different perspectives. A third, sizable group was quite new to the organization. As the field reps negotiated among themselves about what to do, the survivors were most vocal about not wanting to mess with success. Others were more open to whatever might come along, although my impression was that a bunch of them were ready to bail out if events took a direction that didn't suit them. Perhaps, before the reorg, they had been considering quitting anyway and those who had been doing this work for longer had close ties to their clients that meant a lot to them. At any rate, this particular boundary generated heated discussion.

Field reps are a group, not a network. Networks are diverse—a real hodgepodge of people—so you could expect more fragmentation and more boundaries.[17] As a way of organizing, what makes networking manageable, if still challenging, is that each participant has a small, personal network. Connected to relatively few people at any time, he or she has a limited number of relationships to worry about and boundaries to negotiate. While networks are extensive, participants' stakes are in the people with whom they work and have relationships (Jeff reminds us that project work is both collective and personal), which makes networks and networking personal.

Even in small networks, however, there is potential for fragmentation and, wherever it occurs, boundaries need attention. Participants aren't always clear about their commitments and where their priorities and responsibilities lie, because they have varied and sometimes multiple affiliations to individuals, groups, or organizations, both inside and beyond their immediate network.[18] Even when they belong to the same organization, they may report to bosses who have different interests. Some are part of a network for a brief period only (giving a talk or delivering documents), while others have already spent months on a project and feel they have a good sense of what is going on. Besides their diverse experiences, participants have widely different skills and capabilities, as well as more and less knowledge of what others are doing, what they expect, or how they respond to pressure. Also contributing to boundaries are: their attitudes to their work and each other (relationships could range from casual acquaintance to intimate confidant to rival); their areas of specialization (e.g. whether they work in IT, HR, or PR); their positions, ranks, and roles; personality differences (shy and retiring or bold and aggressive); and the fact that they work across departments and divisions. Such formal boundaries, like those between principals and subcontractors and superiors and subordinates, are potential fault lines that could fracture at any time.

Multitasking makes connections tricky

I want to highlight one more set of factors, on top of this diversity, that makes network connections both fragile and tricky. Unlike factory workers, who generally have more clearly defined roles and specific tasks to do, knowledge workers multitask. As a result, they are literally and figuratively all over the place, mentally as well as geographically. This has to do with the nature of their work. Assignments are often quite open-ended and aren't easy to schedule. It can be hard to know whether you've completed a project or a task and are ready to concentrate on the next one, because work you thought was almost finished may take on new life if a client isn't satisfied or because project priorities change when your client's organization hires a new CEO.[19]

When called away to do something else in the middle of an assignment, finding themselves in an unfamiliar situation, in new networks, dealing with different people, knowledge workers have to scale back their existing commitments to give more attention to their new responsibilities. Or, without warning, network connections can grow like Topsy and they find they have a long and expanding list of people to contact. In either case, they're using all their energy just to stay abreast of their immediate concerns, but are unable to keep up with what is going on elsewhere. Meanwhile, their new commitments begin to cascade all over the network as their colleagues, who have to take up the slack and have more work than they'd bargained for, reschedule and reorganize.

Put it down to wicked problems

No matter how much negotiating, creating, or networking people do while they organize, unless they agree on their problems and what to do about them, there'll be little constructive action. Donald Schön explains that today's professionals' biggest challenge is pinning down (i.e. defining or framing) the problems they are dealing with, which he calls "problem-setting."[20] The toughest problems of organizing have to do with differences of opinion over what is important (values), who should bear the costs (interests), what to divulge to co-workers, and who is fit to lead (relationships). These have to be addressed through *collective action*, meaning that a *group* has to "commit themselves to undertaking a particular effort together." Clay Shirky explains that collective action is the most difficult of the three types of activities he associates with group work.[21] With the field reps' situation fresh in our minds it is easy to see what he means.

What exactly are the field reps concerned about? We know they are dealing with a strategic reorg and new job descriptions and we also know the problem isn't the content of those new job descriptions. Unpacking these, line by line, activity by activity, and rewriting them, probably won't solve anything. Do they have one problem or many? Apparently, the field reps' problems aren't confined to this group, but have to do with their connections to others–both individuals and groups–they work with. But, which others? Is it management, meaning everyone who is a manager, or is it specific managers? Has the strategic reorg, initiated by management, created a series of interrelated problems for them? Perhaps some of those problems are between them and their managers, others have to do with their clients, and still others with their colleagues in finance, planning, and so on.[22]

You'll notice that the questions have broadened: from *what* the problems are to *where* the problems are. This is a signal that they're dealing with "wicked" problems. Horst Rittel and Melvin Webber invented this term to explain that the problems of urban planning are not technical, or "tame," as they put it. As there is hardly a problem to do with organizing that isn't wicked, their distinction is just as useful here.[23] It has us thinking, again, about the importance of social spaces at work and it brings all the issues of networks—fragmentation, diversity, and relationships—into focus at once, revealing more clearly why boundaries emerge in organizing and why they need special attention.

There are many examples of tame problems to be had, but few that have to do with managing or organizing. I want one to contrast with wicked problems, so I'll settle for a car that won't start. These are some of the considerations that make this problem tame. It is a situation where you are certain you have a problem. The engine is supposed to come to life when you turn the key, but it doesn't. You also know where the problem is. It is in the car. Then, as a limited number of things can go wrong with a machine (it has to be an electrical or mechanical failure, or something similar), you can work your way through the possibilities systematically, until you get to the source. This is how you deal with a tame problem. It is what expert technicians do. Once they isolate the cause, they are normally able to solve the problem, meaning that, after they have replaced a part or changed some settings, the car will start and the problem will no longer exist.[24]

Problems to do with organizing are very different. Suppose you are asked to design a questionnaire (i.e. an "instrument") to be used for employees' annual performance appraisals. This may sound like a fairly technical task and a tame problem, but it isn't. One of the questions you'd no doubt have to ask is what "performance" means. Another is how to assess performance; and a third might be how you measure it. None are easy to answer because each is a matter of interpretation and meaning. People disagree about what to measure, how to measure it, and whether it is being properly measured, which is why performance evaluations are controversial and why designing an instrument is a wicked problem. If everyone involved saw eye to eye on the whats, whys, and hows, we wouldn't have these problems.

The problems take shape in the heat of conversations, so to speak, when people are actually engaged in organizing and are negotiating meaning, and at that point they're already figuring out what to do about them. It is not a case of first seeing the problem then trying to solve it. Jeff Conklin explains that, with wicked problems, problem-setting and problem-solving are one and the same process, because you don't and can't begin to understand the problems until you set out to solve them (and vice versa).[25] It's only when a group, like the field reps, gets together and gets down to the nitty-gritty of talking about what's on their minds, working out what is going on and what to do about it, that the problems start to crystallize. And, while this is happening, they're thinking, too, about how to tackle them. The different parts of the problem being tightly interwoven, it is not clear where one ends and another begins. As it is difficult to separate them, to tackle the problem you have to deal with all of them and they generally don't have solutions in the conventional sense. It's not hard to imagine that the problems surrounding a strategic reorg don't disappear, but drag on and on. Just when you think you have one part resolved, there is a new wrinkle—something you hadn't noticed—or something else turns up to take its place.[26]

These are collective problems

What stands out about problems to do with organizing work—wicked problems—is that they are *collective* problems (and collective solutions), "owned" by the particular set of stakeholders who are actively dealing with them (e.g. field reps, their managers, and perhaps other employees). What they see as problems and solutions, hence the actions they take, depend on how they make meaning, *together*. The problems and solutions, which *both* come out (emerge) in the course of their negotiations, have as much to do with their interests, their attitudes to what is going on, and their relationships with one another, as with data or "objective facts." When they're organizing, questions like whose interests will be served, who has the power either to prevent or permit them doing what they want to do, and whether and how those people are likely to use their power are *at least* as important to the participants in framing their problems as deadlines and financial considerations.

This is not to say organizers can forget about deadlines, budget allocations, and safety regulations. As information to be gathered, assessed, and interpreted, shared and used, these are an essential part of the work of organizing. Though you don't want to lose sight of this sort of information, it's only one type of information and, in terms of what is involved in organizing, other matters are more elusive and more complicated and trickier for an organizer to handle; such as avoiding unclear, overlapping responsibilities or, if it is too late to do that, then dealing with the consequences when the problems surface.

Here is the punchline about the work and problems of organizing. Shaped by relationships, attitudes, and ideals, they exist at the boundaries among people and groups, in the spaces among them (for example, among the field reps, between them and their managers, between them and their colleagues, or between them and their clients).[27] There is a different set of problems at each boundary and, if it is possible to sort out the problems (not all can or will be resolved), it will be because people work on those boundaries, person-by-person or group-by-group, working on relationships, attitudes, and values. Borrowing Ron Heifetz's term, this is what makes the work of organizing "adaptive work" as distinct from "technical work."[28]

In Figure 7.1, I've recycled the picture of people organizing, which I used in Chapter 6, to show them working on their wicked problems. When you are dealing with technical problems, like a car that won't start or a computer that won't boot, you look at the electrical system, the registry, or the hard drive. These tame problems are "out there" in the car or the computer. But wicked ones are in the spaces between them. "Getting organized" means working *on* your connections (not just *with* one

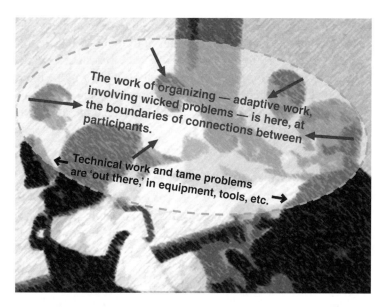

The work of organizing — adaptive work, involving wicked problems — is here, at the boundaries of connections between participants.

Technical work and tame problems are 'out there,' in equipment, tools, etc.

Figure 7.1 Comparing organizing with technical work

another), in your social spaces, at the boundaries of your interpersonal relationships, which hold your conversations.[29]

The work of organizing is messy, not orderly or structured. Organizers live with ambiguity and uncertainty, states of mind that are a "reality" of work life. Problems morph as we work on them and new ones pop up unexpectedly. Work relationships are complex. Our expectations and interests differ from those of the people we work with and while we're organizing we discover their expectations are obstacles to doing things in ways we'd wanted. To prevent our work from stalling, the boundaries have to be crossed in order (a) to get some level of agreement on what to do and (b) to obtain people's commitment to doing it. When it is successful, the adaptive work of organizing orients people in their work so they can agree on what to do (and on when, why, how, and with whom), and that they are committed to doing it. Because the quality of their work depends so much on people cooperating—being open to sharing knowledge, responsive to each other's requests, and committed to working together—I think you can see why I call this work—the work of aligning—the "bottom line" of organizing.[30]

The work of aligning (the "bottom line" of organizing)

Aligning is the process of reaching agreement about what has to be done and how to do it. I say aligning is the bottom line of organizing, because the work of organizing ends with aligning, both literally and figuratively. When people are aligned things happen, while, if they aren't aligned, the possibilities for action are much more limited and it's more likely that things will go wrong: there will be breakdowns. When they're aligned, there is enough common ground for people to cooperate and keep their work moving forward.

What aligning is and isn't

Being aligned is a temporary state of affairs and, quite possibly, a fleeting one. Positions and attitudes shift for all sorts of reasons. Sometimes it is literally just a matter of time before this happens. With the passing of time you see things differently. You acquire knowledge about people or situations that you didn't have earlier, which may be all it takes for you to change your mind.[31] Or, a change of heart may have to do with changing alliances in a group, prompted, perhaps, by someone joining or leaving. There are, of course, no objective criteria to determine whether people are aligned or not. Aligning has to do with the states of mind of those engaged in the collective work of organizing: their feelings about whether they are (or aren't) clear, close, or committed enough to accomplish something together (e.g. to sign a contract, develop a proposal, or handle an instruction from above). Only the parties themselves are able to assess whether they are or aren't ready for this and to decide what to do if they aren't. Will they work at aligning, try to push their way forward anyway, or will they walk away from the situation entirely?

The squaring off that occurred between blacks and whites to bring an end to apartheid in South Africa in the early 1990s is the best illustration of aligning I can think of.[32] Finding common cause among parties with ideologies as divergent as those of, say, the "white" Nationalist Party (NP) and the "black" African National Congress (ANC) was no overnight miracle. It took months of negotiations, including hard bargaining in a variety of situations and, just as important, it required participants to commit themselves to negotiating, to being willing to put their faith in a process when they didn't trust one another.

For clarification, I want to point out that there is a major difference between aligning to do with organizing (i.e. work practices) and a similarly named concept in management. The former is mainly a matter of people agreeing—not necessarily fully—while the latter has to do with fulfilling expectations, meeting requirements, and complying with norms that are all set at the top. A consultant describing the connection between structure and strategy and asking whether they are aligned, or a CEO who wants to see "everyone on board with the mission," isn't looking for alignment in the way I've explained it. At the top, things appear to be under control when people think alike and do what they're told, but appear out of control when they don't. Diversity spells trouble. The way to alignment and control is through a "common culture" and "shared vision." Who is determining the culture and vision? Naturally, it is someone at the top, who knows what is good for the whole organization.

When they're not able to agree on what to do, people get stuck; and if one or two of them act on their own things typically fall apart, so they look for alignment, which simply means that, for the time being, there is enough of a sense of common purpose to take action together or to go along with others. There are few visible signs of alignment.[33] Participants know intuitively whether and when they're aligned. In order to align with one another, team members, clients, and supervisors have get to know what the others' priorities are, what they think and expect, what they're willing to do to take matters forward, and what kind of commitments they're prepared to make. While they are talking—conferring, discussing, and negotiating—they make requests of each other and make commitments to do things. These lead to action. They juggle schedules, arrange meetings, rearrange priorities, shift deadlines, rewrite plans, send off memos, meet with colleagues, organize training sessions, book hotel accommodation, and so on. This is how they move their work along.

Now, let's revisit the nonprofit organization and its reorg, which began when employees, who had been told about management's intentions, received new job descriptions. What followed was dissatisfaction and disappointment all round, but little action; at least not the kind that was expected. Why? No one was aligned. For a reorg to have "teeth," it's not tools you want—directives and plans—but talk (plus tools). A reorg takes shape when it's in everyone's hearts, not a few people's heads. This happens in, or through, their talk. When they engage one another around the issues, problems, and questions they have, eventually you may get people's commitment, then action. In a reorg of the magnitude that was envisaged, there is a lot of aligning to do: both within and between groups, from the admin staff at head office to the field reps in the field and everyone and everywhere in-between, including a number of regional offices, and, of course, between management, the people making the plans, and the ones who are expected to put them to work.

Alignment doesn't mean that everyone has to work with the same sense of purpose or make equal commitments, have the same goals, vision, or values—or reach agreement on every issue—and act in unison. It would be nice to see some of this, but it isn't necessary, and it surely isn't either realistic or sensible to expect it, let alone to try to make it happen. There are at least two reasons why it is unreasonable to expect anything approaching consensus or common purpose among members of a team or project group. One has to do with the variety of circumstances under which people organize (e.g. team members who are new to the job and don't know what their colleagues have been doing, or individuals reporting to bosses who have different agendas). The other is the fact that, in knowledge-work, diversity of skills, capabilities, interests, and points of view is an asset. Differences of opinion and outlook are desirable, even necessary, provided the groups and teams can channel their differences into productive interactions and people can align.

You can see why diversity in networks or teams is both light and shadow to the collective work of organizing. When you think of the benefits that flow from collaboration among people with different capabilities and interests, the light is easy to see. The shadow is where the boundaries lie, which, typically, we overlook. Whether people are working in small or large groups, in pairs, or across groups it is only when there are more bridges between them than barriers that they align and their work gains momentum. Given the mindboggling diversity and movement in networks, sometimes it seems little short of a miracle that stakeholders cooperate at all. Clearly, good relationships and positive attitudes help and, when these are in short supply, which is often the case, in the interests of getting things done satisfactorily participants must be able to coax them out of one another, being willing to hold jointly the kinds of social spaces that make negotiation and aligning possible.

CHAPTER 8

Tools are the empty heart of management or why strategic initiatives fail

Management myopia

If you are looking for the heart of knowledge-work, you will find it in all varieties of talk which make organizing and aligning possible: from calm and open discussion to negotiating, gossiping, bickering, bargaining, haggling, conferring, chatting, and arguing. As management is all tools and no talk, however, our work places have no heart.

The die was cast roughly a century ago. Fredrick Taylor's biographer, Robert Kanigel, explains that early in life he began to believe fervently—to the point of obsession—in "one best way" of doing anything and found his salvation in exhaustive measurements of human effort. His idea for making organizations efficient and more profitable was to formulate, based on time and motion studies, a job description for every conceivable kind of work people did; each a blueprint for the one best way, which included a standard of efficiency in terms of, say, the number of units a worker had to process every day. The standard was "scientific" because it was based on experiments that provided data. Meeting his target, which he needed to do to earn his base pay (the "rate for the job"), would put the worker close to his physical limits, but he would be paid a bonus for anything he produced over and above this.

If Taylor had lived today he would surely have used the clichéd and disingenuous "win–win" when bragging about the impact of his brilliant system, which he was prone to do. He saw it not only as good in every way for workers—physically, morally or spiritually, and financially—but also as the best route a business could take to bigger profits. He had, in his estimation, an almost flawless scheme for advancing society. Yet, in his lifetime, it was obvious his work didn't match his claims and never would. After they were let loose on a plant, for example, executives discovered it took months, even years, for Taylor and his assistants to observe then calculate the "scientific" way of doing only a fraction of the multitude of jobs in a particular plant. On top of this, workers balked at the blatant authoritarianism of Taylor's system. Growing impatient waiting for results that didn't materialize, his clients usually sent him packing after a year or two, during which time he'd made a lot of money for himself but nothing for them. But, while he may have failed to deliver what he promised (his actions, ironically, undermining his exaggerated claims not only for his system but also for science), this didn't seem to deter the many acolytes he collected along the way, including the head of the newly established Harvard Business School. Taylor was so extraordinarily good at marketing himself that he succeeded in getting people to believe that management-by-measurement was the only way to run a business. From his day forward, everyone knew to call a management consultant when they had a problem and to expect an efficiency expert to turn up with "instruments" or "tools" to measure, calculate, and chart some or other aspect of the organization's or workers' performance, before submitting a report on how to solve the problem.[1]

The use of tools remains the essence of management-craft, so, when you learn to manage the MBA way, given any kind of problem, big or small, you know to reach for a tool. You follow these steps; use this template; adopt these best practices; or apply this instrument. Instruments include psychometric tests, like the Myers-Briggs type indicator; "inventories" or "profiles," like "Personal Conflict Style" or "Leadership Style," and "Strength Deployment" inventories and "Success Style" or "Learning Style" profiles. Next you do a follow-up, perhaps by questionnaire, so you have data to tell you how you've done in correcting the problem. Then you can forget about the problem until it pops up again. Listening to management consultants, there isn't an organizational problem that can't be solved this way quite quickly and painlessly, if you overlook the fact that it might cost you an arm and a leg.[2]

The allure and illusion of tools, ranging from strategic plans to mission statements to IT systems and incentive bonuses, is that they make wicked problems appear tame. "Training" and "workshops" are some of the favored ones. Does your workforce consist of people who don't get along? They may be from different countries or cultures. Perhaps there is chafing, tension, and possibly noticeable conflict. Send them to "cross-cultural training" or "diversity training." You can check off the box that says "training completed" and move on. Do you have team members who don't work well together? Put together a two-day team development workshop. Are your senior employees retiring? Purchase this piece of software and you'll be able to capture and distribute the knowledge they have. Do you have a group of employees moving into more senior positions, facing some tough challenges, who will need to deal with complex organizational issues? A smidgen of leadership development is the answer. Is there a "communications problem"? Create a newsletter; or, better still, invite your employees to a "social evening," where you can meet and talk to them over coffee and doughnuts. Saying that these are solutions to the problems is a massive deception, yet we seem quite comfortable with it. Why? Management makes the rules and, if you're wearing management lenses, organizations are machine-like and tools are the way to deal with problems that all seem to be technical when viewed from the top.

Saying knowledge workers are "all talk" isn't a criticism. They get things done, together, by engaging and sharing knowledge. But, when all eyes are on tools, not talk, and a large part of what it takes to do the work of organizing—certainly to do it competently—is out of sight and out of mind, there are bound to be breakdowns. No matter what kind of data or how much of it you have, unless everyone understands what they're doing and is committed to doing it well, data is more or less worthless. Work gets done by interpreting tasks, deciding what to do, and assigning responsibilities. Talk *is* action, and talk is a knowledge worker's most valuable resource. The myopia of management is its failure to see this and to recognize that standard management practices stand in the way of good conversations. You can see that there are problems just by looking at office work spaces. Those rows and rows of cubicles, production lines of knowledge workers designed for "maximum productivity," are arranged so that it is difficult for people working a few feet apart to talk. Through a management lens, it is more acceptable for workers to use an IT tool and to email a colleague who works down the corridor, or even in the next cubicle, than for them to go and talk to him or her. As they're merely "exchanging information," IT tools are more efficient: they keep people at their desks, working instead of chatting.

Work practices that are missing in action

"Tools" and "talk" are my words, but the idea for them comes from Etienne Wenger's views on practices, and no one has written more illuminatingly about practices than Wenger. What are practices? His definition, "the body of knowledge, methods, tools, which [people] share and develop together," is appropriately broad, as it is difficult to think of anything people do that isn't a practice when they do it consciously or deliberately and keep doing it.[3] Clearly, practicing law or medicine qualifies, but so does raising children, cooking food, and even watching sports on TV for those who do it often and conscientiously, with beer and pretzels.

To illustrate the nature of work practices and show what is missing from management, I've adapted a drawing of Wenger's. It is a view from inside work—from practice—of what goes on when people are doing anything work-related. Whether it is a lawyer cross-examining a witness, a doctor examining a patient, a blogger reading the responses of her readers, a sports fan-cum-couch potato, whose family is hassling him about getting more exercise, or a new employee learning the ropes as she works with her colleagues, their practices emerge and evolve in the course of their interactions, when they're negotiating meaning together, as they talk to one another.[4] So, in Figure 8.1, practices are framed by meaning-making. I've added "organizing" which certainly is part—and possibly a large one—of people's practices.

Everyone's practices combine talk and tools.[5] Both are integral to what people do. Completely intertwined, they are interdependent, complementary, and symbiotic.[6] Like *yin* and *yang*, their conversations and the tools that people create or use evolve, together, while they are engaged in doing things together. They interact and talk and, in the course of their conversations, may create tools (such as minutes of their meeting or a PowerPoint presentation) or use ones that are already to hand (like org charts, questionnaires, and software). They'll have more conversations, about the accuracy

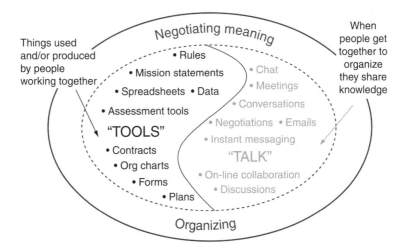

Figure 8.1   Work practices

Source: Adapted from Etienne Wenger, *Communities of Practice: Learning, Meaning and Identity*. p. 63. Used by permission of Cambridge University Press. Copyright © 1998 by Etienne Wenger.

of the minutes they've taken, the impact of the PowerPoint presentation they're developing, or why the org chart needs to be revised. These will lead to new conversations, which involve other people, as well as to the creation or use of more tools; and so on.

Referring, say, to math drills or improving soccer skills, we often use the word "practice" to mean doing something again and again, in order to improve the way we do it, or until we get it absolutely right. But, with knowledge-work, doing good work is more a question of making sure that what we do is satisfactory, which means acceptable to the parties involved, rather than getting it just right. The problems are wicked, so there aren't any right answers, only better or worse solutions; and, there is something unique in every activity. Perhaps it is that you're working with someone new, whom you've not worked with before, or, as you're always learning on the job, your thinking about what is likely to work in these circumstances has changed. As you won't have the opportunity to do exactly the same work again, you have only the one chance to do it well.[7]

Just ensuring that you're doing good work is hard enough. It is quite possible that you'll have to satisfy people with different expectations and requirements (part of the wickedness of organizing is trying to balance different and possibly conflicting interests). Doing good work certainly requires everyone to pay close attention to what they as well as other stakeholders—from colleagues to clients—are saying and to what they're doing. Good work depends on people cooperating and on both talk and tools. This is how it has been through the ages. That is, until the Industrial Revolution, when work practices fell under the influence of high-control management and the idea of efficiency.

You may have noticed that everything in Figure 8.1 is faint and hard to read, except for the piece labeled "tools," which stands out from the rest. This is deliberate. I wanted to show what work looks like through a management lens and, to do so, I grayed out the other parts because, the way management is practiced, getting work done relies heavily—almost exclusively—on tools. The obscured parts mean little and, for all practical purposes, are invisible.

Of course people talk to do their work: they have to. But, standard practice even turns conversations into tools. We all know about briefings, PowerPoint presentations, executive summaries, and formal meetings, where an agenda plus a high-control social space ensures that both speakers and what they have to say are stage-managed. This is *ersatz talk*, a poor substitute for the kind of real talk where people engage one another fully to do the work of organizing together, from making meaning to aligning for action.[8] When you're engaged, you are aware that it isn't just technical stuff you're dealing with, so summaries, agenda items, and bullet points aren't enough. If feelings, relationships, interests, and values aren't on the table and you aren't dealing with them, you aren't getting to what is at the heart of the work of organizing. Then there is no way of aligning for action and, when people aren't aligned, they are just going through the motions. This is when work gets done badly, if at all.[9]

Work that relies on presentations, agendas, and executive summaries, along with spreadsheets, databases, and reporting structures, is two dimensional. Without talk, in which people engage one another around what they mean, think, and feel, there is nothing behind the tools. In this way, tool-oriented practices are a bit like those cardboard cutouts of a film's characters that you sometimes see in the foyer of a movie theatre. They are intended to trick you into thinking that the real characters are standing there. Of course, they don't. Those fakes are easy to spot because they are two dimensional and lifeless. With management tools it's a bit harder. Unless you stop and think about what is missing, you could—as people constantly do—mistake tools for the real thing. But, tools actually keep us from focusing on what really matters: on the ideas, perspectives, attitudes, relationships, and values of the people behind them, using them. I'm going to use Business Process Reengineering (BPR) as a case in point, to explain why.

The genie that turned ugly

BPR became big business for management consultants during the 1990s, even though controversy swirled around it from the beginning.[10] Its champions claim BPR brought great success to some organizations,[11] while equally vocal detractors say that in many cases the impact was little short of disastrous. Tom Davenport is one of the architects of reengineering. In 1995, when this movement wasn't very old, he made a point of expressing his misgivings about the direction it had taken.[12] Lamenting that BPR never realized its potential for improving management processes, he complained, even then, that management viewed BPR very narrowly, using it primarily to justify layoffs (i.e. "downsizing"). "Once out of the bottle," he says, "the reengineering genie quickly turned ugly."[13]

BPR never had a chance to deliver on its promises. It was always destined to become another tool because this is what happens to all ideas once they fall into the hands of executives or consultants with a management mindset.[14] In the early 1990s managements were looking for yet another way to boost their bottom-line performance. The stated goals of business may vary. At times it is "maximizing shareholder value," while at other times it is ensuring that earnings beat the quarterly estimates of Wall Street's pundits.[15] Both objectives tell the same story. A few decades ago corporate management became utterly obsessed with the bottom line, to the point where little else mattered or matters. BPR became the latest in a line of tools for increasing profits, this time by downsizing: replacing people, especially middle managers, with information technologies, in order to slash costs.[16]

BPR at Jet Propulsion Labs

Looking for a study of BPR that I could use to show why strategic initiatives fail, I was fortunate to find an excellent one. In the 1990s, top management at Jet Propulsion Labs in California (JPL) implemented two "change management" initiatives: total quality management (TQM), followed by reengineering (i.e. BPR). In-depth, retrospective accounts of management strategies are rare but, based on a close study of documents and correspondence plus interviews with some of the protagonists in the drama that unfolded at JPL, Peter Westwick has written a detailed and highly illuminating account of what happened there.

It provides just the perspectives I need, because the interviews and his access to memos allow us to go inside work and see the effects of BPR, not from the top, but from and in practice.[17] We get a good sense of the turmoil that accompanied these efforts, the wide gulf between the expectations of senior managers about what each initiative would accomplish (framed by the view from the top) and what actually happened as a result of their efforts (people's practices), and of the ambiguous and contradictory consequences of reengineering. Understanding the reasons for the gulf between expectations and results explains why, inevitably, genies that seem benevolent to "ideas people" turn ugly in the implementation, when translated into management practices.

BPR came to mean many things as consultant writers and managers all jumped onto the bandwagon and, as was certainly true at JPL, people came to different conclusions about these management initiatives, even holding contradictory views about what they meant and what they would accomplish. A successor of sorts to TQM, BPR was supposed to incorporate many of the goals of that movement, including a shift from a hierarchical to a participative organization, where employees or workers "owned" their work (i.e. the processes) and had a voice in how things were done. As far as I know no one used the term "social network," which seems misplaced alongside an expression like "process reengineering," but, if BPR had fulfilled some of its architects' dreams, reengineered organizations might look a lot like highly client-oriented teams in a network. Even in JPL's technical environment there was talk of "enabling" and "nurturing" and an emphasis on satisfying the customer.[18] Sounding like Jeff describing a team's relationship with their client (see pp. 34–5), Ed Stone, JPL's director through the 1990s, used to say "when you do your own job you're actually doing it for somebody else."[19]

Ideas like "participation," "client-centeredness," and "owning the work" (which I take to mean being responsible and accountable for what you do) all have to do with how knowledge workers work together and with their clients, not forgetting their relationships with one another. In other words, these ideas have to do with how they organize their work and how they, themselves, are organized.

Now, as a consultant to JPL seems to have realized, going from hierarchy to participation is a huge leap and would have meant a management-paradigm shift, with the emphasis falling on new organizing practices. (Perhaps this is what Tom Davenport meant by "improving management processes.") But, the managers and consultants responsible for bringing the new ideas to fruition weren't prepared for this sort of paradigm shift: they never are. Both groups are myopic. They don't see organizing, only the organization. So they did with the ideas what their counterparts always do: tried to squeeze them into conventional management practices and make sure they fit. What was the point of reengineering? "Practices" translate into "tools" in management-speak: obviously the point was to use tools—some old ones, like org charts together with some new ones, such as process-maps—to restructure, downsize, and improve bottom-line performance, cutting costs to increase profits. This is when the genie turned ugly.

BPR through a management lens

Imagine yourself as a corporate vice president for strategy. BPR experts have advised that you'll be more efficient and more profitable with less hierarchy. You stare at your org chart, wondering what you can do to "flatten the organization." What options do you have? The top and bottom are accounted for. Top management has to run the show and, at the bottom, workers have to do the work. But, you should almost certainly get rid of the "fat," in the belly of the organization. Those layers of middle management, whose main function is oversight, add to your overheads but don't contribute to the bottom line. If you do this you'll have technology on your side too.

A panoply of IT tools that move information around will allow you, safely, to bypass middle management; or so the IT consultants have told you. As long as you can feed data all the way up, which is what their tools do, you can fire lots of people and, using your "dashboard" to monitor the data, you'll be able keep a close eye on what is happening below. Doesn't having a dashboard tell you that you are in the driving seat? Just like technicians in a power-generating plant, who watch dials and gauges to see that everything is working normally, you'll have the knowledge you need at the top to stay in control. All you need to do now is to reengineer your processes so there is no middle, warning those who are left that unless they "do more with less" they'll go the same way.

What is a process?

BPR experts say you should be paying much more attention to processes, but you haven't heard of "processes" before. What do they mean? It didn't take long for people who were invested in the idea that "practices = tools" to figure out that "processes" meant "process mapping," which meant "flowcharts." Here is Peter Westwick's perspective:[20]

> Reengineering replaced the standard hierarchical organization chart with multiple flowcharts. Flowcharts, of course, were not new to JPL, since systems engineering also relied on them; any historian working on large technical systems in the United States after 1960 will recognize the flowcharts of PERT and similar techniques of computerized systems management. But reengineering raised flowcharting to an art form and new level of abstraction (in addition to its new status as a verb)... These new flowcharts traced the generalized transformation of information and resources as the inputs and outputs of each process.

An important part of the work at JPL is spacecraft design. It is highly innovative and extraordinarily creative work, and the Labs is, without doubt, a knowledge organization. Yet, with process reengineering as the goal, consultants and managers took this imaginative and ingenious knowledge-work, which benefits from tough peer reviews of new designs, to be something resembling factory-work and treated it this way. They erroneously equated the interpersonal connections, in which people negotiate meaning together to share knowledge and come up with new ideas—the "magic of organizing" to use Jeff's expression—with physical production of the type where activity A is followed by B which is followed by C in predetermined sequence, as inputs are mechanically transformed into outputs. Why did they make the mistake of substituting flowcharts for social networking and process maps for the talk that comprises the work of organizing? The answer is a management paradigm that can't see beyond tools. The view from the top doesn't and cannot differentiate between process-maps and social interaction, which is in a different universe. So, *ideas for organizing*, which at heart are what BPR was all about, were rendered sterile as all energy was turned toward creating tools to improve the organization and the bottom line.

Lay down those tools

Unpacking the failures of reengineering is like holding up a mirror and seeing all management practices reflected in it. Reengineering qualifies as a "reorg"; management-speak for "reorganization." Reorgs come in all shapes and sizes: from efforts to reengineer the whole organization, like BPR; to introducing a new technology, like an Enterprise Resource Planning system that is going to require substantial changes in the way people work; or, remembering an earlier case, redefining jobs to get better results and secure more funding.

Spokespersons announcing corporate reorgs, which usually involve lay-offs, say these are both necessary and desirable to "strengthen the bottom line" or to "build a secure foundation for future growth." Seldom do the business media either question these premises or report in detail on the results of reorgs, but they do add platitudes like "new management, showing that it means business, is aggressively cutting costs." Is there a conspiracy of silence surrounding reengineering and other types of reorg? Why do the experts—consultants—not say how difficult it is to "manage change," how small the chances of success are when management tries to move the organization in a particular direction, or what internal turmoil is likely to result and how people's lives, including their work lives, are going to be affected as a result of trying? The fact is that management myopia is a serious, widespread malady and the tool-oriented mindset behind strategic initiatives that fail isn't limited to corporate businesses.

A Department of Homeland Security

The congressional committee which investigated the attacks on the World Trade Center and the Pentagon that took place in September 2001 found that security and intelligence organizations (of which there are a great many in the USA) had not acted as they said they could and should have done to prevent them, because they were not adequately sharing the information they had. They weren't doing this either within each organization or between one organization and the next.

Intelligence professionals have to share knowledge when organizing because intelligence work is knowledge-work and sharing information is integral to it. For example someone, uncovering what looks like a security breech, might say, "I'd better inform my supervisor and talk to my counterpart at central division to find out what they know about it." If you believe they aren't doing a good job in sharing knowledge, the way to reveal where the problems are is to look at how people organize—at whether, why, and how they share knowledge and at what knowledge they do and don't share—then try to do something about it.

Every one of those US intelligence organizations was and, a decade later, still is, highly hierarchical, bureaucratic, and secretive, and it is widely known and well accepted that both hierarchy or bureaucracy are notoriously bad ways of organizing to share knowledge, especially when combined. Hierarchy is useful when you want to control people, for example soldiers during a military campaign, but giving orders isn't the same as sharing information, because it doesn't allow people to make meaning together, which is obviously crucial to intelligence gathering. Bureaucracy is useful when the work is mechanical, in the sense that it involves doing the same thing over and over again, such as processing applications for drivers' licenses. But this doesn't describe either intelligence-work or knowledge-work in general. Then, factor in the question of secrecy and of course there are major issues when it comes to sharing knowledge.

What did Congress do about this? In order to come up with ideas for reorganizing intelligence with the object of sharing knowledge, you have to know—to see and understand—intelligence work *in practice*. Congressional committee members don't have the right lens for this. So, adopting view-from-the-top thinking, they turned to experts, who looked to tools, particularly the org chart, for "improving communications and organizational efficiency." Intending to make information flow through the system more efficiently, they focused on redesigning the overall reporting structure, while tinkering with the chain of command.

It is almost beyond belief that the experts who recommended creating a Department of Homeland Security (DHS) as a way of making the United States more secure could have thought it sensible to combine more than 30 separate, mostly very large, competing, bureaucratic, and hierarchical organizations into a single mammoth one and have employees cooperate and share knowledge.[21] Although, officially, the jury is still out on whether this reorg will work, you don't have to know a lot about the situation to realize that creating the DHS was bad, not to say expensive, policy. The only reason for doing it, that I can think of, is congress was desperate to show they were in control and would quickly do something to improve the security situation. And the only way for them to do this was to find a tool—the org chart—that made the wicked problems of national security seem tame.

Redesigning processes or structures isn't the real work

In every reorg I know of, management says "let there be change" and thinks "if we have a plan, redraw an org chart, and design a process chart there *is* change: we're making it happen." It is all tools, tools, tools for as far as they can see. Once they get started, they depend on more tools: new job descriptions; Meyers-Briggs Type Indicator [MBTI] workshops to help new teams function; and technology, such as knowledge portals, to connect people with the information they need to do their jobs. Tools do have a role in change initiatives but you can create new job descriptions or draw and redraw org charts, process maps, or flowcharts until you are blue in the face and still not move an initiative along, because tools don't *do* the work of organizing and guiding people to new practices. If practices don't change, reorgs go nowhere and the tools end up as wallpaper (process charts) or bookends (strategic plans).

For a reorg to produce movement, the initiative has to "move" from process charts or strategic plans (what is on walls and in documents) into everyone's (not just top management's) conversations, discussions, negotiations and practices. There has to be talk to complement the tools and there has to be *lots* of talk. Practices begin in conversations, in the space between people, as they talk about what they're doing, why, how, and so on. If their conversations continue for long enough they'll stay focused on what they're doing and why they're doing it and eventually the practices will be in their hearts and minds and they'll be doing their work differently.

Going from a chart or a plan or a spreadsheet (someone's ideas about how things ought to work) to action (practices) is what the work of organizing is all about. It is where the work of aligning comes in and it is adaptive work. Ron Heifetz describes adaptive work as "the learning required to address conflicts in the values people hold, or to diminish the gap between the values people stand for and the reality they face . . . It . . .

requires a change in values, beliefs, or behavior." Add "relationships" and you have a neat summary of why the work of organizing is seldom straightforward.[22]

The work of *re*organizing

At the best of times the work of organizing can be a tricky, complicated business, and more so with reorganizations. A reorg layers on uncertainty and ambiguity. Somewhere, someone has decided to change the system and the rules. A formal announcement preceded an all-hands meeting, which was followed by a flurry of emails from the top asking for "patience and cooperation in what will be a trying time for everyone." But, what exactly does "trying time" mean? Formal communications don't and can't prepare people for what is ahead and for what they should do; but they can and do spur their imaginations. As most reorgs result in people being fired, one of the main concerns will be, 'Am I going to lose my job?'

Then, suddenly, changes are taking place in different areas, there is an enormous amount of reorganizing to do. As usual, no one has the blueprint for how to do it, and it's difficult to fathom out what is going on.[23] "Creativity" is now about figuring out situations that don't make much sense and making up what you do as you go. That's what people are doing. They're trying to find out more about what is going on. They're also lobbying for their ideas, forming alliances, staking their claims to positions and roles in the unfolding organizational drama, learning to break old habits, finding and adopting new practices, and so on. Of course, they have different ideas about what is sensible, what to take seriously and what to ignore, who is or ought to be responsible for doing what, and where they can get the most leverage for themselves or their units.

The wicked problems start to emerge when people are actually "in action," making meaning, and doing something—and it's a case of different groups with different problems. "What is expected of *me* in this process? What are *we* expected to do? What am *I* going to get out of it? Are *we* willing or able to do what is expected? What is it going to take? Is it worth the effort? Am *I* up for this? Are *we* up for this?" Everyone is looking for answers but their problems and questions vary depending on who they are, where they are, and what they do, and I've used the sample questions to emphasize there is both an 'I' and a 'we' in what is going on. There is a personal element to change, which involves people's identities, interests, and values and, because the work of organizing is social (collective work), there is an interpersonal element as well. *Re*organizing means new commitments and involves new responsibilities, all of which requires people to *re*align.

With a reorg the executives closest to planning and implementing the initiative are seldom on the same page and if they aren't you can imagine what happens down in the bowels of the organization, where people get fragments of information and disjointed instructions from the top. Speculation and rumors are rife. Disjuncture is normal in work life but, now, employees are dividing into camps based on their affiliations, their interests in what is happening, or their expectations about what will happen and how they ought to position themselves for the future. Should they seek new allies or send out their résumés? Their convictions about what ought to be happening also play a role (e.g. that matters are moving too fast, too slowly, or in the wrong direction), as does the extent of their commitment to the "old ways" of doing things. The more committed they are, the more likely they are to drag their heels and resist change. Finally, consider the consequences of the rounds of layoffs in the course of downsizing and you begin to appreciate why reorgs undermine confidence and why they are often accompanied by cynicism—"no one seems to know what they are doing" (which is probably true)—and an overall mood of resignation—"this, too, will pass eventually. In the meantime I'll sit back and watch."

When management expects movement in one direction or another and doesn't see it, a typical response is to try a tool or two: team-building workshops; departmental off-sites; even a new mission statement. When you're up to your neck in wicked problems, it is appealing to think (and to be told) that another tool will get you out of the mess. (Of course, if we weren't beguiled by tools, we might be more careful about what we get into in the first place.) At any rate, practical movement happens only if and when people realign, so they are working together and organizing their work differently, because they are thinking differently about their work, Real movement is in the organizing and, first and foremost, has to do with talk (i.e. conversations) and with relationships, attitudes, and values; not as the management handbook has it, with charts and directives.

This is how Michael Schrage describes the heart of work:

> The real basic structure of the workplace is the *relationship*. Each relationship is itself part of a larger network of relationships. The fact is that work gets done through these relationships. As Bell and Flores put it, "The ingredients of work are . . . the *questions and commitments and possibilities* that bring things forth."[24]

The Achilles heel of restructuring, reengineering, and, indeed, all strategic initiatives is that, under "old" management, work is without its heart—talk and organizing. Until and unless these become the centerpieces of change up and down the organization, strategic initiatives are largely exercises in futility that are simply disorganizing. But, now we know what is missing and why it matters, we can turn attention to practical questions to do with new practices. What does a heart transplant look like? How do we restore the missing parts?

CHAPTER 9

Practices that break the mold with agility and care

Agile methods and knowledge work

By looking for practices that are good for knowledge-work, which break the stranglehold of management on how to organize work, we can learn a lot from a mini-revolution in software development known as "agile methods." To explain what the revolution is about, the Agile Alliance's Manifesto is a good place to begin.[1]

Manifesto for Agile Software Development

We are uncovering better ways of developing software by doing it and helping others do it. Through this work we have come to value:

Individuals and interactions *over* processes and tools
Working software *over* comprehensive documentation
Customer collaboration *over* contract negotiation
Responding to change *over* following a plan

That is, while there is value in the items on the right, we value the items on the left more.

The crux of this compact declaration of principles, values, and aims is a series of comparisons intended to set agile practitioners apart from programmers who follow a standard approach, known as the "waterfall method" ("waterfall" for short), where requirements, contracts, and plans matter most. "Not so," say agile advocates, "person-to-person interactions, your ability to respond to change, and collaboration with your customer matter more. When you are 'in' the work of developing software, *talk* is more important than *tools*."

If this has a familiar ring to it, this is because you've seen the substance of the Manifesto before—in this book. Jeff reasons in his journal that differences in the outlooks of project teams and management, similar to the two positions outlined in the Manifesto, are responsible for breakdowns at work. It is also hard to overlook the implication that these positions echo my distinction between right-brain organizing (agile programming) and left-brain management (the waterfall method). All this is more than coincidence. Our views intersect because agile advocates have seen the fact, probably without really being aware of it, that knowledge-work and management don't mix.

In the sparest possible language (the Manifesto falls just a tad short of haiku) they are stating what works and what doesn't work for producing good software. In singling out processes, documentation, and so on as less valuable than individuals and interactions, they're talking about the limitations not only of the waterfall method but also of management practices in general, as the two are closely allied. Both are products of the same you-must-follow-rules-at-all-costs mindset. And, as producing software is knowledge-work through and through, for the reasons that management is wrong for knowledge-work ("dysfunctional" is the word I've used), waterfall is wrong for developers. It has programmers focusing on the wrong things: on processes and tools rather than on individuals and interactions; on contract negotiation rather than customer collaboration; and so on.

Because writing software is a complex, collaborative, creative process, it is necessary for developers, as it is for any knowledge workers, to spend time organizing—to share knowledge while they figure out, together, what their clients want, how to build it in lines of code, and whether they're doing it right; not just once, but throughout a project. Yet, just as management is blind to what knowledge workers do to organize, waterfall isn't attuned to an aspect of programming that is vital for producing good software. It wasn't designed for developing software on the fly while they organize themselves. Agile programmers have been devising practices that give them better results, and I've been observing breakdowns in organizations and looking for causes. Each asking "What is wrong with the way we work?" we have come at the issues from different directions, but with similar intentions, and have arrived at the same conclusion. By steering them away from the waterfall method, agile programming lets programmers unburden themselves, avoiding much of the wrong-headed thinking with which management shackles knowledge workers.

Problems with the waterfall method

There are certainly multiple criteria for assessing the quality of software, ranging from aesthetics—economy of design—to ease of use; but for agile programmers one consideration stands out above all the others. A good result means building "working software" that does what the client wants and does it well.[2] (Isn't this essentially what we all want from our work?) As the waterfall method exemplifies linear thinking and a command-and-control mentality, it is too rigid and restrictive and, more often than not, they end up either with something that doesn't work or doesn't work as well as it should.

Waterfall (see Figure 9.1) is based on twin assumptions congruent with conventional management thinking. Every project needs an overarching structure, in the form of a comprehensive plan, and building software is a sequential process which begins with listing all the requirements and proceeds through various separate stages including design and implementation, with verification right at the end.[3] The premise is that once the requirements are identified (depending on the scope of the project, this may take some time and eventually run to binders full of documentation) and the development team goes to work, getting from problem to solution, where you have a complete and working product, ought to be plain sailing, not all that different from transforming materials while they move along a production line. Because knowledge-work is seldom straightforward, however, progress generally isn't linear. More often than not development

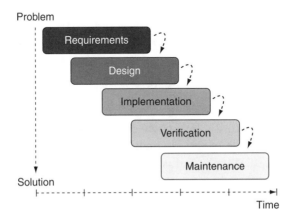

Figure 9.1 The waterfall model

Source: Adapted from a diagram by Paul Hoadley. Used with his permission.

is an iterative process with lots of twists and turns and some inevitable looping back along the way.

Laying out all your requirements at the start, so you know what you have to do and can see the way ahead, might seem like a good idea, but it isn't practical and ends up being something of a sham. Like purchasing all the materials for building a house before you've designed it, a lot of resources—time, effort, and money—are wasted in the process. With software there is no practical alternative to designing (and redesigning) as you build. To see why, take the case of a business that has grown into a diversified conglomerate by acquiring other companies. There are now seven major divisions, each with their own, independent system for maintaining personnel records. Corporate HR, frustrated by the lack of a centralized system for handling personnel data, wants one that will make the same information available across the whole company at all times. With the board's approval, they hire an IT vendor specializing in large-scale, customized systems integration projects.

A project like this probably has requirements in the hundreds or even the thousands, and the problem, when you approach it from the standpoint of a documentation-driven process and have to list requirements, is that many are neither known nor knowable at the start. Designers rely on their clients to tell them what to build but, when they start, their clients rarely know what they want. You can imagine, too, that, with several divisions of the client organization wanting something different, they may not be able to agree on requirements. When interests diverge, defining requirements is a series of wicked problems. This is how Con Kenney sees the situation:

> Customers don't know what they want (until they see it), and developers can't read their minds . . . The problem is customers and developers inhabit different worlds. Sure, we speak the same language, work for the same organizations [referring to "internal" customers], and get paid in the same currency. But don't let these similarities fool you; developers and their customers come from different, and often conflicting, cultures . . . The other problem is that the way customers define the purpose of the IT application is in totally different terms from the way developers define the application itself. The words sound the same, but they do not mean the same things.[4]

Developers know that requirements which are easy to identify and seem straightforward at the start of a project may turn out to be neither, because people change their minds. As their assignment runs its course they may find that they can't build exactly what their client wants, either because it is just too complicated or because it will take too long to do and make the software unwieldy. Another common phenomenon is that, once they see what they are getting, clients ask for a different feature here and a new capability there. So, while software development might look linear and sequential from the top, to developers, building it is an open-ended process. With the scope and anticipated result in a perpetually fluid state you can't frame the project as a set of self-contained elements that allow you to break it into well defined pieces, which is why a highly structured approach favored by management and reinforced by the waterfall method produces poor results. The mindset at the top is that everything ought to function like clockwork, but in the trenches work is untidy—messy. Getting things done often means finding ways of muddling through, so developers need flexibility. They need to be agile. The upshot is exactly the kind of "tension" between management and project teams that Jeff describes.

Agile methods offer a way out of this impasse, with a far-reaching, even radical solution to building good software: break with the management mindset and adopt new practices. What kinds of practices? Agile encourages software developers and their clients to self-organize as they work together.[5] The result, they say, is that they are often able to do things more quickly and, in the end, they find they have software that is better at meeting customers' needs, which is what this work—indeed any work—is all about.

While waterfall completely ignores the fact that developing software is a creative, complex, evolutionary process, surrounded by uncertainty, agile methods recognize that both developers and clients will go down the wrong paths at times—including some that reach a dead-end (although they probably won't recognize this until much later)—and that they will change their minds, meaning that parts of the software they're working on will have to be rewritten. As all this is inherent in the nature of the work (it isn't caused by incompetence), agile methods formalize the kinds of informal work practices that people adopt when they are dealing with ambiguity, uncertain about what to do or what will happen next. When you know you are going to have to revise your plans often, but are never sure how, flexibility is the key. Acknowledging that experimentation, learning-by-doing (through trial and error), adapting, and rewriting are necessary, agile methods encourage developers to create and to hold—among themselves and with their clients—the kinds of social spaces that give them room to organize, learn, adapt, change, and reorganize: so they can align and realign as needed to produce software that works and that people want to use.

"Scrum": an agile method

One of the agile methods, which evolved from efforts to manage cross-functional teams, is "scrum," a word borrowed from rugby. It is both a noun and a verb. A scrum forms when players bind together (i.e. interlock) to take possession of the ball and gain some ground.[6] If you know the game, you might think it superfluous to apply the word "agile" to a pack of beefy forwards who scrum by pushing together against strong opposition. The name is an indication of the intention of agile practices, especially the attention paid to collective action, which is concentrated in short bursts of activity.

Scrumming, like software development, is a combination of individual initiative and collective action, and the scrums that form spontaneously are the mainstay of every game. Once called "loose scrums," but now referred to as "mauls" or "breakdowns," these don't have a set form (and from the names you can tell there isn't much civility in rugby). Though both *ad hoc* and fluid, these cooperative arrangements are structures that provide an effective way of consolidating a movement with the intention of taking play forward and gaining ground. When the player with the ball is tackled and brought to the ground, instantly assessing what others on their own team and the opposing one are doing, in the heat of the moment the players who are close to the action have to decide whether to join the breakdown—jump in—or take up a position behind it, getting ready for whatever follows.[7] What is more, although each side wants an advantage from a breakdown, players from both sides must willingly join in in order for it to form and fulfill its function. So, wherever there is a breakdown, players from both teams are in it for the same reason, aligned around what they're doing.

As a software development process, the essence of scrum is that the participants, including both developers and their clients, plan, self-organize, and build together.[8] Developers collaborate with each other and cooperate with their clients throughout the project, so they spend a good deal of time interacting and talking to one another—sharing knowledge. Instead of trying to create a comprehensive blueprint for the long term, which would quickly become redundant, developers craft the software in a series of "sprints." During a sprint, which lasts for only a few weeks at most, they create and test a piece of the whole and, throughout, they have daily meetings, called "scrums" or "stand-ups," possibly scheduled for as little as 15 minutes, when they discuss what they've done or haven't been able to do.[9] Giving advice on a loose agenda for these meetings, Linda Rising suggests that you "ask these three questions":[10]

1. Relative to the Backlog (list of incomplete tasks), what have you completed since the last meeting?
2. What obstacles got in the way of your completing this work?
3. Relative to the Backlog, what specific things do you plan to accomplish between now and the next meeting?

Stand-ups are invaluable, not simply because this is an opportunity for participants to share knowledge, but especially because, as these questions suggest, this is where they make commitments to each other and are accountable for meeting them. Participants talk frankly about what has happened since they last met (probably yesterday), discuss the problems they've encountered, and update the list of tasks they think they can complete during the current sprint. If they decide to alter the goals for that sprint, which they could do at any time, they know that, after no more than a few weeks work at most, they should have a piece of software ready for testing, and for the rest of the sprint they'll be holding one another to this commitment. Then, if the results are promising, they'll move on, defining then working to complete the next set of requirements. If they've run into problems and need to do more work to finish what they've started, they'll work together on revising their schedules.

There is an odd pretense behind both traditional, plan-driven ways of developing software and management practices in general that people should and do turn up to work (programmers as well as their clients), fully prepared for any eventuality, knowing exactly what they want and what to do, when, and how. If this was just an unrealistic assumption we might ignore it, but it is so much more. From the point of view of doing good work, it is both an absurd and dangerous position which entirely ignores what we might call "the human factor" that is overwhelmingly important in knowledge-work.

Some people are vague, ambiguous, indecisive, and uncertain, not to say vain, ambitious, egoistical, and power-hungry. They are also creative, think imaginatively, learn, take risks, push boundaries, experiment, and, sometimes, fail. Some of these qualities are essential to doing good work but, as all are part of the reality of work life, knowledge workers need practices that foster the essential ones and help people to deal with the more problematic ones. They need practices that both encourage and support people's efforts to align, so they can work together to get good results, even when they aren't sure what to do and in spite of obstacles and boundaries between them. What does it take to thrive and to do genuinely good, human-centered work in a human world of individuals who have failings, foibles, and doubts, a world of social relationships that range from strong to awkward to awful? The answer is flexibility *plus* a sense of responsibility, accountability, and commitment—*it takes care.*

Caring about work

The strength of agile methods is that, as the name suggests, they allow developers to organize and reorganize like rugby players do, without a master game-plan. You can't do this if you are shackled to a set of requirements, or committed to following unwaveringly a plan or a set of instructions, or to meeting an immovable deadline. But it takes much more than flexibility to do good development (i.e. knowledge-) work. Closing the meeting at which the Agile Alliance formed, Bob Martin commented that agile methods were also about "promoting organizational models based on people, collaboration, and building the types of organizational communities in which we want to work." Writing for the Alliance, Jim Highsmith adds his belief that:[11]

> at the core... Agile Methodologists are really about "mushy" stuff about delivering good products to customers by operating in an environment that does more than talk about "people as our most important asset" but actually "acts" as if people were the most important, and lose the word "asset." So in the final analysis, the meteoric rise of interest in and sometimes tremendous criticism of Agile Methodologies is about the mushy stuff of values and culture.

Notice that agile methodologists, as Highsmith calls them, aren't primarily after tighter standards of programming or additional technical requirements. The "soft" stuff they're talking about and want to see more of is human qualities, like collaboration and ways of organizing that value people, the capacity to self-organize, and the ability to deliver good products. It is unfashionable, even unacceptable, in management-dominated work places to put these kinds of issues at the top of a work-practices agenda. Why do they want these? The answer, I believe, is simply that these matter to them: each one *cares about what they do, how they do it, and how others do it.*

I think of care as the secret ingredient of agile practices, in fact of all efforts to do good work; "secret" because no one seems to have hit on the idea that this is what leads programmers to agile practices and away from conventional ones. They want to do good work. They know this takes collaboration and commitment and they're willing to do something about it (i.e. to take responsibility), adopting practices that make good work possible.

When managers complain that employees "aren't willing to take responsibility" or that they "don't show enough commitment"—both are common refrains—they're quite right. What they don't appreciate, however, is that, as managers, they are the custodians of the very practices (including traditional, stick-to-a-script-no-matter-what-is-happening ways of programming) that are to blame. An ethos of high-control infantilizes people.[12] When you are surrounded by regulations you must obey, are required to follow rules, and your work is dictated by a list of requirements you fulfill by rote, checking them off as you go, there is a loud and clear message that "you are not responsible." If anyone is responsible, it is the person in charge, above you, who has authority over you, who sets the rules and/or sees that you stick to them. As a drone, working your way through a list of requirements that someone else has drawn up, or following someone else's plan, without the ability to influence what gets done and how it gets done, you aren't supposed to care. And why would you?[13]

The thrust of management practices is that work is about efficiency, which is very different from caring. In fact, efficiency and care are in parallel universes and couldn't be further apart. One is a technical matter; the other is human-social, and relational. From Taylorism onwards, the organization and control of work has been a pseudo-scientific, technical, or "mechanicalist" discipline; supposedly objective and rational. Organizations are like machines and people are the cogs in those machines.[14] No matter how deep anyone digs below the surface of management practices, they won't find care. Put on your manager's hat, to do things the MBA way, and you shy away from feelings, relationships, and values at work; in fact, from anything human and social. Focusing on efficiency and the bottom line, you put tools first. Management is care-*less* and our work-places are essentially closed to care.[15]

It isn't that people are incapable of care. They work under rules which tell them *not* to care. This won't do for knowledge-work; one reason being that it is collective work and care is the metaphorical "glue" in social relationships. Care leads people to make and keep commitments—and to being responsible for what they do, accountable to one another, and willing to hold each other to account, carefully, for what gets done and what doesn't. If you want agility, meaning the ability to get things done without heavy-handed rules and the need for compliance, it is essential that people are aligned with each other about what to do, why, and how. Responsibility, commitment, and accountability are vital ingredients in ensuring things get done, and you get these when and because people care about what they're doing and care about one another.

Nursing practice: the work of caring

Nursing is a profession of care. Medical practice, like management and for similar reasons, is not. And "managed care" (which is an oxymoron and misnomer), which is used as a synonym for medical practice today, explains why the nursing profession finds itself in a dilemma. Much like programmers, saddled with work practices that are ill-suited to the kind of work they do, they struggle to be good nurses and to do good nursing.[16]

For a long time, there has been friction between nurses and physicians, the "medical establishment," ostensibly over the legitimacy of care against objective science. In fact, as the parties themselves know well, the situation is more complicated and has to do with power as well as practices, with differences in outlook and values and, ultimately, with ways of being. In this regard it mirrors the tension between software project teams and management. Health-care practice by way of medical school training is analogous to organizing by way of MBA programs. Doctors, who have a monopoly on terms like "medical practice" and "medical practitioner," are trained in empirical science (note the similarity between "physician" and "physics") which, in today's world of high-tech medicine and high-pressure marketing by big pharmaceutical companies, means they put machines and medication ahead of the relationship-and-talk-based care that is a foundation of nursing programs.

Although this is a caricature, think of doctors as patriarchal, treating their patients with detachment, as experts who know what's best for them, because they *are* the experts and are "in charge." Nurses, who do their work by establishing relationships with patients, getting to know the "whole person," listening to their stories and gauging their feelings, in addition to assessing their physical conditions, are matriarchal. From an empiricist's standpoint their caring *is* the problem. Medical practice based on data from tests, scans, and other forms of measurement is superior precisely because it relies on "objective facts" and nursing is a second-rate profession: in the words of Patricia Benner, who is a nurse, it is a "cultural embarrassment," because it isn't science.

While the legitimacy of nursing practice as caring practice has been up against empirical science for some time, more recently it has come under siege in the "health care industry" for different reasons. It isn't compatible with bottom-line efficiency. That name, especially the word "industry," says unequivocally that under the control of bottom-line focused "health management organizations" (HMOs)—in this industry the oxymorons just keep coming—management practices rule in hospitals, clinics, and even doctors' waiting rooms. One example is that doctors can't bill for their time unless they are doing something—a "procedure"—that has a billing number. As there are no numbers for counseling, doctors who counsel their patients, talking to them not just about their medical symptoms but, as human beings, about their lives and life-styles, do so on their own (i.e. unpaid) time. HMO's billing practices are another example of tools over talk, which characterizes the whole of this "industry." Officially there is no value in counseling, whether to new mothers on immunizing children or to the elderly on diet and exercise, even though this is almost certainly good preventative practice, which probably reduces the level and costs of medical services later on.[17]

Ted Taptiklis, introducing the ideas of Patricia Benner, whose seminal work on practice centers on her profession and on caring, is careful to distinguish between a common view of caring—associated with "symbols of sentimentality like hearts, flowers, and puppy-dogs" (and giving money to charity)—and one associated with nursing, which Benner brings to light: "a relationship in the 'here and now' in which both mind and body are invested, entailing direct personal engagement . . . a matter of action rather than inclination." "This kind of caring," he says, "is essentially *practical and not sentimental*."[18]

While care is a value and a moral stance—an orientation of people toward each other, to the things they're doing, and to the world itself— the care people show in practice is essential to both social well-being and doing good work.[19] We know instinctively that care plays a role in sharing knowledge. We share knowledge easily with friends, lovers and close confidants: people we care about. Care brings people together, bridging boundaries or narrowing the social distance between them. They're able to talk about all sorts of matters which people who don't care for one another can't or won't talk about, so knowledge becomes "leaky" and moves around more easily. There is no mystery, then, why Georg Von Krog and co-authors, responding to perennial questions from top managers about how to get employees to share their knowledge, advocate care in the work place, claiming that there are four dimensions of care—"mutual trust," "active empathy," "access to help," and "lenience in judgment"—which "enable knowledge creation."[20]

Bringing back care

Whether care is more than these four dimensions and whether it is even possible or desirable to reduce care to specific dimensions is largely beside the point. Good knowledge-work depends on care in organizing and there is no care in management. We need to find a way to put it there, or, perhaps, bring it back with new practices.

I say "bring it back," because care and caring is a fundamental human quality and, in the time before factories and management, when people knew who they were working for, when work was based on relationships rather than contracts and transactions, and work and organizing were indistinguishable and fully integrated into daily life, it is entirely likely that there was care in organizing (or not, depending on circumstances). When it was there it was reinforced by people's sense of responsibility and accountability to the people around them, including those they worked for and worked with.[21]

Going to work in factories and working for eight- or twelve-hour shifts, divided life into "work life" and "home life," with management principles and practices reinforcing the split. Workers, who behaved one way at home, were required to conform to a different "work ethic" on the job.[22] As contractual labor, their commitment was to fulfilling the terms of their contract, not serving their customers.[23] Work became a transaction: so many hours of labor for so much money per hour. There were rules and regulations they had to obey. When you turn over responsibility to supervisors and you, yourself, are no longer responsible, what is there to care about and what is left of care? Listing some of the factors that have contributed to a lack or loss of care helps to know where to look and what to do to bring care to work. Although it might be what's needed, activists, who want to change the way they and their colleagues work, won't be able to change societal norms and possibly aren't interested in doing so. So, the realistic questions include: What does a caring work place look like? Is it practical to organize with care? And, how do you do it?

In search of low-control organizing practices: community, care, cooperation, and commitment

The catch-22 of new practices

Standard management practices and procedures aren't any good for organizing knowledge-work, so we're in search of ones that are. The work of organizing revolves around people making up their minds and aligning: making plans, establishing priorities, agreeing on schedules, and so on. It is often tough to get some consensus on what to do, when, and how, but having done this, they'll change their minds, revise their plans, adjust their priorities, or rearrange their calendars. Work practices that not only allow but also encourage people to respond and adapt to changing circumstances are preferable to fixed procedures, commitments to long-term goals, and rigid schedules that quickly become obsolete. When they constantly have to adapt, it is best for people to organize themselves.

Besides adaptability, getting things done takes a fair amount of cohesion and, as anyone who has worked with groups knows, members typically have different priorities, schedules, interests, and commitments. How do you self-organize, keeping everyone together—aligned—connected, focused on the same outcomes, and intent on getting good results, but prepared to accommodate each other's differences when necessary; recognizing that, often, two (or more) heads are better than one, so differences in outlook and approach are not only inevitable but also desirable?

Alternatives to control and compliance

If you learn to manage the MBA way, it can't be done. Viewed from the top, there is an irreconcilable contradiction between flexibility, or agility, and cohesion. As you must come down firmly on one side or the other, the answer to which is the right side is clear: the one that involves rules, structures, and systems; the side with "control." Having everything under control and running smoothly—like clockwork—is what's important, and compliance creates cohesion. If you have to reign in flexibility and trade off adaptability for the certainty that comes with having control, it's a small price to pay. You start with structures, plans, schedules, and deliverables, specifying what people must do, when, and how. Then, you overlay this with compliance-oriented practices: performance criteria people must meet, ways of measuring performance, and systems and procedures for generating data, so that whoever is in charge knows what is going on and can take appropriate action. Next, add a dash of supervision: to see that workers follow procedures; to monitor data; and to report, upwards, on performance. Finally, you cap the entire apparatus with rewards and penalties, ranging from bonuses to pink slips, to "motivate and incentivize" people to do efficiently what they are required to do.

The general principles as well as many of the practices that define high-control management today go all the way back to Fredrick Taylor. Acknowledging that his ideas fitted more comfortably into an age of machine-dominated industrial production and social circles mesmerized by anything claiming to be science, I still can't explain his conviction that, for the sake of efficiency, profits, and, ultimately, "social progress," managers could and should treat workers, in Matthew Stewart's words, as "mute, brainless bundles of animal muscles . . . subject to minute control from above."[1] Yet Taylor's ideas received an enthusiastic reception in many quarters and, by the time people began to express reservations, which they did, it was already too late. Nurtured by a rapidly growing band of apostles, who, eventually, would turn into the management consulting profession, the practices took on a life of their own and have proved incredibly durable. So far they've resisted the arrival of post-industrial society and all talk about "new science" and "work–life balance."[2]

The practical consequences of Taylor's model are twofold. People who follow orders, locked into what their superiors tell them to do, focused on rules, requirements, and long-term plans, don't pay attention to what is actually going on. They don't need to and aren't expected to. In fact, it is just the opposite. If your goal is machine-like compliance, you want them compliant, not thinking and acting on what they see and hear. If they're doing what they are expected to do, which is to get with the plan, follow the schedule, and deliver on time and on budget, they ought to be functioning—well—on automatic pilot, like machines.

Then, they don't care. It is not that they *can't* care or don't want to care. High-control environments are *care-less* and when there is no reason for people to care about what they do there are breakdowns. There is also no way to "make them care" without restoring their humanity. They will care, act responsibly, and be accountable for what they do when they *are* responsible: when they have authority.

If you aren't happy with the status quo—trading off responsibility and flexibility for control and compliance—then people ought to organize themselves. But, for a lot of managers, the fundamental dilemma would be how to get cohesion. Where does it come from? They believe that without the structures that make compliance possible you're on a slippery slope. It is this belief and, for those at the top, who have power, the additional fear that they will lose it, that are the two main reasons why senior managers won't seriously contemplate knowledge workers organizing themselves.

Executives are usually willing to go part of the way. For example, they'll consider decentralizing decision-making as long as it only involves moving a bit of authority down the hierarchy and changing structures or processes, like taking out layers of the org chart to "flatten" an organization, or altering spans of control. In my experience, however, if a conversation about organizational change moves vaguely toward self-management or self-organizing, they are no longer interested. In fact, they seem to regard the idea as utterly absurd (you get the impression that planning a cab ride to the bottom of the ocean would be less of a waste of their time) and, if there are any questions before you abruptly drop the subject, the one that usually comes up is, "Who will be in charge?"

"Who is going to be in charge?" is the catch-22 for anyone seriously interested in organizing practices that chart the territory beyond management, and it's a difficult question to circumvent because it means the most to "leaders" at the top with the power to support or thwart change. Rigid structures aren't compatible with knowledge-work, which thrives on flexibility and adaptability. But, for many, not just senior managers and administrators, running an organization successfully (i.e. "efficiently") depends on having a small number of people in charge, to do the "planning, coordinating, and controlling," according to one familiar definition of management. "In charge" means "supported by robust structures plus systems of compliance," and for "robust" you can substitute "rigid."

Are we doomed to run knowledge organizations badly, in ways that aren't good for either knowledge workers or their work, that are counter to reason and good judgment, because of what people fear will happen without high-control structures? As far as cohesion is concerned, is there no alternative to compliance? The answer to the first question ought to be "no" and to the second one "definitely no." There are alternatives, but it is difficult is to get anyone to consider them, let alone to contemplate putting them into practice.

Communities of practice

To open the subject of alternatives for discussion I'm going to turn to a topic that has generated considerable interest in recent years: communities of practice, or "CoP" for short. In the hands of Jean Lave and Etienne Wenger, who introduced the idea in a study on apprenticeship and learning-in-action, or through practice, CoP weren't primarily about management or organizations. The authors were interested in the learning trajectories of workers who learn on the job and how they "move" from "peripheral participants," at the edge of the work, to being at the center of it.[3] But, especially after Wenger began writing more extensively about CoP, people took to the idea as something that management, always on the lookout for ways of improving performance, ought to pay attention to.[4]

With the help of management consultants, CoP fell into the laps of executives at the right time, as they struggled to manage knowledge workers using standard management practices, not knowing why they were struggling or what they were struggling with. They wanted high performance from work teams, believing this was desirable and having been told it was possible, but it always seemed an elusive goal.[5] And, with "knowledge management" becoming a buzzword, many organizations where committed to some or other large-scale enterprise resource planning initiative, which promised to make data available wherever it was needed across an organization. But getting people to "communicate and share knowledge" was another matter entirely.[6] CoP seemed like an answer to everyone's prayers.

Few groups actually qualify as CoP. Those that do meet three conditions: their members are actively engaged in the same kinds of practices; they are working together to accomplish something and have a mutual interest in the work and their results; and they have a shared repertoire of routines, symbols, stories, and actions.[7] Usually on the advice of consultants, who sold them as a solution to the perennial problems of team work (and a fast-track solution at that), many organizations began experimenting with CoP, expecting to find them everywhere, or to create them, in spite of Wenger's clear and fairly narrow definition of who qualified. To encourage employees to set up CoP, or something similar but with a different name, organizations continue to provide collaborative technologies, like SharePoint sites, and, via their budgets, to allocate real money as inducements.[8]

Like business process reengineering and for essentially the same reasons I wrote about in Chapter 8, unfortunately, CoP have become another oversold management tool. Frankly, without more fundamental changes in the way organizations are run, the potential for CoP to emerge and change the way people work is limited. But this doesn't diminish the importance of the concept or the practical insights into what makes for good organizing and when, why, and how people self-organize, which come from studying CoP in practice.

There are now a number of instructive, documented examples of CoP that formed spontaneously and lasted. Covering a range of professions and practices, from flute makers to insurance claims clerks to technicians who service office equipment, the studies show the communities as living, breathing, practical examples of people organizing without control or compliance, doing it well and doing good work *because* they organize themselves.[9] While they work inside the usual organizational structures, they do a lot of their work without these, finding ways to skirt them when necessary, inventing their own practices and procedures simply because this is how they do their work best. Echoing Jeff's views about project teams, the studies consistently highlight that members take pride in and are conscientious about doing their work well.

To highlight what they reveal, I'll use Julian Orr's excellent, fine-grained study of an "occupational community" of field service technicians, who repair photocopiers. As they are technicians, you'd probably assume they spend most of their time with their heads inside machines doing the technical work of repairing them. But, as knowledge-workers, much of their work qualifies as organizing. They spend a lot of time in conversation with one another, their customers or clients, or their managers, making meaning, together, of what they are doing, should be doing, or the problems they're having and how to deal with them: generally, "talking about machines," which is how Orr's book got its title. As members' conversations are windows onto their work, including their relationships, interests, attitudes, and motives, the data in studies like Orr's comes from researchers' observations of members at work and from listening to their conversations and the stories they tell in conversation.

Talk, in which members negotiate meaning together as they share knowledge, is the life-blood of their practices and a good deal of it can only be described as storytelling; and, as technicians become more proficient by swapping stories, their storytelling is vital to their work. For example, when one has a machine that continues to make poor quality copies despite numerous visits to the same customer to fix it, another will tell of his experience with a similar model where the usual fixes didn't work and how, eventually, he solved the puzzle. Copiers are complex, quirky, and unpredictable and, quite apart from whether people *do* learn from manuals, there is only a certain amount you *can* learn from a manual which assumes, wrongly, that machines are alike and that electro-mechanical problems can be diagnosed simply by following directions.

Even though the problems are tame, in the sense that they *are* technical and, potentially, can be solved by isolating the fault, without a group of like-minded people, who have similar qualifications and interests, to bounce ideas around, technicians' work would be much harder and take longer. And, whether it is flute makers, who pass their work back and forth, using their eyes as well as hands to tell whether they've got it just right, or technicians, round a table in a diner talking, unpacking their problems with a recalcitrant machine, the things they work with are always in their conversations. The relationship between talk and tools in identifying and solving problems, hence in their getting work done, is unmistakable.

Talk, among members, is always "business mixed with personal touches." This is because their work is social and relational and the line between what is "work" and "personal" is always blurred.[10] Out on the road, early in the morning, technicians are having breakfast together and talking about their work: about problems with machines, about their schedules, and so on. Conversation "flows freely from technical detail ... to people they used to know through the corporation ... The nominally personal and nominally professional cannot be separated ... and may be substantially indistinguishable in their experience."[11] In their talk they make assessments of one another's capabilities that shape their colleagues' social identities and reputations, joking about a technician, known for not making mistakes, who now has others at a client's premises working to solve problems he created.

It may come as something of a revelation that the technicians, "focused on the work, not the organization," are largely disconnected from the corporation for which they work and do their work with little thought for what is happening there. They spend most of their time on the road between customers, or on customers' premises, out of sight and earshot of the organization and they don't have a work space there to call their own. But, the point is that, while they are without constant oversight and reminders about their mission, this doesn't prevent them from doing a good job. Members of this CoP generally do their jobs very well and a lot of their talk has to do with the quality of their work and how they can improve it, though not in so many words.

What is the secret?

We're back, once again, at considerations of control, compliance, and self-organization. Members of this CoP manage themselves. Yes, they do have targets to meet, but in many ways these are irrelevant. Working mostly without direct oversight, their motivation comes from the CoP, from the members themselves who encourage and assist one another in doing good work. Conventional wisdom has it that, if you want efficiency, employees must be bound up in a common culture, believe in a common mission, and share a common vision, and that it's management's responsibility to set these up and weld everything together. Orr says of field service technicians that they "shar[e] few cultural values with the corporation; technicians from all over the country are much more alike than a technician and a salesperson from the same district," adding that "the only valued status [among them] is that of full member of the community, this is being considered a competent technician. In pursuit of this goal, they share information, assist each other's diagnoses, and compete in terms of their relative expertise."[12] Apart from what this says about conventional wisdom, it reveals something about the technicians' secret to success.

Each one probably doesn't come to work with any more, or less, motivation, enthusiasm for their work, or interest in doing it well, than you or I. But, what the technicians have going for them, which many people in high control organizations don't have, is a community of practice, which Wenger defines, simply, as a "group of people who share a concern or a passion for something they do and learn how to do it better as they interact regularly."[13] Orr's field service technicians don't have their own work place, but, as a CoP, they do have a rather special *social space*: one that they create and hold together because they're a CoP, which is different from the spaces associated with hierarchy and superior–subordinate relationships that are common at work. The secret to their success is community and it's the social space they make for themselves as a community that contributes to their commitment to their work and their effectiveness in doing it.[14]

Caring relationships make the difference

What makes their space different is the combination of elements you find in a CoP, including a shared repertoire of practices and genuine, mutual interest in one another's work; in what they do, how they do it, and what they accomplish. What is most important is that CoP spring from *caring relationships*. You can tell from how they engage and talk to one another and from what they talk about that the members care both for each other and for their work.

When there is rivalry it is friendly rivalry. They set up contests to find ways of solving problems or of reducing mistakes. When they rebuke one another it's a gentle rebuke and if they criticize one another it isn't to show up a rival but to guide or teach. There are recognized experts as well as novices in the group, but there are neither big egos nor slow learners and there isn't any aggressive competition. They're not only good to one another but also, together, are good at what they do. They'll walk one another through ways of solving problems and dealing with difficult customers and, when things are quiet, they will make courtesy calls on important customers: all this without a set of directives or regular briefings from management about what to do, when, and how.

For people who believe that compliance is the only reliable way to get things done properly, the way CoP work is too good to be true—but that is a cynical position. Most of us have little to no experience of an alternative. When you have, you know what is possible and it doesn't take a full-blown CoP for people to organize together well. As I've said before, it requires caring relationships and a sense that "we're in this together, jointly responsible for what happens."

Caring relationships enable "an open process of communication and responsiveness," which I'll refer to, simply, as "openness."[15] Openness, together with their personal pride in doing good work (various authors, including Wenger and Orr, explain that individuals' identities are linked to their work), is vital for cooperation. Add to this the sense that they're participants in a joint enterprise, which is reinforced when they engage each other as *peers* every time they make meaning together about their work. With these factors in play, members want to align and, as they talk together, they make and get commitments and establish accountability. The upshot is that, as a group, they are intent on doing good work (this is in their commitments) and, because they each feel accountable to one another and are willing to hold one another to account, they keep each other's attention on their work.

The spirit of *ubuntu*

Of course, communities of practice aren't perfect. At one extreme it is possible that their joint enterprise is morally offensive. There is nothing to say that crime syndicates or drug cartels can't be CoP, although, because of members' attitudes and behavior, not least their competitiveness and lack of care, not to say their disregard for the lives of anyone they consider opponents, these are unlikely to be good examples. Under more conducive circumstances, where participants have much in common and are willing to cooperate with one another, breakdowns still happen. Perhaps someone feels her team has let her down. In another situation, someone else's stubbornness is to blame. When personal animosities that have simmered for a while eventually boil over, everyone treads lightly until things settle down or somebody steps in and tries to patch up relationships.

With or without the occasional bad press, CoP help us to answer important questions about organizing, in particular illuminating the kinds of circumstances in which people are good at self-organizing. You may know Ubuntu as a brand name for a version of the open-source operating system, Linux.[16] It's a name that suits software produced by a large network of mainly voluntary programmers and which is freely distributed, because the word is an abbreviation of a very old expression that, to the indigenous people of southern Africa, expresses their communitarian philosophy of life. To understand why members of CoP are good at self-organizing, it helps to understand the spirit of *ubuntu*.[17]

Ubuntu stands for a human and humanist way of life. Words like care, accountability, responsibility, friendship, consideration, charity, and love (or domination, carelessness, and heartlessness) all describe human qualities that are expressed in interpersonal relationships. One meaning of *ubuntu* is that we are human (and distinct amongst all species) because we live our lives showing charity, making commitments, caring for, and being accountable to, one another. A life without relationships is a less-than-human life. In Xhosa, the expression from which *ubuntu* comes is "*ubuntu ungamntu ngabanye abantu.*"[18] It says that people achieve their humanity through other people. So, *ubuntu* is also the idea that we fulfill our human potential through our relationships, in cooperating to do things together; and that, together, we know more and are much more capable than we are alone.

From this perspective, organizing, which has to do with the fact that we are social beings and live our lives with others, epitomizes human values, human relationships, and human capabilities. We organize to be of service to one another: to help or to care for others or to provide something—food, fun, money, jobs—for someone, a group, or even a whole community. When we organize we do so out of consideration, a sense of commitment or responsibility, or in order to please them. Members of CoP may or may not embrace these sentiments but, whether they intend it or not, if their practices reflect these values, which they usually do, you are going to find the commitment and responsibility to each other and to their work that makes for good organizing.

The kinds of practices that support good knowledge-work—engaging, networking, cooperating, sharing knowledge, aligning for action—come down to attitudes, values, relationships, and the social spaces that people hold collectively. It's important, too, that they are adaptable, are willing to embrace uncertainty, are forgiving of genuine mistakes, and are open to listening to and learning from one another and to relearning. I think you'll agree that the values and relationships associated with the spirit of *ubuntu* are very different from those associated with conventional management practices. Although we might like to believe that these are universal human values, they aren't values that management practices encourage and reward. In some cases the differences are quite blatant. Cut-throat competition ("aggressive" is the preferred word in management-speak) is the antithesis of cooperation and collaboration. In general, though, community and care, with consideration, commitment, and cooperation, is a universe apart from hierarchy and competition, both of which are self-centered.[19]

Crossing boundaries

It is clear, now, why abandoning compliance-oriented practices in favor of ones that support knowledge-work and good organizing isn't a technical matter and certainly isn't about tools. It takes a shift in values, to openness and showing care, both for the people we work with and for the things we do. This, in turn, is contingent on *being responsible*—having responsibility, both individually and jointly—for the things we do, knowing that the work we're doing is *our* work and that we can do what we want to do on our own (joint) authority.

If you're an activist, if you like the sound of new practices and think you are willing to take on the kinds of responsibilities that go with them, there are at least three obstacles to actually making this shift. One is simply the difficulty of kicking old habits. The values we know, like being efficient, being task oriented, being an expert (having the answers), and being in charge are values we believe in and respect (otherwise they would not be our values). Giving them up, which is what a shift in values means, is hard, but that is what it takes to get into new practices.

Another obstacle has to do with the politics of new practices. Knowledge-work—organizing—doesn't respect job titles, departments, or other formal boundaries. To do it well, you may have to network with all sorts of people up and down your organization and organize across organizational boundaries. But, working in organizations that combine hierarchy with bureaucracy, most of us have limited authority, so any time we wish to step outside our narrow spheres we are supposed to get permission. Negotiating with superiors to be allowed to assume additional responsibilities is an unwieldy and unsatisfactory process for a variety reasons: one being that you are asking someone else if you can take on and take away some of his or her authority. This kind of request will not endear you to your boss.

A third obstacle is perhaps the most obvious one: how do I—we—make this shift. We understand we should be doing things differently, but how do we get from "here"—conventional management practices—to "there"— practices characterized by openness and care, which enable people to self-organize and align for productive action? And what is "there"? How do we know if we've made the shift successfully? What does work look like on the other, organizing side of management? I can address the first and last of these, kicking old habits and how we get to new practices, at the same time. This is what I'm going to do next. Afterwards, I'll get to the politics of changing practices and getting permission when I discuss how we can take on the work of organizing. They are especially wicked issues.

CHAPTER 11

Taking on the work of organizing

Closing the divide between work and organizing

The industrial-age management practice that casts the longest shadow over knowledge-work is the division of responsibilities between managers or administrators—authorized to organize work and responsible for setting goals, making plans, drawing up schedules, creating rules, and so on—and workers, who are not. Fredrick Taylor, who portrayed workers as dull-witted and competent only to take and follow the most basic instructions, had a hand in shaping the division.[1] Yet it is difficult to imagine that his particular brand of misanthropy would have amounted to much were it not for circumstances (factory systems designed to make humans function like robots) and the fact that his prejudices tapped currents of intellectual life, meshing with attitudes (like patriarchy, hierarchy, bureaucracy) and ideologies (individualism, colonialism, and scientism) in favor at the time. Other factors contributed to the division too. An us-versus-them mentality had support from economists, who still claim that competition promotes efficiency, but are silent about the importance of cooperation.[2] Then there were the armories managed by graduates of the West Point Military Academy using military-command-like structures. These were among the first mass production operations in the USA and, as the management practices spread to other kinds of factories, every org chart replicated their basic "chain-of-command" structure and the implicit division between officers and enlisted men.[3]

A vestige of a defunct ideology and an indication of how industrial practices persist in today's organizations, the traditional division of authority and power is an anachronism that blights the work of public-sector employees as much as private-sector work teams and nonprofit project groups, amongst other things, encouraging the attitude that workers, like little children, should do as they're told, not think and be seen, not heard. It needs to be eliminated.

Knowledge-work is everything factory-work isn't. Collective and collaborative, the work itself is creative, improvisational, open-ended, emergent, uncertain, and fluid. It is done through social networks, or connections built on interpersonal relationships, which have many of these characteristics too (if you recall Jeff's metaphors of lightning and clouds forming, we ought to think of networks as social spaces filled with energy and in a state of perpetual movement). Beneath that movement, "inside," people are feeling their way, together, toward agreements and decisions on what to do, when, why, how, and with whom. The process, which I've called aligning, is intensely social (not a semi-technical procedure like getting customers through the checkout line as quickly as possible), which means allowing for discovery and accommodating slippage. It is when they engage, talk, and make meaning together that participants discover that their egos, beliefs, or something else entirely is a barrier or perhaps a bridge to aligning, and this is when they realize the depths and limits of their relationships. This is also when they learn about the extent of one another's commitment to and interest in the work they're doing and uncover wicked problems. Sometimes, to negotiate their way through these and reach agreement, they have to reframe their tasks or goals, or perhaps start all over again.

What is a sensible way to organize in these circumstances and what contribution can activists make to promoting practices that bring together work and the authority to organize it? It is sensible to follow the example of software developers who've adopted agile methods. When organizing work is so much a part of doing it, it is both necessary and practical to organize *while* you do it. The people doing the work must be the ones to organize it. It is much less useful to have a comprehensive plan of action, an expert to consult, or someone with a title or position who can open doors, than to have hands-on know-how (the kind that comes with being intimately involved in the work) and people who are ready and willing to work with one another to frame the tasks (and reframe them as needed) and get things done together—who are committed to aligning for action.[4]

Where to begin

Conditions for aligned action include open social relations that foster cooperation and care and encourage commitment and accountability.

Where does an activist, who is serious about establishing a good environment for knowledge work, begin? We know, now, not to begin with tools. Terms like "decentralization," "participative management," and "the devolution of authority" have been tossed around in management circles for decades. Each sounds like something you could do to close the management/worker divide, but, because of shallow thinking and limited commitment, all that has happened is old management practices got a superficial make-over. If you look carefully you might see a new org chart and perhaps an embedded matrix structure, but you won't be able to tell the difference between organizations that are "decentralized" and those that are not.[5] They continue to function as they did because decentralization is supposed to be about new organizing practices; and practices change only when people have a change of heart, decide they want to do things differently, and take action. Tools, alone, won't do it. It takes new talk: not just new words or new language but new conversations. New practices are possible when people can make new meaning of their lives and work, which opens the door to new actions.[6]

My shorthand for replacing management with practices that are good for knowledge workers and knowledge work is to say we are going "beyond management." Whatever we call this work—"reorganizing," or even "unmanaging"—we're contemplating enormous changes in work practices, so, surely, the way into the new practices has to be spectacular.[7] The idea that the work of unmanaging starts with talk, or new conversations, is probably not what you were expecting and, far from spectacular, it seems altogether mundane. "Where are the pyrotechnics?" "Is 'new conversations' all he can offer?" My response is never to underestimate the power of language and conversation, either to keep us doing what we've been doing all along, or to change the way we think, see, and act.

Like being on a trapeze

To explain why new conversations are the way into new practices and what this means, I want to begin by illustrating the predicament of activists and other knowledge workers. From running organizations the MBA way, relying on tools and number-crunching, to taking on the work of organizing, is like crossing from left-brain "old management" into right-brain organizing (see Chapter 5). You can't walk the infinite distance between parallel universes. You have to leap (possibly at warp speed), which brings to mind performers on a flying trapeze (Figure 11.1).

Figure 11.1 Letting go!
Drawn by Ioana Belcea. Used with her permission.

Letting go while catching on

When you are on one trapeze and want to get to another, you must let go. There is a moment, as you let go and before your partner catches you, when you are on your own, flying, free. It may be the illusion of flying, but it thrills the crowd below, and if you don't catch on more or less simultaneously you're probably going to be in deep trouble. Getting from management to organizing is a bit like this.

You *must* let go of high-control management to take on low-control organizing. These are different paradigms and, like trapezes, paradigms won't let you hold steady in the middle, between them. Each is a different way of being. In each, you think, speak, and act differently. You can't help it. This is the nature of worldviews. Each has us constructing our world—being, seeing, speaking, and acting—differently.

If you're into left-brained management you strive for efficiency through technical-mechanical precision and have a complementary language of measures, benchmarks, results, and so on. Atoms and cells might satisfy the requirements of mechanical exactness, but human life won't; certainly not social life as we understand it. So, feelings, emotions, ideals, or relationships don't fit the management universe and, as they don't have a place, you're not interested in them. The same goes for the language people use to talk about them: a language of "meanings," "commitments," "responsibilities," and "good," "bad," or "indifferent" work. Because managing is neither exact nor a science but has to do with people, hence ideals and relationships, people do try to wedge this kind of language into management, which is why there are terms like "value propositions" and "accountability" in management-speak. But, as we're aware, the language doesn't really belong and people don't know what to make of it, which is why it is difficult to get traction around notions like responsibility, commitment, and accountability. As expressions of relationships, attitudes, values, and ideals, these ideas, like "joy," "frustration," and "good" or "bad" work, belong with right-brained organizing, which is deeply human, full of life, and includes collective action tied to people's attitudes to work and their feelings for and relationships with one another.

Knowledge workers in a management-dominated culture really know what it is like being stuck in the middle, between management and organizing. It is unsatisfactory and uncomfortable: not a place to be if you look for meaning, satisfaction, and collegiality in your work. Discouraged from sharing knowledge, they are expected to do things that, they are well aware, don't make sense; and they have limited scope for exercising judgment and making decisions. While organizing demands responsibility, high-control practices say: "You aren't responsible and must defer to people above you, even though they don't have your first-hand experience."

There is no play-book for knowledge-work, but you are supposed to do things by the book. Complying with someone else's rules, regulations, or requirements means you can't be creative or resourceful when you're in the middle.[8] Because it is what management wants, you pay attention: to structures, not relationships; to tools, not talk; to people above you, not your clients or customers; to the organization, not your work—not to organizing. And, though you are aware of the importance of relationships, attitudes, and feelings at work, you can't do much about these (for example, getting commitments from colleagues or holding one another to account), because your authority has been usurped by people higher up the chain of command. The problem is they don't know what goes on below, and they use compliance in place of accountability. Like everyone else, you're not to rely on your (human) capacity to act with responsibility, but must stick to rules, meet targets, fit in with other people's requirements, all of which stand in the way of your doing a decent job of work.

Relationships and accountability

It takes a combination of desire or will, reason, and aptitude to accomplish most of what we humans do. These don't just come from "inside." Our relationships make us whole beings, nurturing heart, mind, and body. This is the spirit of *ubuntu*. Our desire, as well as our will, aptitude, and even mental facilities, shaped by relationships, are forged and honed through partnerships whenever we collaborate. Like trapeze artists, without partners knowledge workers would fly into a void.

As a trapeze performer it's quite easy to see the need for collaboration. You practice not only to sharpen your own skills but also to teach and learn from one another. You have to learn to think and act as one to make a performance seem effortless and reduce the chances of mistakes. So, getting to know one another's rhythms, reactions, and responses, observing and coaching, making suggestions and giving advice, you encourage each other to try different moves and explore new realms of physicality, all the while learning to adapt and respond to your partner's distinctive requirements and limitations.

There are equivalent reasons why knowledge workers ought to get to know and learn from each other. Problems turn wicked because project participants' interests, perceptions, and priorities diverge; and, the chances are, you're working with people you've never worked with before on something you've not done before. There is very little data to be had, anywhere, to help you make meaning of your circumstances or to guide you through tricky questions. Your work has the feeling of being tentative, experimental, creative, and somewhat risky in nature. Your job is to improvise and, while feeling your way, as much as they rely on your instincts, imagination, and intuition, you want to count on your partners—collaborators—to help you "find answers." Partnership—collaboration—is your safety net.

Using this analogy, officially you don't have a safety net at work.[9] The management mindset doesn't recognize or value partnership. Competition, not collaboration, makes organizations efficient, by greasing the wheels of the machine. "Aggressive" competition is expected and people are "rewarded" for this. In the management universe you either swim alone or sink. Individuals are answerable for work that, in theory ought to be, and, in practice, is a collective (i.e. group) effort. The result is that individuals feel isolated and adrift. Apart, perhaps, from a few close colleagues and/or friends, is there anyone you can really turn to?

When you are improvising, divergent or even contrary points of view are often valuable, so the fact that you are working with people who don't always see things your way isn't necessarily bad, but it complicates the work of organizing. There is so much more to collaborating than finding, joining, and working with people who think like you and act like you. To settle differences of opinion and find a way to bridge contradictory values you may need to ask probing, sometimes deeply personal questions. Is this a sensible view? Can we trust them? What does she want out of this?

Even when people are inclined to help one another, aligning for action takes negotiation and compromise. How much more important it is, then, to be willing to negotiate and to reach compromises when you are working with people who, your intuition or experience tells you, aren't on your side to begin with.

What are the prospects for negotiating when you have hierarchy and, in a bureaucracy, what are the prospects of comprise? In the interests of good work—good organizing—you want people to hear one another out and you want flexible working arrangements. How many bosses listen to their subordinates? How easy is it to bend or just ignore the rules if this is what it takes to get agreement? Is it ethical to bend rules, even if there's general agreement that they aren't doing anyone any good? Looking for a practical alternative to control-with-compliance, trapeze artists, again, provide an analogy. When they're in motion, there is no top or bottom, or the top becomes the bottom and vice versa in short order. The practical alternative to high control is to have people make commitments and be accountable to one another, which means taking superior–subordinate relationships, bureaucracy (employees are in separate boxes, with distinct roles, as the org chart shows only too clearly), and competition ("I have to prove I'm better than you") out of the picture. Only when they are able to organize and work as peers, do you open the door to partnership, with people accountable for their commitments.

Talking the talk

One-half of taking organizations beyond management is letting go of a high-control mindset and helping others do the same. The other half is "catching on" to a new one, of working collaboratively, accountable to whoever you work with. There is no practical way to do both, going from managing to organizing, from competition to collaboration, from charts and requirements to questions and commitments, and from compliance to reciprocal accountability, than to begin by changing the language of work: to let go of management-speak and "find" a new language. Both, as I'll explain, are difficult to do.

What keeps us compartmentalized, with work and workers in one box and managing and management in another, is the managerial culture at work. And what keeps this mindset alive is that, collectively, we believe in it and act accordingly. We believe in it because, whether we're conscious of this or not, it is our way of seeing or thinking about work. And it's our way of seeing/thinking about work because when we talk about what we're doing and make meaning of our work we use management-speak. Whether we like it or not, management-speak is the dominant language and it is the official language, in the sense that if you want to get on in your organization, or if you want support for your plans, you talk this talk. People used to be "personnel," then they became "human resources" and, now, even more distressing and dehumanizing, they are "human capital" or "knowledge assets." At work, you dare not talk to others about how they're doing unless it's in the context of a "staff performance and development review," described by organizations as "part of their ongoing dialogue between managers and their employees . . . designed to be a flexible tool for facilitating communication." And no one should do anything unless it is an established "best practice," a "technique, method, process, activity, incentive, or reward that is believed to be more effective at delivering a particular outcome than any other technique, method, process, etc. when applied to a particular condition or circumstance ."[10] With so many "best practices," you're entitled to wonder whether there is still be room for "continuous improvement."

Social constructionism, a major current in contemporary, postmodern thought, explains that our conversations are parts of stories—constructed narratives—that "hold" our worldviews; that we come to see the world as we speak about it; and that we act in ways that match our speaking-and-seeing. In other words, talk has incredible power to shape attitudes, beliefs, values and relationships and, of course, action. In this sense, talk *is* action. As I explained earlier, talk isn't just words. It involves making meaning with others, or, more accurately, negotiating meaning. The meanings we make together shape what we do together. Amongst other considerations, their talk influences how people get along with one another and work together and has a bearing on what courses of action they consider feasible and acceptable and how they prioritize tasks, shaping what they are willing to do, how they do it, as well as who does it, when, and where.[11]

If you tell the story of work one way—for example, that work is about efficiency, goals, rewards, and profits, which is what business books say—then when people "get it," they'll act accordingly, setting up systems to measure efficiency, requiring employees to set "stretch goals," and so on. Now, it is *their* story, their way of seeing the world, and their guide to action. If you tell the story another way—saying work is a manifestation of the human spirit and is about accomplishing things for ourselves and serving others—then those who are drawn to this version make it *their* own and believe in it, they will see and do things differently or will try to do so. As they've embraced different values, they will probably handle their work relationships differently too.

There is irony and a wonderful symmetry, as well as synchronicity, in changing the way we work through conversation. The irony is we say goodbye to the utterly misguided notion—a big part of the ideology of management—that talk is a poor substitute for work. The symmetry has to do with the fact that knowledge-work—sharing knowledge while building relationships to organize and align—is in talk. Using talk to take on the work of organizing is to adopt precisely the kinds of practices that are good for organizing and for knowledge-work. It makes perfect sense, too, that talk contributes to transforming high-control management into low-control, participative ways of working, or that, by speaking together (a most human and social phenomenon) and organizing themselves (a quintessentially human and social act), people become responsible, collectively, for organizing work. This is synchronicity. Through talk, the quest for participative work practices becomes a grass-roots movement, with everyone, everywhere, responsible for encouraging new organizing conversations, creating and holding spaces for those conversations, and fashioning organizing practices to take them beyond management.

Cultivating a new narrative is tough

New language opens the possibility of new conversations, or stories, that allow for new meanings that make possible new ways of seeing and doing things and of enabling new actions. When new language is in the air it is as if people have given one another permission to do things differently. But new language doesn't lead to new practices unless they take the ideas to heart and, in large measure, whether they do or not depends on whether the ideas dovetail with people's circumstances and experience. If the ideas and their circumstances are congruent, some are likely to be receptive to them and act on them. Think about "texting," "tweeting," and "Googling." Many factors have contributed to making these technologies commonplace in a very short time. Among them is the large number of technically savvy youngsters who are enthusiastic about technology, are keen to adopt the latest fads, and can afford to do so; plus developments, such as low-cost mass storage, faster transmission rates, and more bandwidth, which have made sharing content like music and videos practical. These set the scene (most weren't in place until quite recently). Undoubtedly, however, it was getting word out, in conversations, which provided the impetus for people to adopt new practices. Here, "conversations" cover word of mouth, for example among kids at school, plus saturation media coverage, as well as many invitations to "text me," and people advising friends or colleagues who've asked for information to "Google it."[12]

Where and what is the story that is going to help cultivate the language, narratives, and work practices that, in the fullness of time, will replace management-speak, the story management books tell, and management practices? The story of organizing in this book isn't new. It is the story of people getting things done. Although it has been around for a long time, for a few generations we lost its essence in the shadow of management. In the hands of activists, the object is to spread it around, giving it life at work by making it everyone's story of work. To catch a new story, which means taking it to heart and being willing to do something with it, you have to let go of what you already know and, like a trapeze artist deciding whether it's worth crossing over, this is where the new story has to make sense. Part of what helps is being able to see what's new, or different, why and how this is useful to you, and why you don't want to stay where you are, hanging on to the old one, doing things the way you've always done them.

In the hope that it guides knowledge workers toward new practices, I've tried to cover all these issues: telling a story of work that includes both the "old" management narrative and a "new" one, about organizing; explaining why old, here, means obsolete. Going "inside" to find out what knowledge workers do, I've come up with the bones of a narrative about how to organize work in ways that help knowledge workers to do what they do. One's vantage point makes all the difference. Work seen from the top seems perfunctory and dull, like an instruction manual. Viewed from practice, it is meaningful and profoundly social. Seeing the kinds of problems knowledge workers deal with and how they deal with them reveals why knowledge workers have to organize themselves and what values (such as care and accountability) and practices (negotiating boundaries and aligning) enable them to do good work. The story of organizing is deeply human throughout, about narratives (conversations), meaning, relationships, and social spaces.

Chauncey Bell and Fernando Flores remind us that, while they are plugging away at an agenda, arranging a meeting, discussing their plans, or analyzing a budget, people are making requests and commitments, questioning motives, assessing options, asking for permission, and accounting for what they've been doing, while quarreling, joking, coaxing, flattering, and persuading. It's their questions, requests, commitments, and promises that are the substance of work (not the meetings or agendas or plans). The "ingredients of work," Bell and Flores say, "are not ... bodies and tools . . . but the questions and commitments and possibilities that bring things forth."[13] New conversations about work will make talk, to "bring things forth," the heart of the matter, which is why good social spaces are so important to knowledge workers, and everyone should have their minds on what they are doing to "bring things forth."

New language for new conversations

In spite of what I've said about symmetry, synchronicity, and synergy— nice sounding words—if you suspect there is a catch to changing the way we work through new conversations, you are quite right. It is a double whammy. People don't and won't readily let go of the narratives they know. These are part of their paradigm, and everything they know and do, from their identities to their bank balances, is connected via this worldview. As I've explained, changing conversations means changing worldviews. It's also difficult to engage people in new conversations at work and have the conversations stick, because organizations aren't good spaces for new conversations. The mindset that talk is unproductive makes organizations anything but conversation friendly. When they aren't flatly discouraged, conversations aren't high on a management-approved agenda of things people should do more of at work. A bigger obstacle, however, is the tried-and-tested repertoire of "official" work talk. Changing conversations means, somehow, getting past management-speak, and this is tough: like making yourself heard over the deafening noise of a jet taking off or of 80,000 spectators all blowing vuvuzelas at a World Cup game.[14]

Walking a tightrope

Think of ideas as seeds. A group turns ideas into action by talking about them and taking them to heart. But it is a long way from ideas, through talk, to action. When they are new ideas it's often a challenge to have the seeds germinate. If people don't hold onto them because they can't make sense of the ideas or don't like them, nothing changes. Because the discourse of management is so dominant, many believe the MBA way to be the whole truth and nothing but the truth, so they have difficulty hearing anything else. The further ideas are from what they know and believe to be right, the stranger they sound, the less likely people are to accept them. The last thing you want when you are trying to draw a group into new conversations is to have them turn a deaf ear to what you're saying, but it can happen if they don't recognize or just don't like the sound of what you're saying, which includes the language you use. You probably won't get anywhere if you try to convince senior executives that knowledge workers organize themselves and need the latitude to do so, but they're usually quite willing to talk about "eliminating silos." The trick is in knowing how far you can go and then to stretch slightly people's tolerance for new ideas.[15]

But it is hard to get and hold people's attention. Orienting them to organizing, then keeping their attention on it so they stay in a conversation (ultimately, one about commitments and responsibilities that leads to new practices) is a delicate balancing act. The image that comes to mind here is that of activists walking a tightrope (Figure 11.2). You want to tread a path that enables them to align around new practices, with a story that makes a solid case for letting go of management, includes good reasons for taking on the work of organizing, and offers practical ways to do so. But a misstep makes bringing people to the work of organizing that much more difficult: step to one side or the other and your colleagues are liable to either lose interest or misinterpret what you're doing.

A conversation about organizing, which begins "our goal is to achieve measurable results, showing greater productivity and an improved bottom line" is a step to the left. Now you're really in the management universe, giving your colleagues a view from the top. The chances are they won't

Figure 11.2   A delicate balance

Drawn by Ioana Belcea. Used with her permission.

blink an eye. But, as this sounds just like management-speak, they won't know you are after something different. Hearing the same old stuff, they won't be able to see you're trying to take a new direction, so won't be inclined to think different or have the urge to act differently.[16]

Tell a team it's their job to "create and hold social spaces for productive conversations, which make for good work" and you've probably lost them. You are giving them a view of work from practice, and while it's a step to the right, into the organizing universe, the chances are they won't have a clue about what you mean. While "social spaces" probably sounds like gobbledygook, to anyone raised on a steady diet of "productivity," "performance," and "quality" the whole message will seem dodgy because it is not hard-edged enough.

What is your story?

So, what is the language and story to take you down the narrow path? It is no use looking in the usual places, where you learn how to manage. Business books and programs are purveyors of stories based on a view from the top, about the necessity of high control; and many consulting firms, which depend on top management for patronage, are heavily invested in these too. In fact, there isn't a recipe for concocting anew a narrative of work and organizing, which is just as well or we would end up turning talk into another tool and tools are the last thing you want to be thinking about for getting into organizing. If you're going to adopt new practices, the work of organizing has to live in people's (collective) heads and hearts, which happens only when they are constantly talking about it.

A good question for activists is: What can I do to help people I work with to see that self-organizing is desirable, viable, and practical? What will turn my colleagues on to organizing? We live by the narratives we believe in and vice versa. When it's a question of what narratives encourage people to take on *collaborative* work practices, the only consistent answer is "ones they invent themselves: ones they *co-create*." Groups have to find their own stories, collectively, in conversation, tailoring them to their circumstances and to one another's interests, attitudes, and values. What issues are they drawn to? What stimulates and inspires them to do things differently? What sticks? Is it seeing new possibilities for action, understanding the limits of the way they've been working, or, perhaps, realizing how big a task this sort of reform really is? To complicate matters, what turns one lot on may turn others off. Where some see almost any change as desirable and are keen to push the envelope no matter how unorthodox the practices sound, for others the only acceptable change is gradual, "managed change," with them in charge. Perhaps you see why it is so desirable for activists to be able to read people and why it is important for them to possess a quality like emotional intelligence and to develop close working relationships, so they know how their co-workers think and what they do and don't like about the way they work.

To tell my story about the work of organizing I've deliberately stepped quite far to the right. To distance myself from management-speak, I've invented a few words like "social spaces" when I couldn't find any that fit, borrowing others, like "making meaning," "networks," and "aligning," some associated with organizing and fairly familiar, while others are not. I chose them to paint a picture of knowledge-work, management, and organizing as I see it and wanted to tell it. But, there is more than one way of telling a story and it might be more sensible to craft new work language around words like "networks" and "aligning," which probably resonate with anyone accustomed to the technical language of management. There is then the risk, however, of them losing sight of the humanness of organizing. In short, it's the risk that we'll soon be right back in management-speak.[17]

Three words that must go: management, organization, leadership

It's clear to me that management-speak has to go and it is clear why it has to go. Words like "efficiency," "performance," "productivity," "training," and "capital" are factory-talk, devised to make meaning of "factory management" and "factory-work." Factory-talk legitimizes the view from the top and perpetuates practices that treat work as physical and mindless, which, in factories, turned workers, the subordinates, into largely helpless, hopeless extensions of machines. When you walk factory-talk, albeit unconsciously, you are either a factory manager who holds the key to making workers more productive, or you're a factory worker waiting to be told what to do, when, and how. In the age of knowledge-work, neither of these is acceptable.

Language allows us to make distinctions. When we have them, see they matter, and change the way we talk about people or events, we're inclined to do things differently. So, to evolve new practices, we need the words, or a new language, to distinguish factory-work from knowledge-work and old from new management, not only to see that they are different but also to understand how they are different and appreciate why this matters.[18]

In this vein, there are three words in particular that need to be jettisoned: "management," "organization," and "leadership".

"Management" has to go because every time anyone speaks it they breathe high control into the conversation. It is impossible to separate this word from industrial-age practices and doing things the MBA way, because this is what everyone associates with management. What should we put in its place? I propose that "organizing" becomes the new "management." Organizing is what knowledge workers do and it makes sense to use it, at least until another one comes along. Anyone who does this work, irrespective of their official title or role, is an organizer, as we all are.

Moving "organization" from centerstage to backstage is another priority. Its prominence in work talk is a combination of high control and the view from the top: people's desire to be in control; the mistaken belief that there is something to control; and the equally spurious idea that everyone ought to be doing in lock-step fashion, whatever is going on (e.g. buying into the same "vision" or "mission"). Everywhere you turn, people claim to be doing something because the organization needs it (e.g. a strategic plan, an integrated IT system, or a mission statement) or because it's in the organization's interests (e.g. to give executives exorbitant remuneration packages, to seal a merger, or to have a uniform culture). An organization is abstract and definitely inanimate. Organizations don't have needs or interests and paying all this attention to the organi*zation* distracts us from thinking about how and how well people are organi*zing* to get things done. It's the *zing* not the *zation* that really counts, so, here again is a case for having the word "organizing" centerstage in the new language of new management.[19]

"Leadership," unfortunately, perpetuates the idea that organizations have tops and bottoms. The word doesn't have to mean this, but, by convention, leaders are at the top. Reuniting work and organizing means shaking off the old "top-and-bottom" mindset and jettisoning leadership in the process. In the new work stories, the answer to "Who leads?" has to become: "It depends on circumstances and on matters such as people's experience, their support, and cooperation, but not on their positions or titles."

The kind of leading I'm describing isn't from the top, the bottom, or the middle, as these are all view-from-the-top images, which tell us there is a set structure to work and that organizing and leading is more like baseball than rugby or football. Think of what I'm describing as leading from "inside," from action, or from practice, or as stewardship.[20] The essence of stewardship is that it speaks of a relationship between a leader and others: a relationship of responsibility and care. You are responsible for your actions and are committed to taking care of their interests. Responsibility and accountability, which describe people's willingness to meet their commitments to one another and to hold each other to these, are watchwords of stewards, and it is useful, in this context, to recall a traditional meaning of the word. "Stewardship" has to do with the responsibilities of all humans, because they are human, for taking care of the world they inhabit. For animists, responsibility is reciprocal in that the earth will take care of good stewards, providing them with everything that sustains them.

So, whether it's a simple task or a major undertaking, anyone with suitable experience, who is responsible, capable, and shows insight and foresight, who is in a position to make sensible decisions and take practical action, could and should guide what the group does, with the support and encouragement of those he or she is working with. As it's his or her job to find support and his or her colleagues' job to give it to whoever is in a good position to lead, everyone needs emotional intelligence, with the savvy to appraise people and situations and, seeing what is possible, assess whether to step into the role of leading or to encourage a colleague to "take the lead" and then support them.

Activists, willing to take on the work of organizing, put themselves in the role of stewards, leading from inside and committed to encouraging others—everyone else—to do the same. In hierarchical organizations, what I've described is completely unnatural, which means you need a variety of out-of-the-ordinary skills, as well as conviction, courage, and cunning to win through. Besides thinking and acting cooperatively, which may take some getting used to, your job is also to dismantle the pyramid of management from the inside, while working with people whose positions, power, incomes, and identities are tied to this structure. Some will be amenable to taking a new direction, others skeptical, and still others passionately opposed to anything that appears to threaten the status quo. As stewards, activists also have to learn to recognize when to put or to leave the ball in someone else's court, because he or she either is better placed to offer advice, give guidance, and make decisions, or can help you to do all this. In the spirit of cooperation which is so important for good organizing, they have to learn to be generous about allowing others to help them, too, by putting their colleagues—their partners—in the best position to provide guidance or offer help. And they need to be skilled in rhetoric, because the work of organizing begins with new conversations.

CHAPTER 12

Conversations for aligning: openness, commitments, and accountability

Aligning

Organizing is often hard work. Aligning, which I've called the "bottom-line of organizing," takes experience, ingenuity, and, sometimes, tough bargaining. Assignments that seem perfectly straightforward turn out to hide wicked problems that reveal themselves only when you are trying to clarify something or when you are looking for agreement from the team about what still needs to be done. Reaching agreement may take all kinds of compromises and could depend on knowing: which rules and procedures to follow, which you can bend, and how to circumvent others entirely; when to sidestep long-winded procedures even though you've been told "this is the way we do things here"; what you can do to free up funds, yet stay within budget.

When a diverse group of stakeholders is trying to align, however, semi-technical matters like these are not usually the toughest nuts to crack. Some of the really taxing ones include: reaching consensus about the problems you are dealing with and how to tackle them; settling on whose position to support; obtaining permission or approval; ensuring that associates in diverse locations, with different affiliations and interests, follow through with the commitment to their work and one another required to do a good job. Even when their activities and roles intersect and they need to collaborate, the chances are that participants aren't all on the same page. Perhaps, it is those varied interests. One or two just don't seem particularly involved. It is hard to get their attention and, when you do, they have their own ideas about what needs to be done. There are more headaches when something goes wrong in the middle of an assignment or project and you have to reorganize to put things right. Who is responsible? What do we do about them and the breakdown, and prevent this from happening

time, a lot hinges on having good conversations throughout a network, just as there is a lot to lose by not having them or by having sanitized or superficial ones, which, unfortunately, happens all the time.

Illustrating the framework

At various places in this book I've used a picture of a group around a table to illustrate aspects of organizing. Here it is again, in Figure 12.1, to help explain the three domains of conversation. The group in the picture could be a departmental committee formed to honor a colleague for her achievements; or it could be representatives of major stakeholders in a large building project (contractors, city officials, environmental protection groups, and so on), meeting to go over a proposal. As before, I've put a circle around them to represent their social space. Their conversations do more than fill the space. They actually influence the quality of it in terms of what gets said and, then, what gets done.

Perhaps I should remind you about social spaces. Simply by getting together, a group of people creates a space that "holds" their conversations. Their space, which both influences and is influenced by whatever

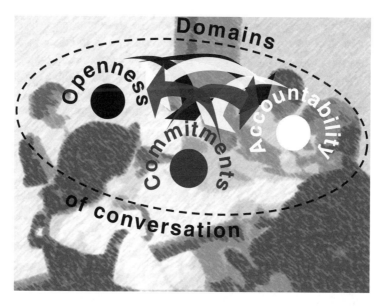

Figure 12.1   Three domains of conversation: a framework for organizing

they think, feel, say, and do (Chapter 6), is shaped by their attitudes (i.e. how each shows up) and their relationships. Filling their space with conversations in the three domains, as I've done in Figure 12.1, suggests that whatever they have to say to one another (whether they're talking shop or chatting about what's going on in their lives), belongs in one or more of these domains. In this regard, the three domains of conversation are just a way of categorizing work talk: that is until I add the stipulation that, whenever people work together, *they need to have conversations that cover all three domains*. Now the scheme is a framework for organizing work—for action—and it doesn't matter what people are actually doing, as long as it is collective work and they have to organize it. Once they are aware of why and how conversations in each domain matter to the work of organizing, provided they think about the domains and conversations, they should do a better job of organizing and do better work.

What to do with the framework

Now that you have seen it, there are three things to remember about this scheme. It is holistic, which is why, in the picture, there are arrows connecting all domains. Next, the domains form a unity. They can't be separated. Finally, no domain takes precedence over the others. When they are organizing in departmental meetings, negotiating contracts, or having online discussions or water-cooler conversations, participants, particularly activists who are out in front in taking charge of work, ought to ask themselves whether they have covered the ground in each domain properly. To do this they should be able to associate conversations they've had, or are having, with domains. Are there specific conversations they ought to have but haven't had yet—missing conversations? If there are, why are they missing? Are they trying to move matters along too quickly? Are there things that they don't, won't, or can't talk about? Is it that the issues didn't seem relevant until now? Have they talked openness, commitments, and accountability, or are there whole domains of conversation that haven't been covered? What are they going to do about it?

Who is responsible for keeping an eye on what people are talking about, for assessing whether they need to "get into" particular conversations in order to align, and for deciding whether it is openness, commitments, or accountability that they ought to be talking about? A short answer is "everyone, jointly." Organizing is everyone's business, as Figure 12.1 is intended to show. If I were tossing these ideas about domains of conversations into the management ring and someone thought they were useful, you could bet they would end up as one or more tool. To start with, the framework might be handed over to "experts," say to the training group in HR, with a directive to design an intervention to "improve communications," "enhance collaboration," or "increase knowledge sharing." Then, as part of a day-long training session on the "Three Domains of Conversation," one-by-one teams would be taught and told to use it and that would be the end of the matter: they'd been trained to have the right conversations.

As a way of crossing between the universes of management and organizing, however, I'd expect groups letting go of one and catching on to the other to treat the scheme as *theirs* and something that *continually* influences how they think of their work (seeing it as conversations in these domains) and *continually* has a bearing on how they work with one another. This is a scheme to keep people: in the work of organizing, talking to one another and not being distracted by tools; focused on what matters to doing good work; engaged, making meaning, and aligning. As there is no beginning or end to organizing, we are always in a conversation in one or more of these domains. The scheme is a way of identifying, differentiating, and naming our conversations. Its purpose is to make us conscious of and familiar with them. Then, in taking on the work of organizing, it is our responsibility to be conscientious about getting into the conversations needed for aligning, deliberately drawing one another into conversations in other domains if necessary, whenever it is appropriate to do so.

Missing conversations

When there are breakdowns in organizing, you'll usually find that missing conversations are the Achilles heel and you can put the problem down almost entirely to management practices. In meetings, planning sessions, and so on, whatever people have to say about the six Ds of documentation, data, directives, deliverables, deadlines, and dollars, their attention is almost exclusively on getting commitments, narrowly defined as "coming up with tools," like agendas, budgets, plans, and lists of requirements. There is so little room for proper conversations in this culture of action-over-talk that even talk about commitments gets short shrift. "Stick to the agenda" and "focus on the outcomes and requirements" is the kind of advice you expect to hear; and you can more or less forget about any discussion of openness or accountability.

Impatient to "get on with the work," people would rather not take time to clarify, and then resolve, who will be doing what, when, and how. Especially if it's a newly formed group, however, to align their intentions and actions it is going to be necessary for them, first, to clarify *how* they want to work together; for example, what they'd like to see from one another, or what they expect to accomplish. No doubt they have different expectations of what constitutes "success," which means they go into their work with varying degrees of commitment to the task as well as to who they want to satisfy and how.

Many missing conversations have to do with those "elephant-in-the-room" situations, when people don't *want* to talk about something, because it's hard for them to have the difficult conversations. Often, the most difficult conversations have to do with accountability. Perhaps the problem is a colleague who isn't holding up her end. Tensions in a small team that is under a lot of stress are now aggravated by members having to cover for her. She hasn't been available to do interviews, never turns up to meetings (but phones at the last minute to say she won't be there), and is always busy with something else. No matter that they've discussed and got agreement on their responsibilities, her assurances just don't seem to mean anything.

They'll whisper to one another about the situation, but no one will speak up to name aloud the matter they aren't willing to talk about and no one will talk directly to her about the problems they're having and what to do; perhaps because they'd prefer not to appear confrontational or because they aren't sure how to handle the situation. High-control management bears much of the blame for this. By perverting "responsibility," turning it into a set of technical tasks, such as administering rules and overseeing requirements, bureaucracy appears to remove both personal and moral considerations from the picture. For many, it is easier on their conscience to "follow directives" and fire someone, say, for "poor performance," because "you haven't met our minimum standards," than it is to hold him to account as a fellow human being whom, you feel, has broken promises or not met commitments he made and, generally, has fallen short of your expectations. The problem is that you can't have bureaucracy, or rules, regulations, and compliance, without someone to enforce them: hence high-control. Especially when it's combined with hierarchy and competition, bureaucracy encourages a not-responsible-for-anything and blame-someone-else mentality. Without conversations for accountability, the team's ill-will toward the person who isn't meeting her commitments will fester, adversely affecting their willingness and ability to work together; and there is a good chance that, if they don't talk about the problem, sooner or later this matter will contaminate her work relationships with others.

It's tough to have conversations of accountability when you aren't accustomed to doing so, but it may help if groups are in the habit of asking about, then getting into, their missing conversations, which brings me to the question: What is the purpose of conversations in each domain? Answering it will explain why conversations in all three domains are necessary, why openness is at the top of the list when it comes to aligning, and why conversations for accountability, which remind us of our joint ownership of and collective responsibility for knowledge-work, are essential to organizing.

Conversations for openness

Openness is a precondition for good conversations in all domains, so I have conversations for openness first on the list; not because they are more important than the others, but, above all, because these conversations influence the "quality" of the social space people hold together. The openness of their space influences what they say to each other; what they feel they can talk about (and shouldn't talk about); what they actually talk about; and how they talk to one another (whether, for example, they are willing to listen, patiently to one another or, on principle, are dismissive of what others say). Knowing how difficult it can be to talk to your spouse or life-partner about how you organize and live your lives together—telling him or her that he or she regularly goes to bed too late, or that you feel that leaving a trail of clothes on the floor is being inconsiderate—it isn't hard to understand why organizing work is often difficult, especially when working with people we hardly know.

Social networks are a hodgepodge of people organizing in different places, doing different things, for different reasons. So, whenever individuals interact to talk, there are lots of potential, invisible boundaries between them; a result of their varied affiliations, relative positions in the hierarchy of bosses and subordinates, and different experiences and personal interests, as well as their attitudes to each other. For good organizing, participants should be able to engage easily, without these considerations becoming insurmountable obstacles, so they can get into good conversations, share knowledge, and align in action. If the obstacles are already there, as many usually are, they need a space, *which they create and hold jointly*, where, because everyone is paying attention to their relationships and to aligning, they can still engage productively. This way, when they spot boundaries that are barriers to aligning, they can name them and negotiate them with the object of turning the barriers into bridges. "Openness" describes social spaces with these qualities.

Openness is a relational idea, which speaks of people's way-of-being with others. Openness refers to a space—a context—where they can readily participate in organizing if they wish to. Openness describes how they "show up" when organizing. It refers to the stance of participants toward each other. It signifies their willingness to "receive": to listen, to pay attention to other people and other things, and to participate with them in what they are doing. Openness is a value. It comes from caring about and trusting in others and being committed to "groupness": Jeff's term for the idea that, when they collaborate, people, together, can accomplish things they cannot do alone, as individuals. In this respect openness is completely compatible with *ubuntu*; the idea that people fulfill their human potential through (their relationships with) other people.[2]

Although openness comes from individuals' attitudes—their hearts—it is seen (or demonstrated) in their interactions and it takes *reciprocal commitments* from participants to experience openness. You foster openness by example, not rules, and, as you do with every aspect of organizing, you have to work at it. For organizers, sustaining openness takes continuous effort and energy, always being conscious of the spaces of organizing, paying attention to how people interact, and responding to what is going on.[3] Without a long, detailed explanation, but leaving it up to you to connect the dots, openness benefits from the following personal attitudes and practices, beginning with lots of "Cs":

- Cooperation, consideration for others, and conscientiousness (without being fanatical) about your work.
- Being careful (literally "full-of-care") about what you do and in how you deal with others.
- Caution (i.e. being cautious) is helpful when you don't know exactly what you're doing or what the consequences will be, which is always true of knowledge-work.
- Flexibility (compared to rigidity) is a necessary quality for the same reasons.
- Reflection and thoughtfulness stimulates the imagination, promoting inquiry, probing questions, and intelligent guesswork.
- Lightness of spirit, or not taking either yourself and others too seriously—lightheartedness rather than flippancy or impertinence—encourages a creative spirit, experimentation, and learning.
- Leniency in judgment, as well as patience, encourages people to experiment and be creative.[4]
- Open or deep listening as opposed to being closed-minded and dogmatic in your views.
- Responsibility, which relies on good judgment, self-control, and accountability to others.

Sharing knowledge and aligning are top priorities when you take on the work of organizing in a high-control work environment. Setting the climate for talk, conversations for openness invite participation, encouraging people to ask questions and express their opinions. When there is openness, people talk and listen, so these conversations, which foster inquiry and collaboration, help to create social spaces that are host to multiple points of view, which is particularly important in dealing with complex, wicked problems. Conversations for openness influence the way people approach their commitments when they're nailing down the work. They also influence whether they are willing to talk about accountability and acknowledge their accountability and, when it comes to action, on how they handle accountability: whether they are confrontational or conciliatory, hot-headed or restrained, and prefer open accountability or want it done behind closed doors.

Conversations for commitments

People quickly get the idea of conversations in the domain of commitments. A typical reaction is, "I understand that these have to do with the details of work: making plans, formulating budgets, negotiating contracts, listing requirements, identifying deliverables, scheduling the work, assigning tasks, and so on. But, the word 'commitments' is confusing. 'Conversations for action' makes more sense." I've called these "conversations for commitments" because this is a better description of their nature and purpose. Certainly, the object is to establish what has to be done, which includes getting acknowledgement from those involved that they know what they are supposed to do and are on board. Yet, when people make plans and produce schedules, they do a whole lot more than detail what they'll do, how, and when.

In conversations for commitments, they actually *negotiate the meaning of the work itself.* "Adaptive work" is Ron Heifetz's way of saying the work of organizing is about how people see things, what they value, and what they believe. Identifying what has to be done and who is going to do it (i.e. assigning work) is one thing, but it is quite another to get commitments and have them "stick"; meaning that participants are willing and able to follow through on what they're committed to doing.

To have their commitments stick, because knowledge-work is collective work, whether they are colleagues or clients, people must agree on what they're doing and why and how they're going to do it. In conversations for commitments organizers do the adaptive work of framing problems and identifying the solutions or outcomes they are looking for, intent on getting commitments that stick. In the process, which I've called aligning and which is all about negotiating the meaning of "what," "why," "how," and "when," they grapple with one another's expectations, values, attitudes, and interests, rather than with facts and data.

While work on the factory floor is generally precise, the issues at the heart of knowledge-work are fuzzy. They revolve around interpretation and meaning-making. How should we focus this proposal? What can we offer which others can't? As a government agency, what does it mean to be accountable to the public? What is "transparency"? How does what we do differ from the work of private contractors? Who exactly is our client and what do they expect? Although some of these might look like strategic considerations, they aren't just for top management. All knowledge workers handle wicked problems and, with them, questions like these. For some, the issues are about what their clients or the public want and, for others, they have to do with their bosses or their colleagues in another department; but everyone is involved in the adaptive work of framing their problems (and solutions) in order to get to commitments. The only way to do this is through conversations for commitments.

It's helpful if you're taking on the work of organizing to be able to separate conversations into domains, but, in practice, as I've said, all the domains and conversation are interwoven. When you're used to seeing work through a view-from-the-top lens and high-control management practices, where tools are valued, not talk, it may be difficult to appreciate how the work of devising plans, drafting budgets, negotiating deals, drawing up contracts, and assigning work is tied to conversations in the other domains, but you can't do good knowledge-work or good organizing without them. Why? Because you don't get aligned action and commitments that stick without a space that invites and enables participants to speak their minds, identifying obstacles and expressing their reservations, even those that have to do with their relationships (i.e. conversations for openness); without them saying what they hope to accomplish (i.e. conversations for commitments); and without them encouraging each other to "stick to the plan," and warning of what may happen if they fail to reach agreement (i.e. conversations for accountability).

Conversations for accountability

The work of organizing continually evolves as people network to get things done. It has no structure in the usual sense of the word. If you are looking for structure in organizing, it is in taking action that is timely, appropriate, and effective. Do people know what is going on? Are they aligned around their work-related responsibilities, committed to fulfilling those responsibilities, and doing good work, like a well-functioning team? Good social spaces for organizing, supported by conversations for openness, provide one pillar; conversations for commitments provide another. But this is not enough. What people do, collectively, in their spaces is what matters, and what we want in particular, because it is the keystone of good work, is to have them observe and honor the commitments they've made, cooperating with and supporting one another in their work. The third pillar for timely, appropriate, and effective action is *mutual accountability*, created and maintained by conversations for accountability.

With openness as one side of a coin, accountability is the other side, which is why I have drawn conversations for openness and accountability flanking conversations for commitments (Figure 12.1). Open spaces invite people to participate in work conversations, setting a context for productive discussions and interactions. When they make and negotiate requests and offers, they begin to align as they define their work, establish priorities and, with further discussion and negotiation, make commitments. This is all to the good. But, without accountability you have the potential for unfulfilled requests, empty commitments, vague promises, and careless behavior. Accountability is what "makes things happen." To use another hackneyed expression, "it is where the rubber meets the road."

Accountability to others—mutual accountability, peer-to-peer accountability, or, for convenience, just "accountability"—when you allow others to hold you to account for things you've said you will do, is the public face of taking responsibility. It is an age-old way of organizing. People depend on accountability whenever there is too much happening or so much that needs to be done that no single person can take it on, take charge, and handle matters effectively. For knowledge workers these situations are the norm rather than the exception. Before those involved decide what to do they have to come to terms with their varied and possibly conflicting responsibilities or dissimilar interests and resolve them. Then, once they've decided, they have to make sure that everyone plays their part in doing the work.

As an organizing principle, the premise of accountability is that effective collective action begins with people recognizing and acknowledging their interdependence. While everyone is capable of taking responsibility for his or her own work, they are responsible *to* one another and look out *for* one another. As colleagues assisting and guiding colleagues, treating one another as peers, they remind each other of their joint responsibilities, hold each other to the commitments they've made, and enable one another to fulfill these commitments. As an organizing practice, reciprocal accountability only works when each person cares enough about what others do (and don't do) and cares about what they say to take their views to heart and take their advice seriously.

Accountability has become one of the "in" words of management-speak and, probably because it is tossed about at work with abandon, everyone seems comfortable with the idea of conversations for accountability and the need for them. When managers say "accountability," however, most of the time they mean "compliance," which makes a big difference.

Accountability as a way of being

Accountability is actually a way of being, rather than something you do. It has to do with relationships. When you interact with others, you "show up" in a particular way, exemplifying certain principles and values in your dealings with them:

- You make commitments to do things *knowing that others expect you to meet your commitments* and will hold you to them.
- You also *allow others to hold you to account* (i.e. you give them permission to do so).

As both a human and social phenomenon accountability is "bi-directional." When there is accountability, people make commitments to each other, saying what they will do or take responsibility for. They also allow their peers to hold them to account. Allowing others to say what they think about your efforts and, in certain situations, to caution, reproach, reprimand, or discipline you if you don't meet your commitments, is probably the hardest part of the bargain for most people. Clearly, however, it is a necessary part of being accountable. What does it take to assess someone else's work and to want to do so? You need to know them and be interested in them and their work, which means you are relatively close to one another and have enough of a stake in the work to be affected by what they do. What does it take for people to give you the authority to hold them to account? The answer is they need to know that you are interested in them and their work and to feel that whatever you're doing you are in it together, as peers who cooperate rather than compete. Amongst other things this means they can ask for help in meeting their commitments, can expect to get it if the request is reasonable, and they can expect to be treated fairly and considerately (i.e. carefully), even if they are being criticized or reprimanded for not living up to the commitments they've made.

All in all, relationships are paramount, with care, fairness, consideration, and trust playing an important role in fostering accountability.

Accountability ought to be present in all social interaction. It is about how people "are" with one another and the way they work with one another, which means conversations for accountability ought to be part of everyday work talk and nothing out of the ordinary. You practice accountability as you organize together when you "check in" or pause to recognize one another's contributions. "How are things going?" "Are you up to date?" "I hear that you did a great job with the training material and that everyone was happy." "Why are we still waiting for approval?" There is nothing unusual about these questions or comments. People ask similar ones all the time. This is how they stay organized. With these examples, you can appreciate that practicing accountability is part of being jointly responsible for the quality of work, identifying problems together, and cooperating in getting work back on track if necessary; and, also, that it takes constant negotiation around commitments with lots of give-and-take.

People practice accountability when they negotiate or talk about the commitments they've made and what they have to do to meet them. If it seems to some of his colleagues that someone isn't living up to his commitments their first step is probably to remind him of his responsibilities. If, after that, they feel he is still letting the side down, taking their cue from social norms or from policies they've agreed to, it is up to them to decide whether to take additional action and what to do. They might reprimand him or punish him in some way or, as a last resort, tell him that they will no longer work with him: in other words, fire him from the team or work group. Whatever they're planning to do, in the spirit of accountability, they will remind one another that openness is a counterpart of accountability and that care for others, patience with one another, and leniency in judging each other are just as important as ensuring that the work they're doing is done well.

Compliance is quite different. This has to do with following rules, regulations, laws, or policies. It is a one-way street that runs from the top of the pyramid down and a technical process that is meant to obviate negotiation and avoid give-and-take: "Rules are rules." Someone sets these, usually for others to follow, and people are assigned to monitor whether they are doing so and to enforce the rules if necessary. Monitoring and enforcement typically takes place at regular, often scheduled, intervals by someone who isn't involved in the work and doesn't really know what is going on. Quarterly and annual reports, end-of-contract assessments, annual reviews, and even those dreaded monthly staff meetings, where the chair works his way through his own agenda and from time to time permits individuals to speak for a few moments, demonstrate that compliance is ever-present. Come the annual review, or when it is time to submit a financial report, there is a scramble to ensure that everything is "in order," everyone is in compliance, and, taking a cynical view, to hide what doesn't look right. In-between, no one seems to care much about what anyone does. It is generally a lot easier to hide things from enforcers, who don't know much about what is going on, than from peers, who do, especially when you know both what they're looking for and when they will be looking.

There is a place for rules

As you'll have noticed, practicing accountability doesn't negate the need for rules and regulations. It is all a question of who makes them and for what purposes. In many situations rules that guide people or circumscribe what they can do are both useful and necessary. In some situations they are absolutely essential; for example, when people are going to come into contact with hazardous materials, are doing things that could injure others, or may not understand the potential harm to themselves of certain actions.[5] Rules are easier to formulate and to work with, however, when the circumstances under which they are going to be applied are well known, when there are a limited number of clearly identifiable things people can do, and when the consequences of each option are understood. Obviously, this means rules and knowledge-work make poor bed-fellows. So, when they're needed, whenever possible, the people who understand best the need for them and the specifics of the situations in which they will be applied, should both make the rules and apply them. In practice this means having knowledge workers make rules to suit themselves, so they can coordinate their activities and align their actions in the interests of doing good work.

In high-control environments everything about rules and rule-making is the complete opposite: from why they exist and for whom they exist, to who devises them and when and how they are applied. Typically, the people who devise the rules aren't the ones who have to follow them. If they aren't actually devised at the top, then it is usually done in the name of someone near the top ("this is what management wants"). Bureaucracies rely on a lot of general rules, which are supposed to apply to almost everyone. Seen in a positive light, this is democratic. It minimizes the role and influence of special interests. But, in practice, it means that the rules serve hardly anyone's purposes, especially since the object is more often control than guidance.[6] The rules are there to limit people's authority and autonomy so that, in spite of not being able to see what is actually going on, the top can determine what people do and don't do. None of this is good for knowledge-work.

The irony is that, although they mean something quite different (they actually mean "compliance"), managers who grumble about there not being enough accountability at work are quite right.[7] Top-down control, with the combination of hierarchy, bureaucracy, and compliance, is completely at odds with accountability. Accountability depends on people caring about one another's work but, in high-control organizations, there is no reason to "take an interest" unless you are a supervisor and it is part of your job. If you aren't a supervisor and do take an interest in what others are doing they're liable to be offended, claiming that you are sticking your nose in where it doesn't belong.

Conversations for accountability serve a dual purpose

In taking on the work of organizing, where it is absolutely vital to get away from compliance, conversations for accountability shift the weight from compliance to accountability. In fact, they have two purposes. We typically recognize the one closest to compliance, which has to do with keeping an eye on each other to see that we are on track and fulfilling our commitments. But it is the other purpose that is actually more important from the standpoint of aligning for action and making commitments stick.

Talking to one another about our responsibilities, reiterating how important it is to let each other know when we can't do things we're committed to doing, or when we're unclear about what is expected, or uncertain about what to do next, reminds us that we are accountable to our peers and that at any time they may ask us to account for what we're doing. When they know their peers intend to "keep them honest," people are likely to *be* more honest: more realistic about making commitments, more moderate in their assessments of what is going on, more careful in their estimates of costs and in incurring expenses, more thoughtful in the way they deal with one another, and possibly less prone to exaggerating their achievements or the impact of what they are doing.

Conversations for accountability are essential to aligning and getting work done. They are necessary for trying to ensure that breakdowns in organizing don't occur and for dealing with the breakdowns that do. It is in conversations about their mutual accountability that people: perform their own quality checks; ensure that the goals they set and commitments they make are realistic; keep one another's attention on what they are doing, what has been accomplished, and what needs to be done; make assessments about whether they are on track in terms of meeting their commitments; and, if necessary, reassign work or ask people to leave and find replacements for them.

The problem is that, like so many things, it is easier to talk *about* accountability, why it is important, and how to practice it, than it is to walk the talk—living your work life being accountable to others for what you do—especially since there is such a small price on accountability (as opposed to compliance) at work.[8] The antithesis of high control, you can't properly practice peer-to-peer accountability as long as people are separated by superior–subordinate relationships, which means that, if you value accountability, hierarchy has to go. Also, mutual accountability relies heavily on good working relationships, evidenced by showing care, consideration, and respect for the views of those who work most closely with you and who know what you are up to. Conversations which foster and sustain accountability emphasize values like care and respect, making accountability and openness inseparable.

Keeping talk and tools separate

Now that I've looked into conversations in all three domains, I'm suddenly conscious that a many-headed monster, which usually haunts management consultants' offices, is hanging around. This one loves tools, hates talk, and tells a beguiling story about turning the ideas people are working on into tools to solve others' problems. The monster is trying to convince me that the three domain framework would make a nice tool box of conversations. All that is required is for me to identify and list all the good or necessary organizing conversations and explain when and how to use them. Organizers, using this as a checklist, would be able to spot the conversations they need to have to get them or their groups past a roadblock, to broaden or narrow negotiations, or to bridge boundaries and bring people together. Organizers would also know what do next, in terms of getting into the right conversations. As seductive as this might sound, I'm sure this isn't a good idea at all.

Tools and talk, which are both essential to our practices, are complementary but different, and we need to keep them separate. There is no substitute for good conversation, in which people engage one another, speaking and listening in a spirit of openness. We need to have those kinds of conversations at work. They are the way to deal with complex issues. Skilled facilitation may be useful, but not a recipe book of conversations. Amongst other things, a checklist approach implies that particular conversations are necessary or appropriate in particular circumstances, and we can establish which are necessary because there is a one-to-one relationship between conversations and problems or circumstances. None of this is true.

When I phone a client to discuss a proposal that has been going back and forth for some time, hoping at last to get her acceptance, we may well talk about stuff that seems to have nothing at all to do with the proposal and commitments, but, in fact, has everything to do with the *work of organizing*. I may ask her about her kids or she'll ask whether I've seen a film she recommended. Organizing revolves around relationships. The object is to align our actions to get the work done together. This kind of chit-chat shows we are interested in each other as one human being to another; it helps us to connect, build relationships, and bridge boundaries. "Shooting the breeze" comes under the heading "conversations for openness"!

Organizing conversations are woven into the social fabric of our lives. They certainly are not like Lego blocks of specific sizes, colors, and shapes, neatly arranged in a box, waiting for instructions about how they should be assembled. There is a sense in which conversations are both organic and seamless, with each emerging in the moment, shaped by the particular social space that holds them, while growing out of ones that have preceded them (even though participants may not be conscious of connections between their conversations then and now). And whatever they are discussing, conversations in other domains are always in the background, never far from what they are talking about, "waiting to happen." The intimate relationship between accountability and openness is an example of this.

One of the things an activist can do is learn to ask questions or make suggestions that help to "bring out" conversations "waiting" in the background, which should come out in the interests of doing the work of organizing well. To see that they do happen, organizers need to train their technique, paying close attention to what people are saying. Particularly useful is the ability to identify themes of conversations and to note where—in which domains—conversations belong. When you're organizing, asking each other what conversations are missing, or what you should be discussing, but aren't, is good practice. Apart from practicing your accountability to each other, the question "What is missing?" gets everyone into the habit of reflecting and may create an opening for some of the more difficult conversations.[9]

CHAPTER 13

Organizing moves

We are still short of an answer to "how"

Knowledge workers make decisions on the spur of the moment and act on the fly. To figure things out they use their imagination and, to get things done, align with one another. They look out, to their networks, including their clients and customers, for ideas, advice, and guidance. When it is *their* work, it is personal. They know what constitutes good work and want to do the best work they can.[1] When the human spirit is paired with collective judgment, decision-making, and action, and you combine a sense of personal responsibility with commitment and accountability to others, you have a sound combination.

The combination of bureaucracy plus hierarchy is hopelessly and irreparably at odds with responsibility, collaboration, imagination, flexibility, and accountability, hence with knowledge-work. It is also both expensive and inefficient. Instead of looking out, everyone below the highest level looks inward and up; and the resources and effort that go into ensuring compliance—those layers of oversight—can hardly be called productive. What is more, satisfying compliance-oriented requirements, including writing reports, completing questionnaires, and gathering data, diverts attention from productive work.

When it's obvious that standard practices are deeply flawed, "business as usual" is not an option: it is time to develop new ones.[2] This is why activists commit to taking on the work of organizing. Notice that, in the title of this chapter, I've called the actions for getting into organizing "moves," not "steps." I'm not splitting hairs. Words are important and "steps" usually imply easy answers. "Sign up for this five-step program. You follow these steps and are assured of success." That most step programs are the snake oil of the information age doesn't stop lots of people enrolling, and Peter Block reminds us why. As a culture, he says, we constantly hope for, look for, and expect to find simple answers to complex problems; but the bad news is there aren't any. The right and practical thing to do is to keep probing—asking, examining, debating, and negotiating—until you have workable solutions.[3] This is exactly the spirit required to turn management into organizing.

I've written about some of the most important moves, explaining that new conversations are the key, and I've described the kinds of conversations people need to have to organize well, but we're still far short of knowing *how* to turn "managers and workers" into "organizers." This is because, if the wickedness of problems was measurable, the ones associated with this particular "how" would be at the farthest end of the scale. Yet, this is the most important organizational issue of our time and is tightly interwoven with other major concerns, like climate change, destruction of the planet's ecosystems, political corruption, social inequalities and injustices, handling incredibly complex technologies, responding to poverty, and dealing with crime. It's intuitively obvious that the solutions—whatever that means—have to do with how we organize our lives, our communities, our districts, and so on. So, the right and indeed the only practical thing to do is to keep probing, intent on gaining a deeper understanding of how to take on the work of organizing and do it well.

Because this work starts in hierarchical organizations, where activists stand or sit, whether they are coming at organizing from "above" or from "below," makes a difference to the moves they have to make when they take it on. If you are moving into the role of organizer from above (and remember that there are many "tops" in organizations) your commitment is to get out of *managing*. From below (and there are just as many "bottoms"), it is to move away from *being managed*. Though the moves involved are somewhat different, it takes commitments both from people above and below to make organizing work: commitments to engage peer-to-peer, organizer-to-organizer, not manager-to-worker or superior-to-subordinate. Which is why, whether you are above or below, these moves may mean radical shifts in work practices.

Organizing moves from above

From above, there are three basic moves involved in taking on the work of organizing:

- Speaking metaphorically, letting go of control.
- Treating subordinates as peers (transforming your relationships with them), by moving aside to make way for them (and you) to do the work of organizing collectively.
- Promoting peer-to-peer accountability instead of top-down compliance.

These moves are commitments. Everyone getting into organizing has to make commitments, but the first is what differentiates people when they're doing this from the top or bottom (the other moves are somewhat similar wherever you are).

Letting go

"Control" is a frame of mind (that it is necessary as well as practical to direct the whole enterprise), coupled with procedures and practices (such as positions or grades, rules, rewards, and penalties), which give certain individuals both formal authority and power over others.[4] Together, they delineate the view from the top. A commitment to organizing means relinquishing the mindset and the practices, which explains why the first move is possibly the most difficult. Letting go takes sacrifice and courage, especially because people who dislike what you are doing will try to thwart you. Earlier, to dramatize what it takes to get from management to organizing, I used the metaphor of a trapeze, suggesting that there is a moment when you let go in mid-air. At that point you have nothing to hold onto except your faith that what you're doing is right, that others have succeeded, and there are still others who want you to succeed and you will do so with their help.

The fact that organizing means *sharing* responsibility for handling tasks and solving problems should make the first move much more appealing if you're one of the many who find themselves saddled with responsibilities that are basically impossible for one person to fulfill and are depressed—literally, weighed down—by this burden. In high-control organizations the combination of hierarchy and bureaucracy makes every problem an individual's responsibility. When you understand the distinction between tame (technical) and wicked (adaptive) problems an obvious downside of this arrangement is that individuals are responsible for things they don't control and cannot and should not handle alone, which can cast a huge shadow over their lives, both at work and at home.

Work-related problems are truly collective and social. Whenever there are differences in attitudes or beliefs about what needs to be done, when, how, or by whom, the problems are wicked and, the higher you are, the more likely you are to feel the burden of not being able to handle problems effectively because when you carry more formal authority the problems you deal with seem to get wickeder. But feeling that problems are too big and one's responsibilities are too onerous isn't reserved for people at the top. When a "routine" task becomes unexpectedly complicated and a backlog of work starts to accumulate, so it is no longer practical for one person to handle "his or her work" alone, the most obvious thing to do is to ask for help, guidance, or advice. But under the rules of management you can't. Saying "I can't manage this on my own," "I could really do with some help," or "this is too much for me to handle" is admitting that you aren't competent to do *your own* work.

Give up control and the burden of being a superman or a superwoman disappears! Organizing practices cater to the collective nature of knowledge work. Activists commit to being jointly responsible and accountable for what they're doing, open to asking one another for help or advice, and expecting to get it.

Transforming relationships

As long as there is hierarchy, organizing cannot be a fully cooperative practice and collective experience, with joint accountability. Hierarchy takes away the voices of those "below," robbing them of responsibility and accountability. Subordinates are supposed to listen and comply, but not speak, except to acknowledge and accept instructions and, unless they have cleared it with their superiors and have their permission, they aren't supposed to think or do anything for themselves. So, the second move involves sweeping away superior–subordinate relationships. Your personal commitment is to give back others' voices and let them take responsibility again, by cultivating social spaces where everyone around the table who is involved in the task or problem can speak and act and expect to be taken seriously.

Promoting accountability

How do you spread responsibility around when organizations aren't geared to assigning collective responsibility? The answer is in the third move, replacing top-down compliance with peer-to-peer accountability. A necessary counterpart to the second, it includes putting yourself in a position of accountability to the people you work with, just as they are accountable to you.

Replacing compliance with mutual or peer-to-peer accountability highlights the riskiness of taking on the work of organizing. If you were coming at it from the top and knew everyone else was fully behind the idea and had the same kind of commitment, you'd only have to think of your responsibilities and commitments to and relationships with those further down the ladder. You'd be asking questions like, "What is the role I play now—what can I do differently—so everyone participates?" and "What concrete steps can we take to achieve mutual accountability?"

It is difficult enough to find answers to these kinds of questions, but getting into organizing from the top is never simple or clean. There is always another layer of hierarchy above you to deal with, and the chances are that, whatever you do, you'll find yourself sandwiched in the middle: between subordinates-turning-peers who are taking on new responsibilities and need support for what they're doing, on the one hand, and people above you who are into high control and not willing to let go. You'll be working both sides of the room, so you can create a space for movement, via conversations for aligning, in the middle.

Organizing moves from below: extricating yourself and your work

From above, your personal commitment in saying "yes" to organizing is to give up high control. From below, it is the other side of the coin: extricating yourself from hierarchy: saying "no" to having your work directed by remote control and saying "yes" to taking responsibility and being jointly accountable for what you do.

Accepting this challenge requires just as much of a commitment, courage, and sacrifice as getting into organizing from the top. One important difference, though, is that, in my experience, at the bottom there is less push-back from one's peers. People at the top, who feel they, personally, have a lot to lose by letting go, are upset when they see their colleagues doing just that. At the bottom, people are usually quicker to appreciate the possibilities of saying "no" to top-down control and keener to say "yes" to taking responsibility. There the problem isn't finding support among one's peers but, rather, what to do about your bosses.

When I think about who could and should make this commitment and why, my clearest image (now conjuring up an org chart) is of a sizeable band of mid-to-upper level administrators in government departments (who, in the USA, would qualify for GS 9 or 10 administrative positions and above). Most are making careers in the public sector and some have many years of public-service experience. They understand, well, how government departments and agencies function and are keen to "take charge" in their departments or units (i.e. to have responsibility for what they do). All are fit to do so, too.

The combination of rigid hierarchy and unyielding and uncompromising bureaucracy, created originally to regulate and control work, takes away responsibility from everyone except the person in charge, so these government employees live with decisions made higher up (in some cases, much, much higher up), and they follow rules. The combination is pernicious. Without a say in what gets done or how it gets done and unable to do things that they know will make a difference, they stand by, often frustrated. They know this because they are in the thick of the action, able to see what is being done and what is not; or how it is being done and how it could be done.

Getting into organizing from below (and out of being managed) is about extricating yourself, others who work with you, and your work from this straitjacket, in the interests of doing creative, productive, and useful work. But, in government, the buck is supposed to go all the way to the top before it stops: all the way to elected officials who—the theory goes—are responsible because they are accountable to taxpayers, the electorate.[5] From above, this is too far from the work that the majority of employees do to know what they are doing and too far to care. From below, it means that, to take responsibility, you probably have to move aside layers and layers of hierarchy while working your way around all manner of bureaucratic red tape. The predicament shared by thousands of public servants makes it clear that, while it is vital to take on the work of organizing, there are no instant solutions or even short cuts to changing hierarchical relationships into collaborative ones from below.

Once again, three moves highlight the personal commitments for getting into organizing:

- Speaking metaphorically, "moving up" and taking responsibility for organizing.
- Holding a space for anyone in your network, including supervisors and bosses, to engage and interact as peers.
- Encouraging people you work with to allow the others to hold them to account and have them hold each other accountable and being willing, yourself, to do both.

Moving up

Coming from below, the first move is still the most difficult: both tricky to handle and potentially risky. Your goal is to show up as a peer, not a subordinate, as you work with others, so everyone is engaged, participating in the work—talking, listening, and doing—on the same level, as it were. I use the expression "moving up" because control-oriented and status-conscious bosses and supervisors are the main obstacles, not your immediate colleagues. It's the former, who insist on your using their titles when you address them, who use these and their formal positions to maintain a distance between you, who see your efforts to take on the work of organizing as "stepping out of line."

One way of keeping people in their place is to require them to get permission. It is a means of ensuring compliance, which is why it is a vital principle and practice of high-control organizations. Anyone who is going to do anything out of the ordinary is expected to ask permission before hand. But having to follow protocol is a problem when coming at organizing from below. As you aim to take responsibility for your work, get out from under high-control management practices and structures, and change the way things are done, the act of asking permission is deeply contradictory. By asking permission, you would be encouraging and supporting precisely the practices you wish to change! Whether or not to forgo getting permission is often a major dilemma.

Shortly, I'll describe how people struggle with this dilemma when dealing with hierarchy. But a dilemma it is, and there are only two options. Either you negotiate your way into a role you don't usually play or a position you don't normally occupy. (You have to be prepared for disappointment and there is the possibility that, if you don't succeed, you'll be at an additional disadvantage for having declared your ambitions to move up.) Or you are willing to eschew authority and press on regardless; acting as if you have permission when you don't and, if it comes down to this, asking for forgiveness and hoping you get it.

With these considerations in mind, moving up involves a declaration to yourself and others working with you that you'll do what is sensible and appropriate in order to do your work well. You'll take on the work of organizing by negotiation, talking to people above you who now have the formal authority to make decisions and, if you judge it to be the sensible thing to do in the circumstances, you'll act without permission, taking responsibility for doing things that you don't have permission to do.

Facilitating open discussion

Here is another dilemma. Let's suppose you've seen an opportunity to promote knowledge sharing inside your organization. You have no doubt that it is the sort of initiative that management will support, but on what terms?

This is a project without borders, which touches on the culture, embraces IT, and runs right across formal boundaries and layers of authority. To take on the work of organizing and get it off the ground you are looking for lots of latitude, or, as you are in a high-control environment, a lot more authority. The challenge in negotiating your way into a new role, with new authority and responsibilities, isn't in defining your role (although management, always with an eye on structure, may see it this way). Roles come later. They are defined and redefined as people interact. The initial crunch in taking on a new role has to do with something more basic: negotiating from below in an environment where most of what happens is not negotiated—but is directed—and it isn't normal for superiors to negotiate with subordinates.

You know you could put together a team to start the work, but what is missing is a social space where everyone has room to discuss and debate options and negotiate positions, so it's possible to gauge people's interest, identify the level of support, and reveal roadblocks, all part of the work of organizing. What is needed is a space where superiors and subordinates, departments and units, aren't automatically set against one another. What do you do? One of the commitments you make in getting into organizing is to act as facilitator, creating and holding an open space that enables people to talk and align. And how do you create that space? This, too, isn't easy but, essentially, by getting into conversations for openness: conversations about "what we would like to see," "what is possible," and, moving in this direction on delicately as you need to, "what is likely to trip us up."

Negotiating accountability

The third move, the counterpart to the second, is a reminder of how closely interwoven are organizing moves and the conversations for organizing (which I discussed in Chapter 12). In moving up, negotiating your way into new roles, the question organizers invariably get from above is "Who is going to be responsible?" Coming from above, it is a fair question. With high control the answer is clear in principle (although never in practice): "look for the chain of command on the org chart." To make low-control organizing work there has to be a practical alternative to compliance, where individuals are not put in a position either of having to ask or give permission.

What we're looking for may sound like a contradiction. Knowledge-work thrives on independence and openness. These serve the creative spirit and the need for people to share knowledge. At the same time, work practices have to acknowledge and satisfy the collective nature of knowledge-work. Knowledge workers depend on one another to get things done. The practical way of allowing people a great deal of latitude in deciding what to do, when, and how while, at the same time, trying to ensure they act responsibly by supporting one another, meeting their commitments, keeping their promises, and doing a good job in the process, is to have them acknowledge that they are accountable to each other and have them actually hold one another to account whenever they feel it is desirable to do so.

So, the third commitment you have in coming into organizing from below is to try to talk both peers and bosses into allowing the people they work with to hold them accountable and everyone into taking joint responsibility for holding others to account. This is usually a tough sell. Among your peers, the reason for this is that the idea of mutual, peer-to-peer accountability is unfamiliar and untried and they're being encouraged to act collectively and commit to practices that go against the ideology of individualism they've grown up with. For bosses, you can add their understandable reluctance to turn over "their authority" (actually power) and their skepticism that mutual accountability is a workable substitute for compliance.

CHAPTER 14

Handling hierarchy and more

Change that pushes all the buttons

Like the word "change", "change management"—meaning actions at the top to change the whole organization ("whole system change")—is a mantra in the world of management consulting.[1] It is also a myth. There is no whole to change. Departments, divisions, and organizations are not made of Lego blocks, which can be rearranged to create a new and different structure.

The kinds of moves I've outlined are the opposite of whole systems change. They are practical, piecemeal, and personal. Responding to the need to organize differently to do their work better, people improvise. They find or create whatever openings they can, as they do whenever they work. Change happens in or through *action*, when they act and speak differently. It is not the kind of change you put on an org chart, saying "look, we changed the organization!" It is neither rapid nor grand and ambitious. It is both gradual and localized, confined to contexts where people are actually doing things differently. You feel (or experience) this kind of change, because it touches you when you are involved or associated with it.[2]

Chipping away at high-control practices is not only about how organizations function and who runs them, but also has to do with people's identities and interpersonal relationships that are tied to titles, roles, and positions on the social ladder, who they work with, and how they deal with one another. In short, we're talking about reforming work culture, which means anything and everything to do with the way we currently organize work, including values and beliefs, pay-scales and working relationships, and the way we speak about our work and talk to one another.[3] Whether it is a directive, systems of rewards and incentives, or the silos that isolate departments, activists will try to alter, circumvent, eliminate, or, possibly, just ignore it. If it stands in the way of working cooperatively, then networking, sharing knowledge, and aligning it is a candidate for change.

But, whatever you do, someone, somewhere, who is attached to the status quo, is bound to feel affronted. As Hamlet might have put it, "there's the rub."

All sorts of people are attached to management practices for all kinds of reasons and, if you are, the idea of moving into organizing can very be troubling. Many have faith in management, believing it is the right way to run organizations (i.e. to organize work). Others, though less convinced, can't imagine a viable alternative to high control, with someone "in charge." Or they are quite content with the way things are and, possibly, are quite determined to keep them this way. Organizing moves seem to push everyone's buttons, all at once. You need an appetite for this kind of work because it takes a lot of effort. Yet organizing is intensely social and calls for cooperation and collective action. Where do you find allies? Let's look at what is involved, including the complications and hurdles.

Handling hierarchy

Handling hierarchy is the trickiest and most important part of taking charge at work. You have to do it. It is no secret that collaboration hinges on good working relationships and that our work environments permit both good and bad ones. *Reciprocal* relationships characterized by mutual respect, care, and collegiality or friendship are good ones for organizing, because people are open to one another's suggestions and criticisms, feel accountable to each other, share knowledge, and align easily. Superior–subordinate relationships, which come with hierarchy, are bad for collaboration—hence for organizing—and it is even worse when hierarchy and bureaucracy are combined.

So for the sake of good work we want to get these relationships and the formal apparatus that supports them (e.g. job classifications, positions on the org chart, and the idea of "going through proper channels") out of the picture when people organize. By "out of the picture" I don't mean toning them down or making them less obtrusive. I mean out of the way completely. This is asking a lot, because almost everything we do under the umbrella of management, from pay structures to parking privileges and who gets to sit where in meetings, reinforces hierarchy. But, with commitment, we can go a long way toward the goal.

What exactly is the goal? Ideally, when people are talking to one another they're thinking about what they're doing and should be doing together, not about structures, regulations, their positions, or protecting their authority or their turf. These become reasons for *not* doing things: shields to inaction, masks to hide behind, and means of avoiding responsibility and accountability. Can they engage one another about the work they're doing as peers and colleagues who are *jointly responsible* for what they're doing, open to the other's circumstances, experience, and suggestions—and able to challenge them if needs be? Are they interested in what the others are doing, and are they willing, as well as able, to hold *each other* to account for what they do (or don't do) together? If they can do all this and do it with the intention of doing their best work, they're handling hierarchy successfully.[4]

"Orbiting" is not a solution

Gordon MacKenzie's book, *Orbiting the Giant Hairball*, is about responding to the dreadful concoction of bureaucracy and hierarchy, which he describes as a "Hairball" of "policy, procedure, conformity, compliance, rigidity, and submission to the *status quo*."[5] He sees this combination as "an originality-suppression agency that permeates our lives," which once "tyrannized Galileo into recanting...put a match to Joan of Arc" and has since colonized corporate governance.[6] His antidote, "Orbiting," is "responsible creativity" that includes "vigorously exploring and operating beyond the hairball of the corporate mind set, beyond '*accepted models, patterns or standards*'—all the while connecting to the spirit of the corporate mission."[7]

The idea of finding "orbit around a corporate hairball...a place of balance where you benefit from the physical, intellectual, and philosophical resources of the organization without becoming entombed in the bureaucracy of the institution" is very appealing.[8] At Hallmark, the greeting cards manufacturer where he worked, MacKenzie tried it himself and seems to have succeeded. The ability to orbit, however, depends on the attitudes of those around you, who have the power to keep you in the hairball, or, if you manage to escape and they don't want you to, to pull you out of orbit and get you back in line. In his journal (Chapter 4) Jeff tells us why it is so difficult to orbit, pointing to perpetual tension between people organizing themselves and (top-down) management. When a single individual like MacKenzie is engulfed and smothered by a hairball, she or he might be permitted to orbit in certain circumstances, but groups, teams, departments, and whole divisions almost certainly won't be allowed to do it en masse. In a hierarchy, where conformity is essential to "order" and "efficiency," orbiting threatens the status quo. Whenever and wherever it is threatened there are people who will do everything in their power to protect and preserve it, and in hierarchies, where a few people have lots of power, they also have lots to protect.

Reframing the problem of hierarchy

Of course, there isn't a definitive answer as to how to handle hierarchy. As this is a wicked problem the options and actions available depend on how you frame it (see Chapter 7). From the top, hierarchy has to do with structure, represented by an org chart. To eliminate it you dismantle it layer by layer, unit by unit, with the kinds of reorgs used for smashing silos or attacking stovepipes: merging departments, changing the chain of command, or something in this vein.

When you're looking at hierarchy with a view from practice, however, the structure isn't what catches your eye, which is why reorgs don't eliminate organizational stovepipes. Relationships and attitudes, or the way superiors and subordinates see and treat one another, are much more important elements of hierarchy, and when you see hierarchy in relationships, rather than structure, you've reframed the problem. Now, handling hierarchy is about boundaries in social networks. Whenever people on different rungs of the ladder work together the superior–subordinate relationship could be an obstacle to them cooperating and aligning. A lot depends on how they carry their positions in the social spaces they create and hold together. But, even when their positions are least visible, it's possible that one or the other will pull rank, perhaps to lean on a subordinate who seems to be wavering, or to evade responsibility, claiming he or she doesn't have enough authority to do what others are asking. Whether you are coming from above or below, much of the work of organizing is at these boundaries. Boundaries emerge, re-emerge, and have to be negotiated and renegotiated whenever and wherever people interact, so they call for special attention and care from everyone. You have to be constantly on the alert and prepared to wrestle with them when you find them.

The object is aligning

Every connection in a network is an interpersonal relationship of some sort, where attitudes, values, beliefs, hopes, intentions, and interests come into play, making every relationship-connection a boundary, which helps or hinders people's work together. As a rule, the boundaries that form at the intersection of layers of hierarchy are barriers, not bridges. If it is not exactly unnatural, it is quite unusual for subordinates and superiors to collaborate fully: to engage, talk, and share knowledge in a spirit of openness. Subordinates are expected to "give their full cooperation," which is code for complying with whatever instructions and assignments they are given. Superiors aren't supposed to yield authority, which means you don't tell them more than they need to know or allow them to move without getting your permission. Neither contributes to good knowledge-work.

When knowledge workers organize, the object is to have everyone aligned: well organized, committed, and accountable. It all comes down to their ability to form functional, sound, working relationships. Hierarchy gives one party power over others. This is intentional. It is a means of control. So, no matter how high or low you go in the organizational pyramid, or how large or small the "distance" between them on the ladder, there is a barrier to sound working relationships whenever a superior and subordinate meet. But "meet" is hardly the right word. The problems of handling hierarchy are compounded by another barrier: an aversion to person-to-person interactions.

The distaste for talking face-to-face seems to stem from a conviction (a feature of bureaucracy) that it is easier for a superior to maintain formal authority, which is the source of his or her power over subordinates, if he or she remains aloof. If you don't bond physically or emotionally, but hold an impersonal social space, then whatever comes down from the top is "just business, nothing personal."[9] Can you imagine an HR assistant being invited to participate in the meetings of senior administrators who are assessing a compensation plan? They are much more likely to ask for a written submission than talk to him or her. Talking face-to-face makes the work personal and has a leveling effect that undermines hierarchical authority and bureaucratic control. To open their doors and invite him or her in would be a tacit admission that they can learn from this person (who has something they want), undercutting their authority and the façade that they are fully "in charge and in control."

With a view from practice, we know that "tools," such as reports, are no substitute for conversations. Both are necessary for organizing. We want to encourage talk because it builds relationships and leads to new possibilities for action, but how do you break the logjam? How you handle boundaries depends in part on whether, at the point of intersection between subordinates and superiors, you're coming from above or below.

If you're the boss or an oversight committee, you are a symbolic center of the network and the people below are on the periphery. Your moves are a response to how to connect with and "draw in" the periphery, because you have fuller participation from everyone when they are aligned. In terms of fostering new organizing practices, one of the most important considerations will be cultivating accountability at the periphery. The contradiction you have to resolve when you're getting into organizing from above is that you are asking subordinates to take responsibility, but from their peripheral positions they don't have authority; you do. If they're going to be responsible and accountable, they must have it, hence your commitment to giving up control. One of the things you can do from above, too, is provide cover for organizers below. In addition to giving them the latitude to do their work without having to get your permission and getting directly involved in it as a peer-participant, you can become the point person in negotiations with people higher up the chain. Switching roles, you can wear your position as a cloak to cross boundaries, lending formal authority and weight to requests that wouldn't get very far if they were believed to come from further down the chain.

When you are coming to the work of organizing from below it's a question of how to connect at the center. "What is the best I can do from the periphery and how do I do it?" It is going to be vital to foster accountability, but, from below, you'll want "the top" to *share* accountability, which sounds very much as if you're asking them to surrender their authority. What is in it for them? What is the trade-off? And if they're willing to do it, presumably they'll want to be reassured that you are responsible, even trustworthy: hence your commitment to "moving up" from your peripheral position.

Conversations for openness, accountability, and commitment

Since I know of no other way of handling hierarchy than to treat it as you would any other boundary issue, whether you're coming from above or below the three domains of conversations outlined in Chapter 12 are your framework for action. You have to get into conversations, talking together—in practical terms, negotiating—about what you intend to do, why, how, and so on. And, with the object of aligning your actions across the levels of hierarchy, you'll need to give a lot of attention to openness and accountability. Whether you are negotiating a new political dispensation, as the parties in South Africa did to end apartheid, working to reduce carbon emissions, or settling a labor dispute, organizing is a continuous process of give and take while you negotiate meaning and align for action. There may be much more at stake in some situations than in others, but it is always tricky. Like an unrehearsed dance, you need to be aware of your partner(s): who they are and where they are and what they are doing and thinking. Even when you do, it is highly likely that sooner rather than later you are going to stand on someone's toes; so you need to be prepared to handle the fallout, which is where openness comes in.[10]

From the dance floor and balcony

Explaining that leading is "adaptive work," which (like the work of organizing in general) is largely about attitudes, values, beliefs, and relationships, Ron Heifetz makes a distinction that is just as germane to organizing across boundaries. He writes about the need and ability to view what you're doing from two perspectives, which he calls the "dance floor" and the "balcony."[11] To do a good job of organizing, organizers need to know, first hand, what is happening in the action on the dance floor: to hear what people are saying, to make suggestions, to watch their responses, to feel the tension build or sense the relief, and so on. At the same time, because what is going on there is related to and has a bearing on events and actions that are happing or will occur elsewhere, it is important—not just desirable, but necessary—for organizers to adopt a reflective stance. In their imaginations, for a moment, they detach themselves from the here-and-now of their immediate surroundings as if they are observing the dance floor action from the balcony, where they have a "wider" view.

What triggered this "crisis"? Who are the major stakeholders in the status quo and what is at stake for them? Who is going to be most affected by what we are doing and in what ways? How are they likely to feel and respond? And, in particular, what can, or should, I do about it? You don't ask questions like these when rushing headlong into action or are in the heat of it. You have to step out and stand back.

A view from the balcony is necessary both for strategic and political reasons as well as for tactical (or operational) ones, not least when you are trying to avoid stepping on others' toes. It is from the balcony, rather than the dance floor, that you are most likely to "see" the boundaries between people and/or groups and decide how to handle them. It is the work you do from the balcony that leads to new alliances and continually transforms networks. Who should you talk to, because you need to have them aligned in order to get things done? What kinds of approaches are likely to work? What are you going to do about those who are probably not open to talking about these issues at all or who you are unlikely to persuade?

Negotiating an end to apartheid

The reconciliation that took place in South Africa at the end of apartheid, amongst political groups representing blacks and whites, is a vivid example of the adaptive work of organizing across boundaries, reminding us of how crucial relationships and attitudes are as to whether people cooperate and align, and how far they can go to do so. Fortunately, attitudes and relationships are not necessarily fixed. If the participants had been completely wrapped up in their power-struggle maneuvers on the dance floor and had not kept an eye on the future, from the balcony, it is highly unlikely they would have reached an agreement. Once again, fortune played a part here. During negotiations the major participants were given scenarios to consider, both optimistic and pessimistic. They were encouraged to look, from the balcony, at what role they could play, individually and together, in contributing to a positive future and what role they would play in contributing to a negative one if they dug in their heels and their talks stalled.[12]

Finding common cause among parties with ideologies as divergent as those of the "white" Nationalist Party (NP) and the "black" African National Congress (ANC) was no overnight miracle.[13] It took months of negotiations, including hard bargaining in a variety of situations and, just as important, it required participants to commit themselves to negotiating and being willing to trust the process even though they didn't trust one another. In retrospect, it seems that a successful outcome depended on three considerations. Were leaders of the NP prepared to accept they could and probably would negotiate away whites' hold on power (were they willing to "let go")? Were the parties open to talking and listening to one another? Was it possible to create and "hold," collectively, an open social space conducive to productive conversations? (Were their talks contributing to openness?)[14] Then, would they talk and listen for long enough to overcome some of their biggest differences (so they could align and get binding commitments)?

There was a crucial period, early on, when anyone who could claim to represent a reasonable-sized group could join in open-ended "talks about talks." Without stipulating a time frame, the only agenda, then, was to decide who would be represented in further talks and to come up with an agenda for those talks. What happened is what we see over and over again in conversations. When people interact (and negotiate meaning) and some participants are whole-heartedly committed to talking across whatever boundaries there are, both their relationships and attitudes shift and change. As these evolve, the space between them, which is as real as their values and relationships, may open, to enable them to find common cause and even, eventually, to ask for forgiveness and, perhaps, grant their adversaries amnesty for past actions.[15] Or, their attitudes could harden, so the space closes and no further talk, or progress, is possible.[16]

Slow and steady or bold and brave

Experience tells us that organizing across boundaries, where you are establishing relationships, building confidence, even trust, and, eventually, negotiating responsibilities and shared commitments, takes care, personal commitment, openness, and imagination.[17] People align conversation-by-conversation, usually in small steps and, if they get it right, achieve small victories, with conversations creating openings for more conversations. Timing is often a crucial consideration. Is this the right time to be raising these issues? What is possible under the circumstances? You have to be able to read others' moods, assess their attitudes and beliefs, and respect their values, which points to the importance of a personal quality, "emotional intelligence," which is getting more and more attention. How much do people trust one another? Who is willing to go out on a limb? Are you? Who can you count on? Is your supervisor actually encouraging you or just making the right noises?[18]

The adaptive work of changing the way we work, from working as superiors and subordinates to working together as peers, means transforming attitudes and relationships and is inevitably a gradual shift. A "slow and steady" approach to handling hierarchy usually wins the day. You wait for an appropriate moment, look for an opening, and propose something which isn't too radical: a first step in a new direction, as you envisage it. Depending on the circumstances, however, especially on personalities and relationships, there is also room for some "bold and brave" moves, where you declare what you want to accomplish and how you'd go about it (conversations for commitments), explaining why this is the right and responsible course of action in the circumstances (accountability).

Change "on management's terms" is not practical

Although it *is* a bold and brave maneuver, you should *not* attempt to win support for change by doing it "on management's terms." Here, you declare your intentions, then, quarter after quarter, aim to deliver results that acknowledge your commitment to whatever goals top management sets, proving that your way of doing things is more effective. If successful, this strategy rarely works for more than a year or so, at most. The problem is it pulls you into a delicate balancing act that is impossible to maintain. On the one hand, you want to keep people above you happy, by showing them, on their terms, using their criteria, that your department or unit is successful. On the other, wanting to do things your way, which you believe is better, you are saying "look, I am even more successful than if I followed your rules and took your advice." Because a maverick, even one who is successful in conventional terms, isn't welcome in a compliance-oriented hierarchy, this is sure to make them insecure and unhappy. In fact, success in meeting conventional goals is likely to heighten tensions. You'll be seen, from above, as thumbing your nose at formal authority, saying "experience and ability is more important to success than one's position in the organization." As this is a threat to control and compliance, sooner or later (and it is usually sooner), someone higher up, with the power to do so, will step in to put an end to whatever you're doing. In the meantime, because you've been playing by the rules, nothing fundamental will have changed.

Under the radar

After a few decades in the wilderness, "informal organizations," which exist alongside or inside formal ones, are once more in the news. They are back now because social networks are in fashion.[19] In *Fortune* magazine, Jennifer Reingold and Jia Lynn Yang describe the informal organization as "the hidden workplace." As Jon Katzenbach explains, the notion "encompasses all the connections and relationships that aren't on the org chart but relate to how people ... *actually network to get the job done.*"[20]

I've reintroduced the informal organization here because it is the other way of handling hierarchy: flying under the radar of formal structures, systems, rules, and procedures. Organizers need to find ways around whatever barriers stand in the way of doing things properly. Some are created by superior–subordinate relationships, while others, like those I've listed, are ordinary tools of management. If you think of flying under the radar as deliberately dodging authority it sounds sleazy and perhaps dishonest. But, wittingly or unwittingly, everyone acts without drawing attention to themselves and without getting approval for what they are doing, because spontaneity, along with meaning-making and organizing, is a basic human quality and a condition of knowledge-work.

If we can put aside the blinders of industrial-age thinking for just a moment, we realize that informal organizations aren't aberrations. *Most* of what people do for *most* of the time they are at work can't be found on agendas or lists of deliverables or in strategic plans or any other tool of management. The human way of doing things is to connect and inter-act when someone has an idea or has heard something which, he or she believes, requires action; even if that connection is just a phone call or an email. This is the way knowledge workers work and the way knowledge-work gets done. Up to a point it is also a practical solution to dealing with hierarchy.

How far *can* you go and how far *should* you go when you're organizing under the radar? While these questions aren't entirely separate, they're not the same either. The answer to the first is practical. How far does your peer network reach and what can you accomplish before you need to go up one or more levels and get permission to hire someone or to renegoti-ate an agreement with clients? The answer to the other question is more personal. It may have to do with your attitude toward authority. Some peo-ple like to seek approval. They go out of their way to get permission or to keep their bosses informed, because they feel it is the right thing to do. For others, who may claim that the rules are never clear or that they're there to be broken, it is easier to ask for forgiveness than for permission. How far you go also depends on whether and to what extent you can trade off following rules for getting things done properly and whether you feel you have to choose between asking permission and proceeding with a clear conscience (even if you don't get it) and not doing so and hoping you won't be found out. Whatever your attitude or motives, you must be aware of the gray areas, where your efforts to circumvent hierarchy in the inter-ests of doing good work will drop you into a quagmire, because you are exceeding your legal authority or undermining someone else's. It's here that mutual accountability matters.

Working under the radar appears to contradict both the spirit and prac-tice of openness, which is vital to good organizing. The problem is that high-control environments don't respect openness and, as you have to start somewhere, under the radar may be the realistic option. The fact that orga-nizations are fragmented, not monolithic, means it is practical to fly low as long as you're not too ambitious and are content to limit yourself to activities and objectives that can be accomplished by a relatively small number of people in your peer network. Their willingness to work under the radar is another reason why it is advantageous to have close colleagues with you when you take on the work of organizing. In general, though, a two pronged approach to handling hierarchy is usually the best. Combin-ing radar-evading tactics, where you side step obstacles when necessary, with the adaptive work of dealing with relationship boundaries, where you negotiate with people above or below, will probably accomplish more and your actions are likely to have a bigger and more lasting impact on the way things get done.

The IT cavalry to the rescue?

In the light of claims that information technology is "revolutionizing work and our way of life," I ought to comment on the role technologies can play in taking on the work of organizing. Distinctions between "management" and "organizing" and "tools" and "talk" allow me to differentiate between types of information technologies in a way we seldom do, but that is useful here.

Many technologies under the IT umbrella are designed to support standard top-down management practices, not organizing. In fact, some of them reinforce top-down practices, whether they are intended to or not. There are tools, period. Their main function is to hold data so it can be moved around, especially to the top, where senior executives, checking their "dashboards," can see what is going on then operate their controls. The ones I'm thinking of include portals, enterprise architecture (EA) tools, customer relationship management (CRM), and enterprise resource planning (ERP) software from Oracle, J.D. Edwards, and SAP; and PeopleSoft, whose names may be more familiar than the products they sell.[21]

It is the other technologies that I'm interested in: tools designed to allow people to interact and "talk"; not simply tools, but "tools-for-talk." Software which provides virtual (online) spaces where individuals on networked computers can interact—posting messages or any other digital media for others to read, see, or hear—or can share documents and other information, potentially is good for anyone taking on the work of organizing, because it enables collaboration. Just as the telephone did a century ago, these tools allow people to "talk" to one another or to groups. By email, by texting one another, or by accessing interactive media like blogs, wikis, and social networking sites like Facebook and LinkedIn, they engage, virtually, in ways and from places they couldn't or wouldn't otherwise do.[22] They allow for what Jay Hellman calls, appropriately, "virtual adjacency,"[23] and, as they help them make meaning together (sharing knowledge) and align, these tools certainly help knowledge workers to organize their work.

Like any tools, however, how good or useful they are depends on what possibilities people see in them and how they treat them. With the wrong vision and in the wrong hands or the wrong places, they become barriers to organizing, distracting people from what they could and ought to be doing to organize successfully. Often their potential for helping people to collaborate and organize their work is simply under utilized, either because they don't understand how they could be used or because they are worried about the consequences of too much unsupervised or uncontrolled sharing.

Most IT departments don't understand collaboration

In the early 1990s, shortly after the Lotus Development Corporation launched Lotus Notes, a client–server software they named "groupware," Wanda Orlikowski, who wrote a revealing article about its roll-out in a large management consulting firm, put her finger on a set of organizational factors that limit the possibilities for virtual collaboration then and now: the mindset and practices of management.[24] Implementing Notes required a centralized IT function that included an administrator to install it on users' desktops and professionals with programming skills to build collaborative tools for them (at the time, these consisted mainly of databases and discussion boards). The main problem was that IT departments, representing a management mindset, didn't seem to understand collaboration, why it mattered, or how groupware could support collaborative work practices.

Two decades on, this is still a common situation in organizations. With no effort to alert users as to how to take advantage of its potential for supporting collaboration, for a long time the software was used mainly in its least collaborative capacity, as an email client. Digging down to find out why, you discover that the true nature and purpose of collaboration are hidden to anyone with a view from the top, so management mistakes communication for collaboration. All that is needed for communication is a system that allows people to send messages, information, and data back and forth. The desire for control is an additional impediment to collaboration if you believe, as most IT departments seem to, that putting collaborative tools into the hands of users is the thin end of the wedge in terms of losing control.

Putting tools in the hands of users

Greater bandwidth, the evolution of the worldwide web (the advent of "Web 2.0"), cloud computing, open source software, technologies like smart phones, and online start-ups with unorthodox business plans have combined to take the ownership and control of applications out of the hands of chief technology officers and chief information officers (titles that are unmistakably "high control") and to put applications into the hands of users via third parties.[25] If work teams or other groups in an organization want to work together online but offsite as it were, there is a range of products that allow them to design virtual spaces to suit their needs. Or they can make use of networking sites with tools they can configure for their purposes. All of which leaves their managers worrying about security and the confidentiality of data.

Given a choice between having to use your organization's IT tools and being able to take the initiative and use web-based ones hosted by third parties, few people seem to want the former. This was illustrated quite dramatically by the efforts of military personnel to share their knowledge in the months after the United States invaded Iraq. At the best of times it is difficult to get and stay organized in completely unfamiliar, hostile surroundings. In Iraq soldiers were scrambling to avoid being killed by improvised explosive devices while driving Humvees that were insufficiently armored to protect them from roadside bombs. Realizing that sharing their experiences and lessons learned could potentially save lives, some officers set up a site (companycommand.com) to do this, using the civilian Internet not a defense department portal.[26]

The importance of being present

As practical and convenient as it is for people to engage (i.e. "talk") with the help of tools, especially when it is dangerous, too expensive, or just impractical to get together, what happens in those virtual spaces is not the same as "real talk," when participants interact directly in the social space they create and hold jointly, with everyone present in the same place at the same time. There is a big difference between being in a virtual space and being present in the social space, although when someone emails a colleague in the next cubicle instead of talking to him or her it is hard to tell whether they recognize the difference or realize that it matters.[27]

There is a chemistry of sorts in being present. We've probably all experienced it when coming face to face with people we've never met before. (Something similar does happen between people who know one another, but it doesn't seem to be as dramatic or noticeable as the first contact.) The chemistry happens both "inside," in how we feel, and "between us," in how we connect. We experience it personally and witness it in others in various contexts, most vividly when individuals who once regarded each other as sworn enemies meet and become friends, or people who've been in captivity and isolated are reunited with their families, or when someone has to break the news that a loved one has died.[28] In each case, the personal and interpersonal quality of being present makes all the difference. Perhaps there is a sense of connectedness, accountability, or responsibility to others that is in our genes and goes all the way back to a time before our human ancestors separated from their animal packs. Whatever the chemistry is, the effects go under many names, from "making friends" to "falling in love" to the idea of "a felt absence of human company."

I'm highlighting the importance of being present because knowledge-work is collective work and both personal and relational, as is organizing. They can collaborate, sharing knowledge, and negotiate meaning together online, but it's not the same as doing it face to face. (Anonymity, it seems, contributes to antisocial behavior, which is something we see more and more of online.) When it comes to *negotiating*—not just telling others what you think and hearing their views, but deciding, *together*, what you are dealing with and whether it is important, so you are aligned—being present can make all the difference. Their combined presence affords people new possibilities for action which is particularly important when they are negotiating boundaries. Collaborative technologies certainly help people to organize, but whether you are taking on the work of organizing from above or below, a good deal of this work has to be done face to face. It is the most effective way of handling hierarchy.

Casting around for partners

You hardly ever pick your own boss and are lucky if you can choose the team you're on. There may be no one else to do the work, so you have to step in; or, in this one instance, you happen to have the most experience; or you've worked with this client before. With so many factors over which we have little or no say, most of the time it is more or less in the hands of the gods who we work with and it's our responsibility to fit in. But, you can't take on the work of organizing alone and, when you are letting go of management and catching on to organizing, having support is crucial. Who do you choose?

Naturally, you want to pick partners-in-organizing who are keen to do this work with you. Being a pioneer doesn't appeal to everyone, especially since transforming high-control organizations into low-control ones often feels conspiratorial. Your intentions for change may seem relatively uncontroversial and low key: meetings where people discuss issues that matter to them and their work rather than someone else's agenda; training that develops critical thinking and people's ability to handle complex problems, which doesn't emphasize the usual "measurable improvements in performance"; preproject planning sessions where you talk about how you want to work together, what you expect of one another, and what each hopes to accomplish; or, when you are working in a different country and culture, spending much more time talking to your counterparts, developing relationships, and looking for common ground, so you can plan together, because this offers a better chance of success. The changes you envisage might seem trivial but, because they *are* changes, at times you will need to circumvent conventions and ignore directives. In which case the people you want to work with as you try to take on new practices are sure to be ones with whom you have, or can quickly develop, good working relationships: people you know because you already work with them or have worked with them; who, you are fairly confident, will push the envelope a bit to do things differently if necessary; will encourage other to get involved; and, especially, partners who show good judgment.

As you take on the work of organizing, you are organizing yourselves and need to align your intentions and actions, which make it desirable to work with like-minded people. When there are differences of opinion, say, over what is worth doing, what is practical, and how far you are willing to go to accomplish it, you should be able to talk openly to one another. When you work with people you know, you can take a certain amount for granted about what they think, how they'll respond in particular situations, and, if you know them well enough, you probably have a sense of what they will and will not be willing to negotiate. Aligning is more complicated when you are working with people you don't know and takes a lot more work. You also want partners with good judgment (and not everyone has it), because taking on the work of organizing is tricky. There are obstacles and boundaries to negotiate.

Keeping an eye on your purpose

When people from one level, team, group, department, division, or organization meet people from another, we surely ought to pay close attention to the social spaces they create because these kinds of encounters are prone to produce breakdowns at the boundaries. But, almost anything, from a phone call to running an eye over the budget, to an email proposing a change in the work schedule, can trigger unexpected rifts "inside" our own teams and work groups. With boundaries and divisions lurking just below the surface, waiting to emerge, both to avoid breakdowns and to deal with them, it's important constantly to take the collective pulse of the group and monitor our own, immediate social spaces.

It's highly likely that in groups which are organizing themselves, the participants are all grappling with questions like: "What is our purpose? How much can we accomplish together? What is success? How should we be accountable to one another?" The answers depend to a great extent on their collective sense of purpose and commitment and, as they feel their way into the work of organizing—*organizing their organizing*—no one should take this sense of purpose or commitment for granted. Every group has to establish and sustain its collective sense of purpose through conversations for commitments, openness, and accountability and, as a starting point, it's as well to understand what moves people, individually and collectively, to do the work of organizing.

Is it the work itself: the pleasure of being intimately involved with people, engaging in a creative process? Or the satisfaction of collegial work relationships? Some people like an intellectual challenge, like looking for patterns in data, or solving technical problems. For those who thrive on personal contacts, work in the territory of relationships, attitudes, and values, as they negotiate their way through and around these, is highly stimulating and rewarding. Is it that you feel you do what you do with more integrity when you are doing the organizing? Is it a sense of having a say in what gets done and how it gets done, or of being able to make a difference? Perhaps it is a feeling of being responsible for the work, or of being an agent of change?

Your motivation, surely, is to be better at what you do but, as a description of purpose, this is too general and vague to be a spur to action. Given that the work of organizing is, at times, challenging, frustrating, and risky, you need something to aspire to, which inspires you, too; and one of the most important things you can do in taking on the work of organizing is keep a collective eye on your collective purpose. This means making sure you talk to each other about what you are doing, to clarify why you are doing it and what you want to accomplish, and to assess whether you're making progress in what you are trying to do, and what you need to work at or do differently. It is all part of the process of aligning. Having a good sense of your personal interest and shared purpose makes "good organizing" real and, if you know what moves you, you will be able to answer better the tough questions needed to negotiate your own, internal boundaries and to hold steady when the going gets tough, as it does when you're trying to influence the way people do things.

Encourage active participation

Good organizing takes everyone's *active participation*, which means they do their work with purpose or good intentions, as well as care, commitment, and accountability to one another. Active participation doesn't mean that everyone, even team members, either can or is expected to do the *same* work, or even the same *amount* of work.

One of the biggest fallacies of managing the MBA way is the idea that everyone on the same level, on the same team, or getting the same pay should be making an identical contribution. Most of the reasons for this unrealistic expectation have to do with an outdated industrial-work mindset. In factories, people in the same department, who received the same base pay, worked the same number of hours on a shift and did identical work. Not only was their output measurable but also they were expected to produce work to a uniform standard or quality. By testing samples of their production, it was relatively easy to determine whether they were or weren't doing so. As we now know, knowledge-work and factory-work have nothing in common, except the word "work." The expectation that individuals will all make similar contributions remains (it is a characteristic of high-control systems) but it is illogical, even absurd, to apply it to knowledge-work.

Jean Lave and Etienne Wenger coined the phrase "peripheral participation" to explain that people do different things and make different kinds of contributions from different places or positions in a network.[29] It is an idea that everyone taking on the work of organizing needs to take to heart because we come at organizing with the expectation of uniform contributions. There is no center of a network of organizers, where things "really happen." The strength of social networks is that loosely coupled action goes on all over the place simultaneously. Wherever they are in the network, people are "at work," but, depending on what is happening, are more and less distant from a particular set of problems or issues at any moment. As networks are in flux, it is important that participants not only have different roles and commitments, but also that they change roles and make different contributions work and action moves "around" the network. At one moment a person's role may be connecting other parts of the network, or other networks, as a kind of go-between. Perhaps, as the marketing department begins to craft the message they'll use for advertising, he or she is explaining to them what the programmers are working on. At another time, when the design team is making some last minute changes to the software, besides his or her design work, he or she may be their liaison with the executive group in the corporate office.

In helping to shift the way we think about work and organizing it, the question for activists is, given their proximity to what is happening, is everyone *sufficiently involved*, or do they need to be brought further into the work by way of a phone call or a knock on the door followed by a conversation? There is necessarily a lot of leeway in these decisions and making them clearly isn't a job for one person because no single person can keep track of the work action as it moves around, of who is "in" or "out" of the action, and whether they are sufficiently involved. This is the job of the network and is one of the reasons why mutual (peer-to-peer) accountability, not top-down compliance, is so important. Organizing is always a collective effort. We keep one another engaged and maintain everyone's active participation through conversations for commitment and accountability.

CHAPTER 15

Good work wanted

Who knows good work?

If you have read this far and aren't sneaking a peak at the end to find out whether I have anything interesting to say, I won't have to remind you that I have been poking around inside knowledge-work and the mindset we call management in order to understand work practices. Whatever they do, you can assume people want to do a decent job and, whether it is cleaning out the garage or preparing a report, they need to be properly organized. So, one-on-one, or in groups, knowledge workers spend much of their time talking—planning, negotiating, and arranging; preparing to do something.

Even when everyone is doing it with the best of intentions, organizing can be a tricky process, requiring persistence and agility. The relatively minor matter of coordinating schedules can turn out to be a small trial in itself. Or it may take a good deal of negotiating and maneuvering back and forth to reconcile divergent interests. Then someone new comes into the picture and you start all over. At work an array of practices makes the circumstances for organizing far from ideal. Bureaucratic rules, for example, limit individuals' discretion and flexibility. Hierarchy makes superiors and subordinates out of colleagues, driving a wedge between their interests. And work-place culture discourages talk, hence sharing knowledge. Vestiges of the industrial era, and devised under circumstances far removed from today's knowledge-work environments, these practices were not intended to help people get organized. Factory-work didn't require it. Knowledge workers, however, who have to organize, are frustrated by an enormous apparatus of top-down control. It restricts their authority and constantly diverts their energy and attention from their work. This is not a recipe for good work.

Knowledge-work is social. On the premise that if you aren't saying it you aren't seeing it, at team meetings, on conference calls, and in emails, whenever and whenever people organize, good work should be high on their agenda. Giving others credit for good work, acknowledging their collective effort, which shows you care about what they do, strengthens work relationships, contributes to better collaboration, and encourages everyone to share knowledge, each a foundation for good work. The other reason is you probably don't have to look very far to find examples of bad work. When you do, you'll want to draw attention to it and nudge one another in the direction of good work. Everyone involved ought to be thinking and talking about whether, why, and how the work they are doing together is either up to the mark or falls short of what they expect. Apart from anything else, these conversations are the lifeblood of accountability. In my experience, you hardly ever hear them.

All this begs the question, just what *is* good work? *Do* we—*can we*—recognize it and how do we know it when we see it? We spend much of our lives "in" our work, so how could we *not* know good work? The answer is it is a work-world of "performance" and "results," not good or bad work and, on or off the record, people say very little about their work. On the record especially, the few exceptions to this rule, when someone actually talks about others' "efforts" or "performance," their purpose is generally to reinforce compliance and control. They are not interested in the work. Here are some examples. Invited to open two days of training on "skills for team leaders," an executive, showing participants a graph of quarterly earnings, will remind them that their jobs depend on improved results. In management-speak he is "motivating them to improve performance." Then there is the annual "performance evaluation," a formal and largely secret affair that takes place behind closed doors, with results known only to the employee and his or her superiors. The idea behind these performance evaluations, which started with piece-work and are as universally mocked and criticized by employees as they are staunchly defended by management, is that work—always individual effort—is measurable and is measured by comparing an individual's productivity ("performance") against benchmarks or outcomes set by management. An upshot of these peculiar assumptions (they have no bearing on knowledge-work) is that the distinction of being a "team player" has little to do with helping other project-team members to do good work and everything to do with complying with organizational norms.

On those rare occasions that someone receives visible encouragement or praise for work done, the object seems to be to remind everyone that patronage is integral to high control. A bonus, merited by an "excellent" rating on your performance evaluation, comes with the "personal congratulations" (sent impersonally, in an email) of someone higher up. Even though she hardly knows her retiring subordinate from a bar of soap, it is still customary for his departmental head to present him with a "token of appreciation" and make a short speech about his years of service to the company. Then there are loopy monthly and annual awards, with faint echoes of military medal parades, which recognize individuals for cooperative work. So few actually receive this sort of recognition, and most don't seek it, that employees seldom pay attention to either the awards or the accompanying "rewards." Like performance evaluations, they are tools of high control. It is instructive to examine the agendas behind them, but the awards are often little more than a diversion and source of brief bemusement, when employees see who has been chosen for their "service to our customers" (more likely, "the boss").

So far I have skirted questions about what it means to do good work and how to encourage it. Now that I want to make up for this, it is difficult to know where to begin. The entire area called "work" sits uneasily at the farthest fringes of the management universe, barely visible in the view from the top. This and the fact that management, claiming to be "scientific" and "objective," steers clear of values, opinions, and judgments and, indeed, of anything that sounds remotely human, means it is no use turning to business books for advice. These are preoccupied with "efficiency and "quality," which is something entirely different. The "values" that matter are monetary ones: amounts in profit and loss statements, balance sheets, end-of-year bonus announcements, and the like. These masquerade as "objective facts" but are routinely manipulated to tell the stories about how organizations are doing that shareholders, investors, and others want to hear and executives want told.[1]

Work is human to the core

Perhaps the main message in Matthew Crawford's homage to craftwork, *Shop Class as Soulcraft*, is that work, and I mean all kinds of work, are inextricably human, bound up with people's perspectives and aspirations, priorities and desires, even their hopes and fears.[2] Listen to how he describes his experience of working as an electrician: "I *felt pride* in meeting the *aesthetic demands* of a workmanlike installation." "I felt *responsible* to my better self. Or rather, to the thing itself—craftsmanship has been said to consist simply in the *desire to do something well*, for its own sake." "The *satisfactions* of . . . manual competence," he says, "have been known to make a man *quiet and easy*," adding that "the work a man does *forms him*."[3] We use words like "joy," "disappointment," "pleasure," "satisfaction," and "anger" to describe the way we feel about our work because we *have feelings* about work. It is part of who and what we are.

Crawford tells of his experience as a beginner, learning mechanics from his mentor and, later, as a restorer of old motorcycles, accessing the "collective historical memory . . . embedded in a community of mechanic-antiquarians."[4] The social side of shop-work may surprise anyone who thinks of manual work like old-style factory-work, as routine, repetitive, mindless, and solitary. But, like apprentices and masters, for the generation of workers weaned on social networking software, who use it to swap stories about their work, colleagues, and bosses, who constantly text one another about what they're doing, offer friends and colleagues advice, and ask for help with some or other problem, the collective nature of their work is no surprise.

Crawford's admiration for shop-work is clear. What is not clear is whether knowledge-work possesses the same virtues. His answer almost certainly would be "no." Knowledge-work has a different character, which, he seems to suggest, makes it less fulfilling, or not as nourishing to the soul. Whether we are talking about teaching, litigating, writing, composing, advising, planning, designing, or censoring, however, I disagree. Both knowledge-work and shop-work have their virtues (as well as vices), because, like all and any work, they are human to the core. Allow me to explain.

Often the most familiar face of work is a brief description of a job, such as "editing scientific articles," "brokering deals," and "keeping the public safe." But neither these, nor more detailed job descriptions that include activities, like typing, writing reports, analyzing data, coordinating others' work, which someone hired to do the job is expected to perform, actually describe *work*. Work is the experience of doing something, which typically engages many of your senses, together with your conscious thoughts, all at once. You are involved in work. You participate in it. (I'm sure you've noticed how, when you become immersed in your work, you can completely lose track of time.)

A job description is as close to work as a menu is to eating food. If an item on the menu whets your appetite it is because, in an instant, you go from reading about a dish to imagining what it tastes like. When you lean across the table to thank your host for a superb meal, you are telling her about your experience, how her food tasted (and, possibly, how good it smelled), how you enjoyed the company and the wine, and, now it is over, that you feel contentment. "Good work," too, has to do with the *experience* of working. For the people involved in it, part of that experience, but only part of it, is a sense of accomplishment.

Work—actually work*ing*—brings people together with other people and with things or "tools," like spreadsheets, plans, and agendas. You are obliged by your work to form relationships with co-workers, advisors, messengers, providers of tech support, and customers, amongst others.

All, in one way or another, participate in doing the work, contributing to how and how well you do it. Equally, depending on what you do, you are obliged to wrestle with an assortment of tools and materials, perhaps using a calculator to try to tame numbers, or a desktop search application to find the reply to an email you are sure you sent a few weeks ago. Where Matthew Crawford takes pride, say, in meeting the aesthetic demands of his work—this is what he appreciates and values in doing the work—knowledge workers fret over inscrutable numbers in a spreadsheet, are surprised by the elegance of a solution proposed by a colleague and frustrated by computer problems they can't resolve, or are happy with a client's enthusiastic response to what they've done and their boss's obvious approval. All part of the experience, these contribute to their sense of work's virtues and vices.

You discover the virtues and vices of work (and it always exhibits both) *in* the lived experience of doing it, encountering tools and materials and interacting with others, while analyzing, deliberating, assessing, drafting, thinking, discussing, questioning, and creating things together, or in reliving the experience, reflecting on what you have been doing.[5] Knowledge workers seldom follow well-trodden paths. Organizing while they do their work, they forge their own directions and, along the way lots of things can hold them up. Colleagues with unorthodox work habits may be mildly irritating. More exasperating is a boss who either can't or won't give a straight answer to questions about what you need to do to complete the contract. Without their knowing it, others may be blocking your way, preventing you from doing something important; or you've missed a deadline you set together; or, watching what your partners are doing, you are concerned that they seem to be on a different track entirely. How you handle these situations, whether and how quickly you resolve the problems, depends in large measure on whether people are able to discuss their problems and others are willing to listen, and, if they are, are willing to cooperate. Saying "this is good work" is an opinion about how their work, together, has gone or is going. It is an assessment of collective intentions, actions, and of what is accomplished by people doing things together.

The goodness of work has to do with people's motives, attitudes, and behavior toward each other; with their integrity and commitment; whether they're being sensible and responsible or reckless; and whether they're using their initiative when the situation calls for it. The goodness of work has to do with our feelings about how they are contributing (and whether they are willing to go out of their way to help) and whether what we are doing is worthwhile or useful for them, as well as our sense of achievement in overcoming obstacles and of success at working through difficult problems, and our ability to get a measure of agreement and alignment when parties are far apart. Goodness also includes our assessments of the intrinsic qualities of what we're doing, whether it's the fact that the report is concise and well written, that the images we've used in the presentation seem to have persuaded others in ways we'd hoped they would, or that we've taken steps to cover all contingencies. All of this, from the aesthetics of the things we create to our relationships with people, is integral to being in the work, where we engage people and things and some or all of it may be relevant to assessing how well we are doing or have done.

In the eyes of the beholders

Encountering others' fancies and foibles, and being reminded of our own, or discovering the qualities and characteristics of tools and other things we work with, is not always pleasing or appealing. People bicker and are willing to fight about issues we may think are trivial. How frustrating it is that they won't budge, even when they are obviously wrong! And, there is the guitar that beckoned to me for so long. Sadly, I've learned through bitter experience that I'll never master it. On the other hand, I get a certain amount of satisfaction when, with minimal assistance from a customer service representative on the other end of a telephone, I find I am finally making headway in solving my computer problem. In the same way, when you learn that the proposal you and your colleague sweated over actually got accepted, you share a small moment of triumph with her.

We learn lessons of life in our work. Whatever you do, you are aware of relationships (both good and bad) as well as your values and ideals. Encountering materials, objects, and tools, you learn about their qualities, what purposes they serve, how difficult it is to use them and, sometimes, not to fiddle with things you don't understand. Whether people, tools, or both surprise or disappoint, help or hinder, inspire or bore, we learn to be tolerant, patient, considerate, responsible, cautious, careful, and committed. In the work—the doing—we learn, too, how creative we can be and how to be creative, how to deal with certain types of problems and with particular people, including who to turn to and who to avoid, and we learn the difference between the right and wrong way to do things and what constitutes "doing good work."

Contrary to what we're generally led to believe, "good work" is not a universal phenomenon. There is no broad or even general definition of it. It is specific to both people and circumstances, tied to attitudes, values, and ideals. For example, what doctors can do and what their patients and the nurses will tolerate and even be grateful for in the field, under enemy fire, or in an emergency room, may be very different from what is practical and acceptable in the operating theater of a suburban hospital. Making "quick and dirty changes" to a spreadsheet may not meet your normal standards of thoroughness, but, when you're a few minutes away from the meeting where you have to present the revised budget, they'll do the trick. And we don't have to be wildly successful to do good work. When it is a big problem, a small breakthrough can be highly satisfying to everyone involved.

A god's-eye perspective and a human one

In the management universe, where the views of financial wizards and technically oriented "experts" carry a lot of weight, everyone seems to have forgotten that "quality" is a matter of judgment and opinion. In fact, listening to what the experts say, you must surely come to exactly the opposite conclusion. Perhaps this is a result of playing fast and loose with words, for, in the management universe, besides being a tool for manipulating attitudes and behavior, in an Alice in Wonderland Caterpillarish sort of way, people use language to mean whatever they want it to mean. "Chief knowledge officer," "human capital," and "talent acquisition manager" are a few choice examples. The experts say it is not only possible but also necessary to have objective, measurable standards of quality. So "quality" now is synonymous with meeting ISO 9000 standards and "doing good work" means adopting lean production practices, or something similar, to "preserve customer value with less work." [6]

In truth, conflating technical requirements and quality, or confusing efficiency, a technically constructed concept of quality, with good work, is hardly new. This is exactly how management got started. Wikipedia describes lean manufacturing, correctly, as "a more refined version of earlier efficiency efforts, building upon the work of ... Taylor ... [and] Ford." [7] Six Sigma, lean production, and quality circles have kept scientific management going and up-to-date. These contemporary techniques for making production more efficient, for example, by reducing variations in the tolerances of machined parts while also cutting costs, are variations of the operating system Taylor invented for industrial production when he started to carve out the field of time and motion studies decades ago. Each of them springs from the same mindset as those studies: the idea that the object of "work" is to make *organizations* more profitable and to be more profitable they must be more efficient. First you need data, including benchmarks for efficiency. Then you need to control production by the numbers.

Taylor was interested in people only because, by experimenting with them to determine what a worker—in his words, "a good man"—could produce in a specified amount of time, he got the magic numbers that were the key to controlling production and costs. "Good," here, has nothing to do with a person's character. He meant "efficient." For, in spite of having apprenticed himself in a machine shop and worked for a number of years in a foundry, where he began as a wage-laborer and moved up, Taylor was contemptuous of workers. Treating them like guinea pigs when he experimented, he ridiculed them in his writings. To get a worker to work harder you needed to use tricks much like those you'd use to train a circus animal, bribing him with a "reward" of higher base pay and/or performance bonuses.[8]

Taylor hosted parties of intellectuals and executives at his home, where he explained scientific management to them, concocting stories of his exploits and methods that caricatured workers as dim-witted, incapable of independent thought, and in need of constant supervision. Matthew Stewart concludes that he "came to see the human component on the factory floor as something comparable to the machines, with properties that could be manipulated in the same way as those of a lathe."[9] Commenting on the significance of these stories, Stewart argues that neither Taylor nor his audiences actually gave a fig about the numbers that supposedly made management "scientific." Instead it was the stories that *both* Taylor and his audience found compelling. So, his "good man" turns out to be confabulation and his standards of good work—efficiency—are no *one's* standards and possibly not even stopwatch-based measurements.

At the end of this book, with the distinction between knowledge-work and factory-work now firmly in mind, the obvious reason for ignoring TQM or lean production techniques when we are looking for good work is that it is hard to see any connection between the tools of "quality management," as these techniques are known collectively, and the work I am interested in. Quality goes with a view of work from the top, which as I've noted is hardly a view of work at all. Quality management has a place, probably an important one, in manufacturing production, where the view from the top is practical and useful, but the ideas and practices, taken out of context, are used indiscriminately and the management mindset is to blame, because all "work" looks the same through a management lens; nonhuman and mechanical, routine, repetitive, and mindless. For management, this is a convenient fiction. It maintains the pretence that management principles and practices are universal. But, it is wrong, which is how a cliché like "what gets measured gets done" worms its way into knowledge-work, even though it is nonsensical. With knowledge-work, the doings you are supposed to measure are largely invisible and unquantifiable.

The problem with the view from the top is that it is definitely not a human's or mortal's view, but, possibly, a god's-eye view and, as the omniscient, omnipotent gods we know presumably don't work, they probably wouldn't understand work.[10] If I had to choose one management construct that symbolizes the view from the top, revealing why it is a god's-eye view, not a human one, I'd pick the org chart. To explain why, I'm going to digress for a moment while I reimagine the org chart as a pyramid-maze puzzle. Keep an org chart in mind when you read my description of the "organization" in Figure 15.1 and consider whether this is a fair description of how you see organizations.[11]

What is most impressive about a god's-eye view? It is possible to see and to know everything there is to see and to know about anything. We are talking about an organization. What would it have to look like in order to know everything there is to know about it? Think of a simple mechanism with a few interconnected parts, like a clockwork motor in a toy car. It has a permanent structure or form, you can see exactly how it works, and, although it shows movement, is predictable. I believe this is what we read into org charts and it is what I want to convey with the maze-puzzle

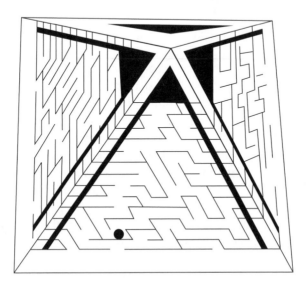

Figure 15.1 A pyramid-maze puzzle

Source: Based on a puzzle marketed by Loncraine Broxton. Used with permission of the Lagoon Trading Co. Ltd.

in Figure 15.1. Structured and, of course, lifeless, it has a top and a bottom and everything in-between has its own, unique place relative to the top or bottom. At the same time, everything needed for it to fulfill its function is present. It is all there, self-contained, complete-in-itself. Nothing is missing. From the structure to the problems you have to deal with to how to solve them, with the eyes of a god you see and know it all.

As to the "work," there is a single, tame problem to solve. It involves moving a ball to a specific place. What could be clearer? All you need to think about is how to do this most efficiently. Through management lenses, organizational problems look remarkably similar. They involve moving resources around and between the obstacles of budgets, deadlines, lists of deliverables, reporting structures, and so on. Doing this efficiently is "good work" in management-speak. What is more, you have information (data) to *tell you* what to do. As you can see which pathways are open and which are dead ends, right or wrong, you will know the difference immediately. Everything is transparent. There is no ambiguity.[12]

Everything exceeds our grasp

Anyone who thinks of an org chart as somehow capturing the essence of an organization, so that redrawing the org chart gives you a sense of how things will look and work after a reorg, has fallen victim to its god's-eye qualities. What a deception this is. If you want to know how and why people do the things they do, you have to see as they see and understand their circumstances and motives. Writing from a human standpoint, the perspective of his "bodily senses," David Abram sees "a world that *exceeds our grasp in every direction*...No thing...appears as a completely determinate or finished object. Each thing...that my body sees, presents some face or facet of itself...while withholding other aspects from view."[13] "Being there," in the work, in the moment (Heidegger's concept, *Dasein*, being human), means there is always a great deal that we *don't* and *cannot* know about any situation. And, while there is a lot we can't and don't see, even the simplest objects that we *do* see hide aspects of themselves from us and, of course, people see things differently. Abram explains that, no matter how hard you try, you can't see the whole of a bowl at once. Break it down into its smallest visible element, powdered clay, and something will still be "missing." You won't see its "bowl-ness."

Time prevents us from having a god's-eye perspective and knowing everything there is to know. The passage of time is a felt (i.e. an experienced) phenomenon. When you are very young, a school term passes incredibly slowly and a car trip of a few hundred miles seems to go on forever, but the older you get the faster time seems to fly. The French philosopher Henri Bergson explains that being-in-the-world means being-in-time and, in a certain sense, being a prisoner to time.[14] Always "in" the present moment, we look "forward" to an *unknown and unknowable* but imaginable future, and think "back" on the past we remember but do not know (i.e. experience now). The fact that the present, past, and future have fundamentally different qualities—the difference between what we know, what we remember, and what we believe we can expect—has a bearing on how we plan and what we do. If we've done the same thing successfully a few times, like going to buy groceries, we will no doubt assume that we'll be able to do this the same way the next time we want to. If, however, because we don't know what will happen, we feel there is reason to be anxious about what the future holds, it is sensible to make contingency plans and act cautiously.

Would organizations undertake as many very complicated projects if people were sensible?[15] Would there be as many failures? How do you allow for contingencies and caution in a contract? From banking to building roads, a panoply of tools, including project scheduling programs and long-term planning instruments, treat time as homogeneous, or a continuum, where the nature and "quality" of the future (using the mathematical notion t_1, t_2, t_3, etc.) is no different from the present (t_0), or the past (t_{-1}, t_{-2}, t_{-3}), fostering the illusion that planners have god-like capabilities. Forecasting tools provide one more example of this deception. Their premise is that data (about the past) will guide you through the future if you have the technology to manipulate it and know how to use statistical methods.

Professionals take this humbug seriously. In the financial sector, for example, they believed, and possibly still do, that replacing flawed human judgment with computations based on complex formulae would enable portfolio managers to "reduce their risk." Until the financial meltdown in 2007 awoke them from their reveries, word was that possessing algorithm-derived "synthetic securities" (artificial assets?), known as derivatives, insured you against market fluctuations, so you no longer had to bother about what could happen in the future.[16] Normal human responses to uncertainty, like prudence and conservatism, or even having a certain minimum ratio of assets to liabilities, were no longer necessary. These "outmoded habits and policies" were inconvenient. They stood in the way of bigger profits.[17]

If you are wondering how people with university degrees could so readily succumb to hocus-pocus, perhaps it isn't as hard as it seems. When you are constantly reminded of management's scientific credentials, whiz-kids with impressive qualifications are showing you mathematical formulae you probably don't understand but half-believe are magical, you possess technology that "experts" claim will free you and your organization from whatever constrains or encumbers you, and you find yourself in a world offering the prospect of impossible riches, where exercising judgment and using your intuition—human qualities—are disavowed, can you resist falling victim to tools and the claims that they make possible what experience and common sense ought to tell you is impossible?

Hiding from the humanness of work

When financial institutions use computers and mathematics to gamble with people's savings *and* their trust, their management having abandoned well-established business practices in pursuit of profits without limit and obscenely large bonuses,[18] we get a glimpse of the kind of chaos that is possible if we don't, or won't, or can't see our work through human eyes, in human terms. We see, too, what happens if we don't stop to think about whether what we are doing is "good work," or to see ourselves in our work and to think about other people and how we fulfill our responsibilities to them, rather than "the killing we can make by aggressively marketing this new product."

Management practices begin with the following assurances. There is a path to perfection, or, as Fredrick Taylor saw it, "one true way"; someone at the top, with enough data, knows what it is; and, when everyone is on it, an optimal outcome is certain. To ensure good work, you need those who know the path to *direct* others to follow it and *keep redirecting* them, as necessary, to make sure they don't stray. High-control practices and tools, like structures, rules, and agendas, all spring from this piece of mythology. But, as Matthew Crawford writes, with them comes "a kind of infantilization at work [that]...offends the spirited personality." To illustrate a "material culture" that promises to "disburden us of mental and bodily involvement...yet...gives us fewer experiences of direct responsibility," he cites the example of faucets designed to turn themselves on and off automatically. Is this a recipe for good work? That god's-eye perspective undermines the human spirit, crushes creativity, dehumanizes work, desensitizes people, and infantilizes them.[19]

The management mindset has us constantly hiding from the humanness of work: trying to avoid the fact that the future is unknowable, pretending it is possible to turn uncertainty into calculable "risk";[20] believing you should cut corners to cut costs and that you can do this with impunity over and over again ("cheaper, better, faster"); treating wicked problems as if they were technical ones that can solved with the right data; looking for exact benchmarks of performance and objective standards for success; believing you can create "value" out of thin air; and insisting, before you approve them, that people show—with financial data—that their proposals are going to be successful.

The trouble is that when you think this way, you lose sight of just about everything that matters for doing good work, you aren't able to tell good work from bad, and, what is more, you don't *care*. The mindset or thought-scheme you're using to organize work doesn't have a place for care. In the aftermath of a "global financial crisis" that sent huge institutions to the brink, which measure their worth in billions of dollars, it seems obvious that we should turn attention to work and why people ought to care. Amongst other things, in the "meltdown," the hopes of many for longer-term financial security vanished; security which the same institutions promised them in advertisement after advertisement. Then in April 2010, on the heels of the turmoil in financial markets, which, incidentally, revealed Bernard Madoff to be the biggest Ponzi-scheme fraudster in history, *Deepwater Horizon*, one the BP oil company's rigs in the Gulf of Mexico, exploded. It took BP employees and many people from other organizations just a fraction under a quarter of a year to staunch the flow of oil from the broken riser pipe that tapped a deep-sea well. No one knows what effects the mixture of oil and gas that spewed out will have on sea life, the earth, and people living near the Gulf. If the consequences are anything like those that followed the grounding of the oil tanker *Exxon Valdez*, they will probably last for generations.

It takes a concatenation of events to bring down a financial system or to cause a pipe to rupture deep below the ocean's surface, but, when it comes to assessing causes, we make a necessary and practical distinction. Either it's an accident, which means it happened in spite of everyone's best efforts, or it's due to carelessness or negligence. Quite often, knowing it's some combination of the two, we try to get to the bottom of things, to figure out how much one, or the other, played a part. As the investigations proceed it is increasingly clear that, in large measure, people's carelessness and negligence are to blame for both these sets of problems, and that these, undoubtedly, were the main causes of the financial meltdown.[21]

Work is complicated, ambiguous, uncertain, and messy, in large part because it involves humans (not gods) doing things together. In the absence of these "problems" and human relationships, there would be no reason to take pride in what you are doing, to exercise care, to act responsibly, to be prudent, honest, tolerant, and empathetic, or to have non-technical standards of excellence. But there is every reason to do so. Compared to what we believe about gods, humans are myopic and, for this reason, good work means, among other things, the ability to deal with ambiguity as you find it, imaging how you'll work your way through a mess, then providing what customers or colleagues want, all the while bridging differences to achieve some degree of alignment among the people for whom and with whom you work. A management play-book won't help you to do this.

The milieu of organizations is little changed from the bad old days of sweat-shops and production lines, where people were treated as appendages to machines. Because Taylorist principles are the norm at work, responsibility, including tolerance and careful judgment, don't get a look in. These signal the role and importance of *relationships* at work. Managing, however, is conceived as a series of *transactions* and a technical process. Time and, above all, money are priorities. Taking care, being considerate, and thinking about the consequences of what you're doing are the enemies of time and money. This "logic" makes organizations moral vacuums.[22] Something has to fill a vacuum, and that something includes egotism and competition amongst executives and employees for the biggest bonuses. Integral to the way organizations are managed, these make a virtue of greed. *Dis*honesty and *ir*responsibility are attractive and commonplace.

Management has colonized life

Just as everything General Motors did was once deemed "good for the country [America],"[23] management practices, were—and, for many, still are—good for work, for organizations, and, therefore, for all of us. In the hundred-odd years that management has been around, it has colonized work life and staked a claim to a universal ideology, spreading to all corners of the globe, infiltrating every aspect of our lives. You'll find management-speak as alive and well in homeowners' associations as school boards. Listening to the radio you shouldn't be surprised to hear an "expert on raising children," telling parents how to *manage* theirs, perhaps listing ways they can become more efficient at parenting, or discussing how they can improve children's "performance" at school, using "tools" that include prescription psychotropic medications such as Ritalin to "help them concentrate."[24] University students who take neuroenhancers like Adderal sound like management consultants, describing them as "good for productivity."[25]

As much as work management, policy management is the instrument of a god's-eye perspective. Institutions of higher learning run policy

programs just like MBA degrees. The skill they prize most in their graduate students is their ability to crunch numbers. To the extent that anyone is
paying attention to climate change or population growth, whether in corporate public relations departments or at the once-a-year meetings in Davos,
Switzerland, a playground for the "world's great leaders" as far from
actual problems as possible, they're doing it the high-control way. At the
top of the agenda is the need for data. All are waiting for "experts"—
the scientists—to agree there is a problem, then for experts, whoever they
are, to find a solution. The savior, everyone hopes and expects, will be
technology, which will allow us to go on doing the unsustainable, making it unnecessary for us to change our lives. If you listen carefully,
you can still hear the old refrain, "give us the tools and we'll finish
the job." [26]

Like good high controllers everywhere, the "solutions" mooted, at the
top, by experts and the executives and administrators in charge, involve
running from the humanness of problems. If you aren't satisfied with the
quality of education, we'll improve it by making everyone pass standardized tests. It doesn't matter that the sea level may be rising, once we're
sure it is we'll move people inland or build dykes. Nor does it matter that
the seas are emptying of fish, we'll construct artificial lakes and farm fish.
Running low on energy reserves, the solution is to develop new extraction
methods. Hydraulic fracturing, or "fracking," is the latest way to produce
natural gas. It involves pumping millions of gallons of chemicals into shale
beds and one result is that aquifers are being polluted by a mixture of this
highly toxic concoction and the natural gas released. Knowing as much as
we do today about ecosystems—the intimate connections between living
things and the systems they live in—how can we possibly look at these as
"good solutions"? [27]

Going topless

With a view from the top, a fake god's-eye perspective, you can't tell
good solutions from bad and aren't interested in doing so. It's a tautol-
ogy when you're at the top, managing, that whatever you do *is* good. The
logic runs something like this. Activities handled with an eye on efficiency
are good ("efficient" means "good"). Financial results are the ultimate
measure of efficiency. You manage activities to get good financial results.
Ergo, when activities are managed, and contribute to the bottom line, the
work involved is good. "Going topless" is my way of drawing attention to
what it takes to jettison this ridiculous "logic." Whether it is building the

next generation of cars or finding a way to save the whales, these are multi-faceted, wicked problems, not only because there are multiple stakeholders with divergent interests, but also because, however they are resolved, they include both good and bad work. We must have the question of what is good and bad work in full view, on the table—in our conversations—at all times; we must have a perspective that allows us to tell one from the other; and we must have ways of encouraging one another to keep heading in the direction of goodness or, whenever we stray, to head back that way.

Now, "going topless" may make it sound as though I'm talking about lopping off the points of pyramids or "flattening" organizations, an ineffectual approach often adopted for "smashing silos" and encouraging collaboration. This is not what I mean at all, because, as I've noted, structure is *not* the problem. Going topless has to do with what is missing at work and what is missing are voices: the voices we need to hear so that we are thinking about our work, are able to tell good work from bad, and that keep us interested in doing good work. These are diverse voices of experience, which come from multiple practices, cover a multitude of perspectives, and from people who are intimate with the work, the people, and the things at hand. They are human voices and stories, capable of "connecting" us with work and everything involved in doing it, not just "results" or "outcomes." Voices that can draw us into conversations and into asking questions about good and bad work—what we're doing and why, with whom, and for whom, how we're doing it, and what are the consequences of what we're doing. I explained earlier (Chapter 5) that the view from the top and the view from practice—management and organizing—are like parallel universes. Management (the mindset) is all models and tools. For experience and talk to count at work, we have to become organizers, banishing high-control practices. This is what I mean by going topless.

Resting on compliance, high-control keeps all eyes on the top. It has everyone looking inward and up, not thinking about what *they* are doing or what is happening in the world "out there," but waiting, anxiously, for the next pronouncement or instruction; waiting for someone else to tell them what to do or how well they are performing. When directives or assessments arrive, they are probably not what you'd expect from super-humans who are above the fray and want to make sure everyone is comfortable, happy, enthusiastic, and doing their best. Despite the constant reassurance that they know and act in everyone's best interests, top-down plans, agendas, instructions, and evaluations are seldom positive, reassuring, encouraging, or constructive. They are usually just the opposite because they are part of a system that serves the interests of people at the top and serves to keep them on top.

Keeping subordinates "on their toes," undermining their confidence, waiting anxiously for another shoe to fall, is one way to do this. Performance appraisals and 360-degree evaluations are favored tools. Another is to divide and rule, pitting people against one another by rewarding competition and discouraging cooperation. And notice how assessing employees' contributions and effort is anything but ordinary. "Rewards" and "incentives" and "evaluations" and "assessments," the carrots and sticks of high control, are reserved for special events like public award ceremonies, where "top performers" are singled out as a lesson to all, or to the annual performance evaluation, where supervisors or bosses can mete out criticism in private, based on "objective performance criteria."

As everything has to be vetted, approved, authorized, or regulated to ensure that whatever actions are taken conform to "our standards/norms/requirements," having all eyes on the top makes it difficult to respond either quickly or effectively to the problems and people you're working with, including colleagues and clients. To make matters worse, remember that as they work their way to the top, which is where "inputs" in the form of data, applications, proposals, reports, recommendations, and, occasionally, complaints are supposed to go, these lurch (the word we use is "flow") through a moral morass. Intended to be technically efficient, "the system" is deliberately designed to be devoid of values, ideals, or principles. It is okay to have "mission statements" and "value propositions" at work. These are tools of management and equivalent to a list of deliverables or a meeting agenda. But no one wants you to have values or express personal preferences. Like genuine mistakes, matters of conscience, or any kind of dissent (which is strange for institutions that promote "aggressive competition"), they are entirely unacceptable.

There are no moral vacuums in human affairs. Somebody "in charge" makes assessments, forms opinions, reaches conclusions, and makes decisions, so ideals, values, and beliefs are always in play. The question is always: Whose ideals and values and what are these? In high-control organizations, they certainly don't reflect the wisdom of gods. It turns out that "up there" people are as myopic as everyone else, preoccupied with their own narrow, often squalid, all too human pursuits. In fact, in the rarified atmosphere of Mount Olympus, because there is so much at stake—so much to gain, or lose, from a personal point of view—people are much more interested in the games they're playing up there than in what is going on among the mortals down below, which they can't see much of, anyway. The games of the gods are games of power and control, including and importantly, "Who has the biggest package?" "Who can I manipulate today?" and "How can I muscle my way in?" While similar games are played out below, with all that power concentrated at the top, once the gods get started, who is going to stop them? And, when they decide to attack one another, whether it's executives from competing IT companies, house committee members confronting industry CEOs, whaling commission representatives, or leaders of opposing sects or religions (who claim power from different gods), the personal stakes being so high, the smackdown can get nasty, with lots of "collateral damage," most often to "small people."[28]

With the ideology of control from the top dominating our vision, we learn to believe—actually are made to feel—that it's superior, both morally and technically. Of course we need administrators, just as we need plans, strategies, guidelines, and budgets. It is a mistake to assume, however, that having these makes for good work. They are not ends, but *some* means of doing good work. Actually we need administrators, who, amongst other things, are well-informed, well-intentioned, thoughtful, careful, sensible, honest, reliable, responsible, accountable, and responsive, who produce sensible, practical, and flexible plans, guidelines, and budgets. This is all possible with the topless option, the way people organize for themselves, by networking, group-by-group, or person-to-person, conversation-by-conversation, which goes on all the time, though, as I've said, we don't see it.

The point, though, as you know only too well from working with people who are organizing themselves, is that "going topless" never works perfectly. On the contrary, getting work done this way is rather messy and certainly not "efficient" in the sense of "neat and tidy and requiring minimal effort," but these considerations don't apply to any kind of human work, which is either sweaty, mentally demanding, or both. Topless is often slow. But, when people are headed in different directions and don't know exactly what they're doing or should be doing, which is often the case in human affairs, slow may be not only desirable but also necessary. Topless allows for openness and accountability, but doesn't guarantee it. Like everything else, if we believe they are worthwhile, necessary for good work, we have to work at achieving both.[29] The main merit of being topless, it seems to me, and perhaps the only sense in which topless is not a completely mixed blessing, is that you work and organize on a human scale: person-to-person, relationship-by-relationship. For the sake of good work, for our humanity, and, perhaps, for the future of humanity this matters a great deal.

Chapter 1

1. Peter F. Drucker, *The Practice of Management* (New York: Harper and Row, 1986 [1954]): 4.
2. Peter F. Drucker, "Management's New Paradigms," *Forbes* 162, no. 7 (1998): 152–77: 152.
3. Peter Drucker published more than three dozen books. His *The Practice of Management*, originally published in 1954, might be called the classic management text of the twentieth century, certainly of the second half. Drucker coined the term "knowledge workers" in *Landmarks of Tomorrow: A Report on the New "Post-Modern" World* (New York: Harper Colophon Books, 1959). See also his *The Age of Discontinuity: Guidelines to Our Changing Society* (New York: Harper and Row, 1969); "The Age of Social Transformation," *The Atlantic Monthly* 274, no. 5 (1994): 53–80. In "Knowledge Workers Are the New Capitalists," *Economist*, September 15, 2001, Drucker claims that the economist Fritz Machlup first used the term "knowledge industry." At about the same time, Galbraith described an emergent class of new knowledge workers, technical and scientific experts, and Daniel Bell foretold the arrival of a post-industrial society where this expertise played a major role. See John Kenneth Galbraith, *The New Industrial State* (Boston: Houghton Mifflin, 1967) and Daniel Bell, *The Coming of Post-Industrial Society: A Venture in Social Forecasting* (New York: Basic Books, 1973). Later, Robert Reich wrote about the global order of the 21st century, with three different categories of knowledge-work: routine, like data processing; personal services, like nursing; and symbolic analysts, like the "wizards" whose legacy is the algorithms and derivatives that created havoc in the financial industry at the tail end of the first decade of the new century. Robert Reich, *The Work of Nations: Preparing Ourselves for 21st Century Capitalism* (New York: Alfred A. Knopf, 1991).

   A conference at Lancaster University in 1992 marks one of the first major academic inquiries into knowledge-work. Papers presented there are published in the *Journal of Management Studies*, November, 1993 and the "Editorial Introduction" includes a brief history of contributions on knowledge-work and the knowledge society from around 1960 up to that time. See Frank Blackler, Michael Reed, and Alan Whitaker, "Knowledge Workers and Contemporary Organizations," *Journal of Management Studies* 30, no. 6 (1993).
4. The etymology of 'management' is uncertain but it began to be widely used and written about at the very end of the 19th century. For one view on the concept and its origins see Geert Hofstede, "Cultural Constraints in Management Theories," *The Executive* 7, no. 1 (1993). On the history of management in the 20th century see Stuart Crainer, *The Management Century: A Critical Review of 20th Century Thought and Practice* (San Francisco: Jossey-Bass Publishers, 2000).

5. The financial meltdown, in 2008, revived controversy over executive compensation; particularly when executives (making a mockery of the fact that "bonus" which comes from Latin and means "good," as in "for good work") continued to receive outrageously large bonuses, although their technically bankrupt institutions had been bailed out by governments on behalf of taxpayers.

6. The charge that managers weren't paying enough attention to processes was made by advocates of "process reengineering," which became one of the tools of management I talk about later. Regarding those views from the Left, under the umbrella of critical management studies (CMS), a loose coalition of scholars has provided valuable insights into management as an ideology. CMS began with the work of Mats Alvesson and Hugh Willmott in the early 1990s, as a synthesis of critical theory and post-structuralism. See Mats Alvesson and Hugh Willmott, eds., *Critical Management Studies* (London: SAGE Publications,1992).

7. Gary Hamel, "Moon Shots for Management: What Great Challenges Must We Tackle to Reinvent Management and Make It More Relevant to a Volatile World?," *Harvard Business Review* 87, no. 2 (2009): 91–8 . 91–2. See also Gary Hamel and Bill Breen, *The Future of Management* (Cambridge, MA: Harvard Business School Press, 2007). In the past few years, bank collapses certainly helped to undermine people's faith in management. Some writers on Hamel's side are even more dogmatic. Recognizing the importance of knowledge in work, Verna Allee says, "changes everything." "Executives and business leaders . . . must completely change the way they think about the organization, business relationships, measures, tools, business models, values, ethics, culture and leadership." Verna Allee, "Knowledge Networks and Communities of Practice," *OD Practitioner* 32, no. 4 (2000) available at *OD Practitioner Online*, http://methodenpool.uni-koeln.de/communities/~%20OD%20 Practitioner%20Online%20-%20Vol_%2032%20-%20No_%204%20 (2000)%20~. htm. Theodore Taptiklis is a fellow traveller. See his *Unmanaging: Opening up the Organization to Its Own Unspoken Knowledge* (London and New York: Palgrave Macmillan, 2008). See also, Lowell L. Bryan and Claudia Joyce, "The 21st Century Organization," *The McKinsey Quarterly*, 3 (2005): 24–33.

8. Writers, increasingly, are questioning whether the MBA is a suitable education for managers: whether it makes good managers and good management. See Henry Mintzberg, *Managers not MBAs: A Hard Look at the Soft Practice of Managing and Management Development* (San Francisco: Berrett-Koehler, 2004); Matthew Stewart, *The Management Myth: Why the Experts Keep Getting It Wrong* (New York: W.W. Norton, 2009); Dev Patnaik, "Reinventing the MBA: 4 Reasons to Mix Business With Design Thinking" (www.fastcompany.com/blog/dev-patnaik/innovation/reinventing-mba).

9. Although he doesn't say so, each of Gary Hamel's "moon shots," like "expanding employee autonomy," "depoliticizing decision-making," and "humanizing the language and practice of business," is a corollary of management practices being incompatible with knowledge-work. Barry Lynn describes the so-called "globalization of production" as "the end of the line," referring to Ford's River Rouge-type of vertically integrated, production-line-manufacturing. The end of the line has enormous implications for economies and societies. See Barry C. Lynn, *The End of the Line: The Rise and Coming Fall of the Global Corporation*, 1st paperback edn (New York: Currency Doubleday, 2005): 16.

10. Wilde, the Edwardian wit, probably never actually said this, but he was fond of dichotomies. He did say "there are only two kinds of people who are really fascinating:

people who know absolutely everything, and people who know absolutely nothing." He also said: "in this world there are two tragedies. One is not getting what one wants, and the other is getting it. The last is much the worst." Topping the original quote, Oskar Kennedy says, "there are three types of people. Those who can count and those who can't" (http://richardwiseman.wordpress.com/2009/03/25/are-there-only-two-types-of-people-in-the-world/).

11. *The American Heritage Dictionary* (4th edn, 2000) defines management as: "1. The act, manner, or practice of managing; handling, supervision, or control. . . . 2. The person or persons who control or direct a business or other enterprise."

12. The "view from the top" is a metaphor which refers to what people know or "see." It is not a literal description of where they stand or sit. The Coen brothers' film *The Hudsucker Proxy* has an engaging visual portrayal of the view from the top, which is important in the film both for the plot and in creating the visual impact of particular scenes. Various sequences either depict "the top" as it might appear to others, particularly to people at "the bottom," or show aspects of organizational life from the perspective of the top. I've used the expression for quite a while, contrasting it with the "view from practice." Recently, I discovered that at least one other person uses it, though somewhat differently. Theodore Taptiklis has a chapter called "The View from the Top" in *Unmanaging*.

Chapter 2

1. The official *Dilbert* website is www.dilbert.com. *The Office* began as a BBC comedy written by Ricky Gervais who also played the lead. It was later Americanized with Steve Carell in the lead. The official NBC website for the U.S. version is www.nbc.com/The_Office.

2. For one view of the social nature of work life see Dennis Sandow and Ann Murray Allen, "The Nature of Social Collaboration: How Work Really Gets Done," *Reflections:The SoL Journal* 6, nos 4–5 (2005): 1–14.

3. An especially egregious case, outlined by Thomas Homer-Dixon, involves IBM and the Federal Aviation Administration's proposed Advanced Automation System for air traffic control. This software development and equipment design project was shut down after more than 10 years of work, when 2 billion dollars had already been spent. See Thomas Homer-Dixon, *The Ingenuity Gap: Facing the Economic Environmental, and Other Challenges of an Increasingly Complex and Unpredictable World* (New York: Vintage Books, 2002): 183–4. Another example, outlined in a story in the *Washington Post*, involves the Commonwealth of Virginia's decision to consolidate its computer operations into one agency and contract out the running of its computer system. See Anita Kumar and Rosalind S. Helderman, "Va. Pays Dearly for Computer Troubles: Northrop Grumman $2 Billion Upgrade Disrupted Services," October 14, 2009: B01 (www.washingtonpost.com/wp-dyn/content/article/2009/10/13/AR2009101303044.html).

4. Edsel wasn't just a brand name or model, but, briefly, was a division of Ford. See the Wikipedia entry at http://en.wikipedia.org/wiki/Ford_Edsel.

5. Military hardware programs that result in technologies that are dysfunctional or anachronistic belong in the same category. For example, programs which produce cold-war-era weapons systems when the military's target is terrorism. The Strategic Defense Initiative, or "star wars program," a still-fanciful missile defense shield, which

was initiated when Ronald Reagan was president, is one example. In one form or another it is still rolling on and might end up costing billions of dollars, although, as I write, judging by what many experts say, it can't and won't provide protection and is certainly not a shield against incoming missiles.

6. Arguments along these lines are exceptionally well articulated by Binyavanga Wainaina, a Kenyan author and scholar, in his interview with Krista Tippett, the host of the National Public Radio Program, *Talking of Faith*, titled "The Ethics of Aid: One Kenyan's Perspective" (http://speakingoffaith.publicradio.org/programs/2009/ethicsofaid-kenya/).

7. The fact that teams exist in name only explains the title of Michael Schrage's book, *No More Teams!*, where he takes a close look at collaboration and how to foster it. See Michael Schrage, *No More Teams: Mastering the Dynamics of Creative Collaboration* (New York: Currency Doubleday, 1995).

8. Zachery A. Goldfarb has a fine example of this type of breakdown in "SEC's Regional Offices Present Managerial Problems, Become an Obstacle to Reform," *Washington Post*, June 10, 2010: A13. He writes that "for nearly a decade, Julie Preuitt told her colleagues at the Securities and Exchange Commission . . . that she had found problems at a fabulously successful investment firm . . . But officials in the agency's enforcement division weren't interested in complex cases, just quick-hit lawsuits that would make the regional office look active, according to a review by the SEC inspector general."

9. According to the Stockholm International Peace Research Institute, in 2010 the United States total military spending of US $698 billion accounted for about 43 percent of the world's total military spending of US$1630 billion. See the Institute's "Background paper on SIPRI military expenditure data, 2010," at www.sipri.org/research/armaments/milex/factsheet2010.

10. The Government Accountability Office that oversees United States government departments.

11. April Witt, "Fatal Inaction," *Washington Post Magazine*, June 18, 2006: 22. Another widely reported set of breakdowns had to do with the shockingly poor way in which soldiers who needed treatment for physical injuries and traumatic stress syndrome were actually treated (i.e. "handled") by various agencies and departments like the Veterans Administration and military hospitals.

12. Two books, by ex-management consultants writing with views from practice, provide good insights into the work of consultants: not least the heavy-handed and self-serving way they wield the "tools" of their profession. See Matthew Stewart, *The Management Myth: Why the Experts Keep Getting It Wrong* (New York: W.W. Norton, 2009); and Theodore Taptiklis, *Unmanaging: Opening up the Organization to Its Own Unspoken Knowledge* (London and New York: Palgrave Macmillan, 2008).

13. Many books and articles define "management" and examine the paradigm. One is Stephen Linstead, Robert Grafton Small, and Paul Jeffcutt, eds., *Understanding Management* (London: SAGE Publications,1996), an edited volume, with a postmodern orientation, in which contributors highlight the complex, social nature of management and managing. See also Dan Growler and Karen Legge, "The Meaning of Management and Management of Meaning," in *Understanding Management*, ed. S Linstead, R.G. Small, and P Jeffcutt (London: SAGE Publications, 1996).

14. Frederick Winslow Taylor, *The Principles of Scientific Management* (New York: W.W. Norton, 1911; reprint, 1967); Frederick Winslow Taylor, "The Principles of Scientific Management," *Bulletin of the Taylor Society*, December (1916). Henri Fayol,

General and Industrial Management, trans. C. Storrs (London: Pitman, 1949). The huge literature on Taylor's work includes these contributions: Gail Cooper, "Frederick Winslow Taylor and Scientific Management," in *Technology in America: A History of Individuals and Ideas*, ed. C.W. Pursell (Cambridge, MA: MIT Press, 1990); Bernard Doray, *From Taylorism to Fordism: A Rational Madness* (London: Free Association Books, 1988); Robert Kanigel, *The One Best Way: Fredrick Winslow Taylor and the Enigma of Efficiency* (New York: Viking, 1997). Matthew Stewart, *The Management Myth*, has a unique perspective on Taylor, arguing, ironically, that it was his ability to tell a good story that brought him both fame and fortune, not "the numbers" he professed were so important and, evidently, was so passionate about.

15. On the evolution of science and the ideas that contributed to the Enlightenment, see Peter Dear, *Revolutionizing the Sciences: European Knowledge and Its Ambitions, 1500–1700* (Princeton, NJ: Princeton University Press, 2001). Hugh Willmott refers to Heidegger's description of the "period we call modern [as] . . . defined by the fact that man becomes the centre and measure of all things." Hugh Willmot, "Bringing Agency (Back) into Organizational Analysis: Responding to the Crisis of (Post)Modernity," in *Towards a New Theory of Organizations*, eds. John Hassard and Martin Parker (London and New York: Routledge, 1994). On modernism in organization and management studies see the following which, as they deal with worldviews and the contrast between modernism and postmodernism, are all philosophically oriented: Robert Chia, "From Modern to Postmodern Organizational Analysis," *Organization Studies* 16, no. 4 (1995); Robert Cooper and Gibson Burrell, "Modernism, Postmodernism and Organizational Analysis: An Introduction," *Organizational Studies* 9, no. 1 (1988); Susan Stanford Freidman, "Definitional Excursions:The Meanings of Modern/Modernity/Modernism," *Modernism/Modernity* 8, no. 3 (2001).

16. Tim Hindle, "The New Organization," *The Economist*, January 21, 2006.

17. The injunction to "be objective" seems far less onerous, technically and perhaps morally, for astronomers, physicists, and the like, who deal with inanimate objects, than for anthropologists, psychologists, sociologists, and even economists, who study people with attitudes, values, and beliefs, who live relationship-filled lives. What's more, if their relationships, attitudes, feelings, and values are what make people tick and make them interesting, wouldn't their efforts to put their feelings and relationships aside make experts less than human? Why would we want less-than-human experts explaining human behavior or human societies? On the whole question of objectivity and subjectivity in science see R.J. Bernstein, *Beyond Objectivism and Relativism: Science, Hermeneutics and Praxis* (Oxford: Basil Blackwell, 1983).

18. *Fantastic Voyage* is not a particularly memorable film. Although it won some awards for special effects, to at least one reviewer it was a vehicle for squeezing Raquel Welch, a leading 1960s sex symbol, into a white neoprene wetsuit.

19. Another difference between knowledge-work and industrial-work is that, in factories, the distinction between "inside" and "outside" doesn't matter as much. If you are watching people on a production line filling boxes of corn flakes or, in rows, at benches, assembling electronic components, you have a good idea of what they are doing just by observing them, no matter that you're not actually doing the same work.

20. Julian Orr highlights the importance of stories at work, in conversations that may not specifically be about work. Julian E. Orr, *Talking about Machines: An Ethnography of a Modern Job* (Ithaca, NY: Cornell University Press, 1996).

21. It is not uncommon, these days, to hear people talking about "knowing" rather than "knowledge." See Frank Blackler, "Knowledge, Knowledge Work and Organizations: An Overview and Interpretation," *Organization Studies* 16, no. 6 (1995). Scott Cook and John Seely Brown make the distinction a theme in explaining the synergy between the knowledge and knowing. See Scott D.N. Cook and John Seely Brown, "Bridging Epistemologies: The Generative Dance between Organizational Knowledge and Organizational Knowing," *Organization Science* 10, no. 4 (1999).

22. The "view from the top" makes the connection with top-down management easy. Remember that the view from the top is a metaphor. In every organization lots of people work from this view and, because it can be very useful, at times it is desirable, even necessary, that they deliberately adopt a view from the top by "stepping back" from their work and looking at it from the outside as it were. The problem is that a management lens only permits the view from the top, which is wrongly presumed to be the view you must have to organize work.

23. The fad for "reengineering" work processes, to make organizations more efficient, is directly attributable to this view. I discuss reengineering more fully in Chapter 8.

24. As you'll see, a good deal of knowledge-work consists of organizing, and much of the work of organizing involves making sense of what happened, such as what people said or did, and then deciding what to do. I'm going to call this "meaning making." Karl Weick calls it "sensemaking" and has written a book explaining that this is mostly what people do in organizations. Work is nothing more, or less, than sensemaking. Karl E. Weick, *Sensemaking in Organizations* (Thousand Oaks, CA: SAGE Publications, 1995); and *Making Sense of the Organization* (Malden, MA: Blackwell Publishing, 2001).

Chapter 3

1. Stephen Fineman, Daniel Sims, and Yannis Gabriel, *Organizing and Organizations*, 2nd edn (San Francisco: SAGE Publications, 2000): 6–7.

2. There is no direct English equivalent for the German word *Verstehen*. Scholars translate *Verstehen* as "interpretive understanding" or "subjective understanding" or (more recently) "meaning-making." See Max Weber, *The Theory of Social and Economic Organisation*, ed. Talcott Parsons, trans. A.M. Henderson and Talcott Parsons (New York: The Free Press, 1964); Max Weber, "Objectivity in Social Science and Social Policy," in *Understanding and Social Inquiry*, ed. F.R. Dallmayr and T.A. McCarthy (Notre Dame, IN: University of Notre Dame Press, 1977); Mario Truzzi, ed. *Verstehen: Subjective Understanding in the Social Sciences* (Reading, MA: Addison-Wesley, 1974). The tradition of interpretive understanding (or meaning-making) actually began before Weber with the first generation of scholars who coined the term "hermeneutics." They were interested in biblical exegesis—how to interpret the Bible. After the Reformation (which coincided with the Enlightenment and the rise of secularism and science), people came to accept that you didn't have to rely on the church hierarchy to interpret the word of God for you; you could do it for yourself. It was not only church teachings but also hierarchy that was being challenged. In the absence of an expert or single authority who told you what to believe, the question was how to draw out the (real) meaning of the Bible. The challenge was the "hermeneutic circle" or the relationship between whole and part. You can't make meaning of

the whole until you understand the individual parts and you can only interpret the parts when you understand the message of the whole. This provided a context for appreciating the subjective and intersubjective character of meaning-making.

3. On the question of how we construct meaning of the social world, see Alfred Schutz, *The Phenomenology of the Social World*, trans. F. Walsh and G. Lehnert (London: Heinemann Educational Books, 1972). The original German title of this book translates as *The Meaning Construction of the Social World*. See also Peter Berger and Thomas Luckmann, *The Social Construction of Reality* (London: Allen Lane, 1967).

4. Renate Mayntz describes a network, succinctly, as a form of governance, "characterized by negotiation and collaboration—purposeful co-operation over time." Renate Mayntz, "Modernization and the Logic of Interorganizational Networks," in *Societal Change between Market and Organization*, eds. John Child, Michael Crozier, Renate Mayntz et al. (Aldershot, UK: Ashgate Publishing, 1993): 11.

5. On the shifts in thinking at this time, see Peter Dear, *Revolutionizing the Sciences: European Knowledge and Its Ambitions, 1500–1700* (Princeton, NJ: Princeton University Press, 2001). Charlene Spretnak argues, convincingly, that it is precisely the kinds of knowing that began to be rejected at this time—bodily (feelings, emotions) and spiritual (beliefs) knowing, as opposed to mental knowing (reason)—which are, for humans, what "real" knowledge is. From her perspective, postmodernism, which relates knowing to the construction of meaning, represents a "resurgence of the real." Charlene Spretnak, *The Resurgence of the Real: Body, Nature, and Place in a Hypermodern World* (Reading, MA: Addison-Wesley, 1997).

6. "Get the beat" is the first step in what Donella Meadows calls "dancing with systems." This is what she says: "Before you disturb the system in any way, watch how it behaves. If it's a piece of music or a whitewater rapid or a fluctuation in a commodity price, study its beat. If it's a social system, watch it work. Learn its history. Ask people who've been around a long time to tell you what has happened." Donella H. Meadows, "Dancing with Systems," Sustainability Institute (www.sustainabilityinstitute.org/pubs/Dancing.html).

Chapter 4

1. For another example of how these types of projects can go wrong see Dan Eggen and Griff Witte, "The FBI's Upgrade That Wasn't," *Washington Post*, August 18, 2006, p. A01 (www.washingtonpost.com/wp-dyn/content/article/2006/08/17/AR2006081701485.html).

2. If you have ever tried to demonstrate computer technology to a group of people you have almost certainly experienced Murphy's law first hand. No matter how many times you test your setup and no matter how many times you check it to see that everything is working as it should, when you get to the actual demonstration you will find that anything that can go wrong has gone wrong. See www.murphys-laws.com/murphy/murphy-true.html.

3. This passage and others remind me of why software developers adopt the agile programming methods which I've written about in Chapter 9.

4. With all the interest in knowledge management, lots of people now know and use the term "tacit knowledge," which is usually contrasted with "explicit knowledge." I believe Michael Polanyi was the first to write about tacit knowledge in his *Personal Knowledge: Towards a Post-Critical Philosophy* (London: Routledge and Kegan Paul, 1973). See also Kazuo Ichijo and Florian Kohlbache, "Tapping Tacit

Local Knowledge in Emerging Markets—the Toyota Way," *Knowledge Management Research & Practice* 6 (2008).

5. Jeff's distinction, between a "contract-is-all approach" and a "people-and-client-centered" one, is analogous to the difference between the "view from the top" and the "view from practice."

6. http://en.wikipedia.org/wiki/Loose_coupling. This article, cites as the originator of the idea, Karl E. Weick, "Educational Organizations as Loosely Coupled Systems," *Administrative Science Quarterly* 21, no. 1 (1976); Karl E. Weick, "Management of Organizational Change Among Loosely Coupled Elements," reprinted in Karl E. Weick, *Making Sense of the Organization* (Malden, MA: Blackwell Publishing, 2001); James Douglas Orton and Karl E. Weick, "Loosely Coupled Systems: A Reconceptualization," *Academy of Management Review* 15, no. 2 (1990).

7. Ron Heifetz and Marty Linsky also use the metaphor of a play-book. See their *Leadership on the Line: Staying Alive through the Dangers of Leading* (Boston, MA: Harvard Business School Press, 2002).

8. Why do people in IT and marketing departments, for example, need a shared vision or mission? Surely, you've noticed that vision and mission statements are interchangeable among organizations. They need to be vague and bland, rather than specific and descriptive, to accommodate the enormous diversity of work as well as interests and outlooks in any organization. It is a good thing employees don't have to chant their mission statements when they come to work, or else we'd hear echoes of the worst excesses of authoritarianism.

9. When I thought about this—the reason for the magic—it isn't just that people's knowledge is tacit, not explicit. As important is the fact that they don't know what they're doing until they actually do it. Their knowledge emerges in the work, through the work, and as a result of the work. The work "calls forth" the knowledge.

10. The story is a folk-tale about three blind men who feel an elephant. One feels the tail, the second its front legs, top to bottom, and the third, the trunk. When, later, they compare their experiences, each claiming to know what an elephant is, they describe different objects: a straw fan, two big trees without branches, and a snake (http://en.wikipedia.org/wiki/Blind_men_and_an_elephant). Blindness is a metaphor for being absorbed by one's own work—whatever it happens to be—and not being able to see things from the point of view of others doing different kinds of work

11. According to Jeffery Goldstein, emergence happens in complex systems when "novel and coherent structures, patterns and properties [arise] during the process of self-organization." Jeffrey Goldstein, "Emergence as a Construct: History and Issues," *Emergence: Complexity and Organization* 1 (1999): 49–72.

12. Quite a few authors have written about the improvisational nature of work and compared it to jazz improvisation. See Frank J. Barrett, "Living in Organizations: Lessons from Jazz Improvisation" and Lois Holzman, "Lev Vygotsky and the New Performative Psychology: Implications for Business and Organizations," in *The Social Construction of Organization*, eds. D.M. Hosking and Sheila McNamee, *Advances in Organization Studies* (Malmö, Sweden: Liber and Copenhagen Business School Press, 2006). Arguing that there are many forms of improvisation, Ken Kamoche and his co-authors explore some that go beyond the often highly structured and competitive improvisation associated with jazz. See Ken Kamoche, Miguel Pina e Cunha, and João Vieira da Cunha, "Towards a Theory of Organizational Improvisation: Looking Beyond the Jazz Metaphor," *Journal of Management Studies* 40, no. 8 (2003).

13. "Dance," too, is now quite a popular metaphor in contemporary descriptions of management and managing. See for example, P. Senge, A. Kleiner, C. Roberts, R. Ross, G. Roth, and B. Smith, *The Dance of Change: The Challenges to Sustaining Momentum in Learning Organizations* (New York: Doubleday/Currency, 1999).

14. Jeff's distinction between plans and planning (i.e. organizing conversations) mirrors the distinction between "tools" (plans) and "talk" (planning) that I introduce in Chapter 8. It is important for understanding organizing practices and the difference between management (which focuses on tools) and organizing (which begins with talk).

15. A lot has been written about social networks and network mapping. I'll discuss this later in the book. See, for example, Robert Cross and Andrew Parker, *The Hidden Power of Social Networks: Understanding How Work Really Gets Done in Organizations* (Boston, MA: Harvard Business School Press, 2004).

16. Adam Kahane makes a similar point about dealing with tough problems in his *Solving Tough Problems: An Open Way of Talking, Listening, and Creating New Realities* (San Francisco: Berrett-Koehler Publishers, 2004): 104.

17. Jeff's "social space" sounds to me like the Japanese concept *Ba*. The Japanese philosopher K. Nishida is credited with introducing the concept in a book published in 1970 (www.cyberartsweb.org/cpace/ht/thonglipfei/ba_concept.html). Working in the area of knowledge management, Ikujiro Nonaka and N. Konno use *ba* in a similar way to Jeff. See Ikujiro Nonaka and N. Konno, "The Concept Of 'Ba': Building a Foundation for Knowledge Creation," *California Management Review* 40, no. 1, Special Issue on "Knowledge and the Firm" (1998). Scott D.N. Cook and John Seely Brown introduce the idea of "affordance." This ties in with social spaces, which allow or afford varying possibilities for action. Scott D.N. Cook and John Seely Brown, "Bridging Epistemologies: The Generative Dance between Organizational Knowledge and Organizational Knowing," *Organization Science* 10, no. 4 (1999).

Chapter 5

1. See the growing literature on brain functioning including Daniel H. Pink, *A Whole New Mind: Moving from the Information Age to the Conceptual Age* (New York: Riverhead Books, 2005).

2. Figure 5.1 can be viewed as a Western perspective on knowledge from about the time of René Descartes onwards. Descartes, a French philosopher of the Enlightenment, was a prime influencer of the view that science and religion are separate, because they are different types of knowledge or different ways of knowing. Science, represented by the left-hand side of the picture, is associated with the mind. It is rational, analytical, empirical, objective, certain, and so on. Religion, on the right, is associated with the body (or spirit). It has to do with beliefs, values, and other non-observable, unquantifiable, hence "subjective" phenomena. When this "Cartesian dualism" took root about 400 years ago, the West began to turn its back on the phenomena of the right-hand side in the course of embracing empirical science. That process continued into the 20th century, with scientific knowledge gaining in stature at the expense of emotions, beliefs, feelings, intuition and other human ways of knowing, which were downplayed and even rejected as being subjective, hence anti-scientific, and not real knowledge. The Cartesian divide explains why we are deeply attached to management and ignore organizing and why students are taught to think about management as a science. Management doesn't and won't have

anything to do with what's on the right-hand side of the diagram. Rene Descartes, *Meditations on First Philosophy*, trans. J Cottingham (Cambridge: Cambridge University Press, 1996).

3. Etienne Wenger, *Communities of Practice: Learning, Meaning, and Identity* (New York: Cambridge University Press, 1998): 197.

4. Words like "spirit" and "creativity" have crept into management-speak, but they don't belong there and are used mainly for show. They are useful to have when you're trying to motivate people, but they don't mean much and people know this and aren't fooled by this rhetoric. As far as management practices are concerned—and they dominate the way we work—it is the meaning of those words on the left-hand side that matters.

5. This view from the top of a network of conversations is the source of "knowledge networks," a construct quite widely used in the field of knowledge management. See Verna Allee, "Knowledge Networks and Communities of Practice," *OD Practitioner* 32, no. 4 (2000).

6. Don Lavoie was a colleague. As far as I know he never put the concept in print, but taught students about "returnability" in the context of how online collaborative tools like SharePoint or Lotus Notes change the nature of interactions and conversations. When you have an online conversation, mediated by these kinds of technologies, you can usually come back to the content, as office workers may find to their dismay when they discover that their employer has archived copies of all their emails. The problem, however, is we never know what another group, or the same people at a different time or in another place—i.e. in a different context—will make of the tools. Although you can return to them, these artifacts don't *have* meaning on their own: people have to *make* meaning of them and, as Brown and Duguid explain so well, meaning depends on context. See John Seely Brown and Paul Duguid, *The Social Life of Information* (Boston, MA: Harvard Business School Press, 2000): ch. 7.

7. I want to acknowledge here that the distinction I'm drawing between management and organizing was foreshadowed by Douglas McGregor's "Theory X" and "Theory Y" organizations and by Tom Burns and G.M. Stalker's "mechanistic" and "organic" systems, as well as other writers, none of whom had the benefit of philosophical discussions about paradigms or worldviews, which came later. Douglas McGregor, *The Human Side of Enterprise* (New York: McGraw-Hill, 1960); Tom Burns and G.M. Stalker, *The Management of Innovation*, 3rd edn (Oxford: Oxford University Press, 1961; reprint, 1994).

8. This doesn't mean there is no room for some of the practices associated with management. It does mean that the main way of getting work done is by people organizing themselves, treating one another as peers and being accountable to each other.

Chapter 6

1. In his highly praised and well-received book on the value of craftwork, Matthew Crawford has a bit to say about knowledge-work, which he contrasts with craftwork. See his *Shop Class as Soulcraft* (New York: Penguin Books, 2009).

2. Stephen Barley and Gideon Kunda note that, from Fredrick Taylor onwards, earlier writers kept a close eye on work, but, in organization studies during the 1960s and 1970s, attention shifted away from the work place. Among their list of contributions that were work-oriented, it is relevant that most were based on the observation of factory-work. See Stephen Barley and Gideon Kunda, "Bringing Work Back In,"

Organization Science 12, no. 1 (2001): 80. As ethnographic research, based on interviews and participant observation, become more acceptable (compared to quantitative research which always was), we are seeing a renewed interest in work, such as Julian Orr's close look at the work of people who repair photocopiers: Julian E. Orr, *Talking about Machines: An Ethnography of a Modern Job* (Ithaca, NY: Cornell University Press, 1996). Some of the most interesting studies in recent years that provide a deeper understanding of work practices, have come from writers who, like Orr, were linked to Xerox PARC and the Institute for Research on Learning.

3. Jared Sandberg, "Modern Conundrum: When Work's Invisible, So Are Its Satisfactions," *The Wall Street Journal, Asia,* February 19, 2008 (my emphasis). See also, Robbie Kunreuther, "Goals, Objectives, and the Everyday Employee," *Fedsmith.com*, March 11, 2008 (www.fedsmith.com/article/1540/).

4. Peter Eisner, "How Bogus Letter Became a Case for War," *Washington Post*, April 3, 2007.

5. Charles Chaplin, *Modern Times* (United States of America: United Artists, 1936) (http://en.wikipedia.org/wiki/Modern_Times_(film)). Fritz Lang, *Metropolis* (Germany: UFA, 1927) (http://en.wikipedia.org/wiki/Metropolis_(film)).

6. Historically important images of factory-work, from the same era, taken in the Western Electric Company's Cicero, Illinois, plant can be viewed, online, at Harvard University Business School's Baker Library Historical Collections website 'The Human Relations Movement: Harvard Business School and the Hawthorne Experiments 1924–33,' 'Western Electric Company Photograph Album' (www.library.hbs.edu/hc/hawthorne/). The famous Hawthorne experiments, conducted in the 1920s and 1930s, which sparked the human relations movement in management, were undertaken at this plant. Researchers, led by Elton Mayo and Fritz Roethlisberger, explaining the outcome of conventional experiments with lighting levels in the plant, which appeared to have failed, argued that what seemed to be perverse results were a consequence of industrial workers wanting and getting approval and appreciation; or, more generally, being treated like human beings not machines. Their published findings contributed to the emergence of organization development, which continues to challenge the fundamentals of management that are still in place a hundred years after they were first articulated. On the Hawthorne Plant experiments and the human relations movement see Fritz. J. Roethlisberger, William J. Dickson, and Harold A. Wright, *Management and the Worker: An Account of a Research Program Conducted by the Western Electric Company, Hawthorne Works, Chicago* (Cambridge, MA: Harvard University Press, 1939). On the history of organization development as a heretical movement, see Art Kleiner, *The Age of Heretics: Heroes, Outlaws, and the Forerunners of Corporate Change* (New York: Currency Doubleday, 1996).

7. For a short but quite comprehensive overview, including a history of the concept, see the Wikipedia entry on "Social Network" at http://en.wikipedia.org/wiki/Social_network.

8. The last 10 years or so have seen a proliferation of material on social networks and mapping social and organizational networks, accompanied and encouraged by the more recent explosion of Internet-based social networks. For a sample of work on networks and organizations see Verna Allee, "Knowledge Networks and Communities of Practice," *OD Practitioner* 32, no. 4 (2000); Robert Cross and Andrew Parker, *The Hidden Power of Social Networks: Understanding How Work Really Gets Done*

in Organizations (Boston, MA: Harvard Business School Press, 2004); Art Kleiner, "Karen Stevenson's Quantum Theory of Trust," *Strategy+Business* 29 (2002); Valdis Krebs, "Introduction to Social Network Analysis" (www.leader-values.com/Content/detail.asp?ContentDetailID=912) and "Knowledge Networks: Mapping and Measuring Knowledge Creation, Re-use and Flow" (www.leader-values.com/Content/detail.asp?ContentDetailID=914); Duncan J. Watts, "Relationship Space: Meet Your Network Neighbors," *Wired* 11.06 (2003). See also Ronald Breiger, "The Analysis of Social Networks," in *Handbook of Data Analysis*, eds. Melissa Hardy and Alan Bryman (London: SAGE Publications, 2004) and Union of International Associations, "Network Visualizations Online" (www.uia.be/sites/uia.be/db/db/x.php?dbcode=vi&year=2006).

9. My arguments owe a lot to Etienne Wenger, particularly to his concept of "identity." Etienne Wenger, *Communities of Practice: Learning, Meaning, and Identity* (New York: Cambridge University Press, 1998). Explaining the work of insurance claims clerks, he says they don't switch off their work and work identities when they leave work and, similarly, they bring who they are at home to work. You don't slip your identity on and off like a coat. It is integral to who you are—your "being-in-the world," which is why everything that happens between people at work is their work. Anything may, and probably does, influence their attitudes in some way, hence what they do or don't do. Just as relevant here is Richard McDermott's powerful and subversive comment that "knowledge belongs to communities." His position, that people acquire knowledge by making or creating it *together*, when they interact, is a radical departure from the standard Western idea that knowledge is stuff that people have in their heads, "between their ears." See Richard McDermott, "Knowing Is a Human Act," *Upgrade* 3, no. 1 (2002): especially p. 9. On "being-in-the-world" see Hubert L. Dreyfus, *Being-in-the-World: A Commentary on Heidegger's Being and Time, Division I* (Cambridge, MA: MIT Press, 1991).

10. This is probably the right place to identify the interpretative tradition in social theory that has shaped my thinking about the work of organizing. Here it is hermeneutics and particularly the work of Hans-Georg Gadamer, *Truth and Method*, trans. G. Barden and J. Cumming (New York: Seabury Press, 1975), especially his argument that meaning is constructed between people or between a person and an object—that meaning resides in the space between them. See Georgina Warnke, *Gadamer: Hermeneutics, Tradition and Reason* (Cambridge: Polity Press, 1987). Besides Max Weber and Alfred Schutz, whose contributions I've already referred to, this line of thinking includes phenomenology (for example: Edmund Husserl, *The Crisis in European Science and Transcendental Phenomenology: An Introduction to Phenomenological Philosophy*, trans. D. Carr (Evanston, IL: Northwestern University Press, 1970); Martin Heidegger, *Being and Time*, trans. J. Macquarrie and E. Robinson (New York: Harper and Row, 1962); Maurice Merleau-Ponty, *The Phenomenology of Perception* (London: Routledge and Kegan Paul, 1962)); contemporary hermeneutics (for example: Jurgen Habermas, *Knowledge and Human Interests* (Boston: Beacon Press, 1971)); and postmodern thought (for example: Michael Foucault, *The Archaeology of Knowledge* (London: Routledge, 1972); David L. Harvey, *The Condition of Postmodernity: An Enquiry into the Origins of Cultural Change* (Oxford:Oxford University Press, 1989); D.M. Boje, R.P. Gephardt, and T.J. Thatchenkery, eds., *Postmodern Management and Organization Theory* (Thousand Oaks, CA: SAGE Publications, 1996); William Bergquist, *The Postmodern Organization:*

Mastering the Art of Irreversible Change (San Francisco: Jossey-Bass Publishers, 1993)).

11. See http://en.wikipedia.org/wiki/Ayers_rock. Another one, to which Ayers Rock is sometimes compared, is Silbury Hill, in Wiltshire, England (http://en.wikipedia.org/wiki/Silbury_Hill). See also Christopher L. C. E. Witcombe, 'Sacred Places' (http://witcombe.sbc.edu/sacredplaces/sacredplacesintro.html).

12. David Abram, *The Spell of the Sensuous: Language and Perception in a More-Than-Human World* (New York: Vintage Books, 1997): 85.

13. An interesting sidebar to writer Michael Hastings's report in *Rolling Stone Magazine* 1108/1109 (2010), which led to the dismissal of the U.S. Commander in Afghanistan, General Stanley McChrystal, is that it reveals all too clearly how places influence what people say and do. An article in the *Washington Post* notes that "McChrystal allowed ... Hastings to join his team all the way, and the reporter witnessed a general far away from Washington and the Obama ethic." "All the way" included a trip to Paris that coincided with the eruption of the Icelandic volcano Eyjafjallajökull [and, with European airspace closed,] ... a bus trip to Berlin and a nearly week-long stay at the Ritz-Carlton. Then came the tourist-trap boozing and insubordinate smack talk." See Jason Horowitz, "McChrystal Violated not just Protocol but Obama Tenets on Media Management," *Washington Post*, June 28, 2010.

14. There is a striking example of collaboration, alignment, synergy, and the magic of organizing knowledge-work in an article by Eli Saslow, a member of the then-President-elect Barack Obama's speech-writing team:

"The writers could sometimes crank out a 1,500-word speech in one or two days, working in Obama's Chicago headquarters almost until sunrise. Sometimes, it took Favreau and his team hours to conceptualize the opening few lines. They gathered in a tiny office and formed sentences out loud, each word mulled and debated, until suddenly—yes!—they could envision the whole speech. '*When we were on, we could finish each other's thoughts,*' Frankel said. 'We knew where we were going next. We were in total alignment on those speeches.' " ("Helping to Write History," *Washington Post*, December 18, 2008, p. A01 (my emphasis)).

15. Of course, the idea of knowledge "moving" is a metaphor. See John Seely Brown and Paul Duguid, "Organizing Knowledge," *California Management Review*, Special Issue on "Knowledge and the Firm" 40, no. 3, (1998): 104. See also their *The Social Life of Information* (Boston, MA: Harvard Business School Press, 2000): 150. And see also John Seely Brown, "Storytelling: Passport to the 21st Century" (www.creatingthe21stcentury.org/JSB14-k-sticky-leaky.html). The source of the idea that knowledge is sticky is probably Gabriel Szulanski, "Exploring Internal Stickiness: Impediments to the Transfer of Best Practice within the Firm," *Strategic Management* 17 (1996).

Chapter 7

1. The threads I've identified are one way—my way—of making sense of the complex social phenomenon we know as organizing. As there are many ways of doing so, it is a good idea to think of these as makeshift categories. The reason for dissecting the work of organizing is to enable people to do it well. And we really want to understand the whole, rather than being preoccupied with parts. Thinking holistically means asking how we are doing at organizing and where we could and should be more conscientious about what we're doing.

2. Etienne Wenger's *Communities of Practice: Learning, Meaning, and Identity* (New York: Cambridge University Press, 1998) is really a book about organizing seen from the inside (from practice) and is all about practices. Emphasizing the socialness of organizing, it is arguably the most original book on organizations and work since management theory was framed in the 19th century.

3. This is one of the central themes of interpretive social theory that includes phenomenology and hermeneutics. See the references in Note 8, Chapter 6.

4. A story that is frequently told about reorgs, by both consultants and managers, is that employees always resist change. Not a single employee I spoke to was against change. They were all concerned, however, about the nature of the reorg and felt it was being handled in a heavy-handed way: imposed on them, without consultation, even though the organization's business is consultation, by people who knew little about their jobs and certainly less than they, themselves knew. Remember that the field reps and management looked at the reorg with different intentions and from entirely different perspectives. One view from field reps (from "practice") was that the planned reorg, which represented management's perspective on change (from "the top") and was naïve and simplistic. It didn't reflect the challenges of working through community-based organizations to improve the quality of life for inner-city communities, hence the practical constraints on achieving more with the existing resources.

5. Etienne Wenger uses the expression "negotiating meaning" rather than the more common one, "making meaning," to emphasize the socialness of meaning-making and the fact that meanings are never settled but always tentative, open to revision and subject to change in conversation or when people reflect on what has been said or done. See Wenger, *Communities of Practice*, part 1, ch. 1, "Meaning."

6. http://dictionary.reference.com/browse/creative.

7. The idea that knowledge-work is ideas built on ideas reminds me of a story about worldviews. As it is usually told, a tribal elder tells a foreigner that one of his island tribe's main beliefs is that their island is supported on the back of a turtle. The foreigner asks, "And what holds up the turtle," and the elder replies, "Another turtle." To the foreigner's follow-up question, "And what holds up that turtle," the elder replies, "It is turtles all the way down." With knowledge-work, it is action built on ideas enabled by conversations "all the way down."

8. When people do get together just to hang out, normally we regard this as pleasure, not work, even though the organizing involved in getting them together certainly means work for someone.

9. The metaphor that comes to mind here is a jazz ensemble, jamming and improvising. See Chapter 4, Note 12.

10. I'm implicitly contrasting knowledge-work with the kind of technical work that is associated with a mechanical or technical system. Although it takes a certain type of expertise, fixing a broken transmission system, for example, is often a matter of following instructions or a schematic. Yet, as Julian Orr explains in a wonderfully instructive book about the work of technicians who service office machines, a good slice of maintenance work would qualify as knowledge-work. Complex machines are quirky and when the technicians encounter problems that are not covered in a manual they depend on one another's experience to solve them. Julian E. Orr, *Talking About Machines: An Ethnography of a Modern Job* (Ithaca, NY: Cornell University Press, 1996).

11. Gordon MacKenzie, *Orbiting the Giant Hairball: A Corporate Fool's Guide to Surviving with Grace* (New York: Viking, 1998). Appropriately, for a book about the

importance of creativity, this book is characterized by quirky drawings and unusual metaphors. Much of the writing on creativity is about the creativity of people—individuals—dealing with topics such as why some people are more creative than others and how to be a more creative person. Few ask the sorts of questions MacKenzie does, about the influence of workplace culture on creativity; although, today, more writers are taking an interest in creativity at work. See Daniel H. Pink, *A Whole New Mind: Moving from the Information Age to the Conceptual Age* (New York: Riverhead Books, 2005).

12. The term "Skunk Works," a registered trade mark of Lockheed Martin, comes from the name of a forest distillery in Al Capp's L'il Abner cartoon that brewed a strange concoction with stranger ingredients. The name was first used by engineers at the Lockheed Corporation, who were developing a fighter jet in World War II using unconventional organizational/management practices based on "The 14 Practices and Rules" of Clarence L. "Kelly" Johnson. See www.lockheedmartin.com/aeronautics/skunkworks/index.html. Also Ben R. Rich and L. Janos, *Skunk Works: A Personal Memoir of My Years at Lockheed* (New York: Back Bay, 1994). Employees in organizations seen as prototypes for creativity, like Xerox's PARC, which is credited with the computer mouse among other inventions (although its parent failed to see the market for them), had a lot of latitude and, for a time at least, the culture of these "labs" was very different to that of their parent companies. The question as to what makes organizations with a track record of innovation, like Apple and Pixar, successful has received a good deal of attention. Not surprisingly, there are few hard-and-fast answers. See Ed Catmull, "How Pixar Fosters Collective Creativity," *Harvard Business Review* 86, no. 9 (2008): 64–72. Arguing that networks support knowledge sharing and are a source of innovation, Sally Helgesen identifies some of the innovative organizations that have adopted unorthodox structures to this end: see her *The Web of Inclusion: A New Architecture for Building Great Organizations* (New York: Currency/Doubleday, 1995).

13. This is the central theme of Daniel Pink's *Drive: The Surprising Truth About What Motivates Us* (New York: Riverhead Books, 2009). He argues that external rewards, like money, which go hand in hand with a carrot-and-stick approach to motivation, are useful only when the work is simple and routine, which describes factory-work. But, when it is complex and requires creative thinking, as knowledge-work does, people want the freedom to create. Then, their motivation, Pink argues is a combination of a sense of autonomy, mastery, and purpose.

14. In an engaging book about the contributions of some of the main figures in OD, Art Kleiner explains why their ideas and actions were, or are, heretical. See Art Kleiner, *The Age of Heretics: A History of the Radical Thinkers Who Reinvented Corporate Management*, 2nd edn (San Francisco: Jossey Bass, 2008).

15. There are important questions here for new organizing practices, especially when the goal is self-organization. Is it possible to have work places that aren't hairballs? The problem of how best to organize is usually framed in terms of balancing "structure," which really means "control and compliance," with "freedom/autonomy/creativity." This is a view-from-the-top perspective. As we'll see, the challenge for knowledge workers is very different when viewed from practice. It has to do with people aligning, so they work together productively, which often hinges on their willingness and ability to form practical—meaning functional or sound—working relationships.

16. I've discussed the notion of a "network" on pp. 67–70. See also Jeff's journal, Chapter 4, pp. 44–6.

17. What is the difference between a group and a network? One way of thinking about this is that the former consists of members: people who recognize that they have some sort of shared identity as a result of working together on something that is of mutual interest. Whereas a network is a way of describing interconnected pairs and small groups of participants. Every participant probably only knows a few others in the network, but as each has some connection to the others, we see them as part of the larger entity. The participants, however, don't identify with the network. Their identities are in groups, organizations, professions, or regions they represent as participants in the network. Sometimes it's hard to tell the difference between a network and a group. As an employee category in a single organization, field representatives are technically a group who identify first with that group and then with their organization. But, in practice, they work from different locations spread across the country and speak to one another only occasionally. When discussing changes in federal policies that affect their work or asking advice on a client-related matter, one-on-one or as a small group, their relationships are more like people who have common work interests than close colleagues in the same department. On the meanings of "network" see Louise Knight and Annie Pye, "Multiple Meanings of 'Network': Some Implications for Interorganizational Theory and Research Practice," University of Bath School of Management Working Paper Series #2006.12, Claverton Down, Bath, 2006.

18. A formally constituted team of a dozen employees, which is part of a health services network and supports sites around the state, may consist of various categories of employees, from area managers, who report to senior management, to regional directors, business managers, and sales and HR specialists. Contacts among team members will vary enormously, with the whole team seldom, if ever, "connecting" at the same time, either face-to-face or on a conference call.

19. The fact that it's difficult to tell whether you've resolved a problem or not is one of the defining characteristics of wicked problems, which "have no stopping rule." Horst Rittel and Melvin Webber, "Dilemmas in a General Theory of Planning," *Policy Sciences* 4 (1973): 162. A wicked problem generally comes to an end when circumstances change and the people involved are no longer interested in the issue—they've grown tired of it—or when those who are working on it run out of time, money, or other resources, and not when someone has solved it. See also E. Jeffrey Conklin and William Weil, *Wicked Problems: Naming the Pain in Organizations* (Washington, DC: Group Decision Support Systems (n.d.), [ca. 1992] available at www.accelinnova. com/docs/wickedproblems.pdf. Jeff Conklin, who introduced me to the distinction between tame and wicked problems, has done more than anyone to spread the word about the importance of Horst Rittel's work and has recently published his own book which includes a discussion of wicked problems. Jeff Conklin, *Dialogue Mapping: Building Shared Understanding of Wicked Problems* (Chichester, UK and Hoboken, NJ: Wiley, 2006).

20. Donald Schön, *The Reflective Practitioner: How Professionals Think in Action* (New York: Basic Books, 1983): 40.

21. The other two are sharing (the easiest) then cooperation. See Clay Shirky, *Here Comes Everybody: The Power of Organizing without Organizations* (New York: The Penguin Press, 2008): 49–51.

22. At a two-day retreat, organized by their managers when it was clear that there was more work to do on the reorg, field reps were asked to look for a way forward. After some discussion they realized that, as jobs were so intertwined, they would not be able

to do so without talking to lots of other people, both in the organization and beyond: to a whole network, in fact.

23. See John C. Camillus, "Strategy as a Wicked Problem," *Harvard Business Review* 86, no. 5 (2008). An article in the *Harvard Business Review* is a sure sign that Rittel's concept of a wicked problem and his distinction between tame and wicked problems has entered the mainstream.

24. See Rittel and Webber, "Dilemmas": 160 on the characteristics of tame problems. It is worth noting that there is a difference between wicked problems and complex (but tame) problems. While spacecraft, including the space shuttle, are very complex pieces of machinery, the technical design issues—engineering problems—are tame, but complex ones. The problems which caused the destruction of both the Challenger and Columbia space shuttles were known in advance and could be fixed (solved). The fact that, in both cases, solutions were found only after lives were lost in two disasters shows that a wicked problem of organizing almost always accompanies the tame (technical) problems: do people have the will to deal with them and are they willing to put aside enough money to do so? Those are wicked problems. In the case of the Challenger, engineers at Morton Thiokol, which built the solid-fuel booster rockets, knew that there was a potentially fatal design flaw in the seals of the tang and clevis field joints on the boosters. They'd apparently tried for some time to get NASA officials to pay enough attention to deal with the problem. All in all, the Challenger disaster makes a first-class case study in the wickedness of organizing. Among many contributions to the case, see Mark Maier, "A Major Malfunction: The Story Behind the Space Shuttle Challenger Disaster" (Binghamton, N.Y: Research Foundation of the State University of New York, 1992) VHS Videorecording with supplemental materials; Paul M. Dombrowski, "*Challenger* through the Eyes of Feyerabend," *Journal of Technical Writing and Communication* 24, no. 1 (1994); Barbara S. Romzek and Melvin J. Dubnick, "Accountability in the Public Sector: Lessons from the Challenger Tragedy," *Public Administration Review* 47, no. 3 (1987); Diane Vaughan, *Lessons Learned in the Challenger Launch Decision: Risky Technology, Culture, and Deviance at Nasa* (Chicago, IL: The University of Chicago Press, 1996).

25. In 'Wicked Problems and Social Complexity' (http://cognexus.org/wpf/wicked problems.pdf). Jeff Conklin has a set of graphs showing the differences between the conventional view that problem-solving is a linear, step-wise process from "problem" to "solution" and how people who are dealing with wicked problems really try to solve them, in a series of ongoing iterations. As they work on a wicked problem, participants' views about both the nature of the problem and how to solve it invariably change. In working on it, they gain perspectives and insights into the problem that they did not and could not have before and are influenced by what others think and say.

26. Rittel and Webber's discussion of tame problems is interspersed with their explanation of the characteristics of wicked problems. See "Dilemmas": 160–7.

27. See Martin Wood, "Cyborg: A Design for Life in the Borderlands," *Emergence* 1, no. 3 (1999).

28. Ronald A. Heifetz, *Leadership without Easy Answers* (Cambridge, MA: The Belknap Press of Harvard University, 1994). See also Ronald A. Heifetz and Marty Linsky, *Leadership on the Line: Staying Alive through the Dangers of Leading* (Boston, MA: Harvard Business School Press, 2002).

29. Phil Brown's case study of lay persons' and professionals' responses to the prevalence of childhood leukemia in a Massachusetts community is a profound illustration of how

wicked problems are created by stakeholders differing interpretations. See Phil Brown, "Popular Epidemiology and Toxic Waste Contamination: Lay and Professional Ways of Knowing," *Journal of Health and Social Behavior* 33, no. 3 (1992).

30. The word "aligning" can be interpreted in a technical-mechanical way (e.g. aligning two pieces of wood), but it shouldn't be. It has to do with interpersonal relationships and people seeing eye-to-eye. I want to add a special note of thanks here to my friend and colleague, Raj Chawla. We've used the idea of aligning in our work together and, originally, I probably got it from him.

31. My perspective on how knowledge changes with time comes from Ludwig Lachmann, a friend and mentor, who writes that "time and knowledge belong together. As soon as we permit time to elapse, we must permit knowledge to change." See "Austrian Economics in the Present Crisis of Economic Thought" in Ludwig M. Lachmann, *Capital, Expectations and the Market Process: Essays in the Theory of the Market Economy*, ed. Walter E. Grinder (Kansas City, KS: Sheed Andrews and McMeel Inc., 1977): 36.

32. Adam Kahane, uses South Africa's transition from a racist state to a nonracial democracy along with other examples to explain what it takes to solve tough problems. See his *Solving Tough Problems: An Open Way of Talking, Listening, and Creating New Realities* (San Francisco: Berrett-Koehler, 2004), in particular the chapter "The Miraculous Option": 19–33.

33. Their unwillingness to sign a treaty, contract, or a bill is usually a good indication that parties aren't aligned, but, as we've seen so often in history, the mere fact that there is a treaty or an accord is not evidence of alignment. These are tools. Aligning has to do with the parties' relationships and commitments and responsibilities to each other, facilitated by talk.

Chapter 8

1. As far as I know the pioneers of scientific management were all men, although, by the 1920s, at least two consultants, Lillian Gilbreth and Mary Parker Follet, were women. From her gender to her ideas Follett, a social worker, was an exception in every way. See the University of Western Ontario libraries' biography of her at www.lib.uwo.ca/programs/generalbusiness/follett.html. References to the work of the foundations of scientific management include: Keith Hoskin and Richard Macve, "Writing, Examining, Disciplining: The Genesis of Accounting's Modern Power," ed. Anthony G. Hopwood and Peter Miller, *Accounting as Social and Institutional Practice* (Cambridge: Cambridge University Press, 1994): 67–97; Hugh G.J. Aitken, *Scientific Management in Action: Taylorism at Watertown Arsenal, 1908–1915* (Princeton, NJ: Princeton University Press, 1985); Stuart Crainer, *The Management Century: A Critical Review of 20th Century Thought and Practice* (San Francisco: Jossey-Bass, 2000); Henry Fayol, *General and Industrial Management*, ed. Irwin Gray (Belmont, CA: David S. Lake, 1987). Robert Kanigel's excellent biography of Taylor describes his obsession from an early age with efficiency related to human motion: *The One Best Way: Fredrick Winslow Taylor and the Enigma of Efficiency* (New York: Viking, 1997). One of the best and certainly most interesting accounts of Taylor's work, including his impact on management methods, is to be found in Matthew Stewart, *The Management Myth: Why the Experts Keep Getting It Wrong* (New York: W.W. Norton, 2009). Stewart argues that Taylor was "unambiguously a workplace 'dualist' . . . laborers are bodies without minds; managers are minds without bodies" (p. 35).

He also makes a convincing case that Taylor's "data," on which he based his claims about the efficiency of his methods, were, at best, no more than guesstimates. Taylor wasn't interested in the kinds of science where data "speaks for itself." He intentionally and deliberately concocted whatever he needed to sway his audience with a good story.

2. Reading books on management is the way to understand the importance of tools. What you get are structures, supply chains, reengineering, and so on, with an emphasis on work-flow processes and the bottom line. You'll also read about org charts, IT systems, scorecards, the kinds of data you need to manage the structure, your supply chain, and the bottom-line. But you'll find little about talk and meaning-making. Together with relationships, attitudes, and values, the latter are about as rare as the Ivory-billed Woodpecker. People may claim to know and to have seen them, but no one can prove that they really exist and matter. Peter Drucker's, *The Practice of Management* (New York: Harper and Row, 1986) has been enormously influential. In it (pp. 343–6) he describes "five . . . basic operations in the work of the manager." A manager "sets objectives," "organizes," "motivates and communicates," undertakes "the job of measurement" and "develops people." Though it would be unfair to blame Drucker for the over-reliance on tools, after only a short time, anyone joining an organization begins to learn that there are tools for each of these operations. Tools for setting objectives include mission statements, lists of deliverables, budgets, and both operating and strategic plans. Org charts, Meyers-Briggs Type Indicators, customer satisfaction surveys, timetables, and Gantt charts are tools for organizing. Work evaluations, pay scales, employee-of-the-month awards, meetings, and vision statements are used to motivate and communicate. When it comes to the job of measurement there is an almost inexhaustible list including performance metrics, balance sheets, executive dashboards, ERP systems, and scorecards. Finally, there are 360-degree evaluations, job descriptions, and training programs for developing people.

3. Etienne Wenger, "Knowledge Management as a Doughnut: Shaping Your Knowledge Strategy through Communities of Practice," *Ivey Business Journal* 68, no. 3 (2004): 1–8, p. 3. It is a definition that says, unequivocally, "practices are social—shared, not individual."

4. Etienne Wenger, *Communities of Practice: Learning, Meaning, and Identity* (New York: Cambridge University Press, 1998): 45–9.

5. Wenger's terms for what I call "talk" and "tools" are "participation" and "reification." "Participation" refers to people interacting in some way. "Reification," from the Latin for "thing," is the process of turning ideas and talk into things, like notes, plans, or spreadsheets, which people do before, during, or after they've talked. Unlike participation, which happens in the moment and is ephemeral, ideas that become reified are more durable and can be stored and circulated. Wenger, *Communities*, ch. 1.

6. The *Encarta English Dictionary* defines "symbiosis" as: "1. close association of animals or plants . . . 2. mutually beneficial relationship . . . "

7. These are some of the characteristics of wicked problems. Rittel and Webber explain that every problem is essentially unique, that solutions to these problems are good–bad, not true–false, and that every solution is a "one shot operation." See Horst Rittel and Melvin Webber, "Dilemmas in a General Theory of Planning," *Policy Sciences* 4 (1973).

8. Using the kind of thinking that shaped industrial management practices, there is no good reason for knowledge workers to talk to one another. Workers performing

routine, repetitive, physical tasks didn't need to talk to each other and, for a variety of other reasons, talk was discouraged. At least one reason was practical. Some hands-on factory work was potentially highly dangerous—especially before safety standards and mechanisms like blade guards were enforced—which required workers to pay careful attention to what they were doing. Like driving while using a cell phone, talking on the job was distracting and reduced productivity, which was reason enough to prohibit it. Although there had been various pieces of legislation about occupational safety over the years, it may come as surprise that OSHA, the government agency in the United States that regulates occupational safety and health, was only created in 1970, under President Richard Nixon (see www.dol.gov/oasam/programs/history/mono-osha13introtoc.htm). See also Mark Aldrich, *Safety First: Technology, Labor and Business in the Building of Work Safety, 1870–1939* (Baltimore: Johns Hopkins University Press, 1997);David Rosner and Gerald Markowitz, eds., *Dying for Work: Workers Safety and Health in Twentieth Century America* (Bloomington: Indiana University Press, 1987); Committee to Assess Training Needs for Occupational Safety and Health Personnel in the United States Board on Health Sciences Policy, *Safe Work in the 21st Century: Education and Training Needs for the Next Decade's Occupational Safety and Health Personnel* (Washington, DC: National Academies Press): Appendix C (http://organizedwisdom.com/helpbar/index.html?return=http://organizedwisdom.com/History_of_Occupational_Health_and_Safety_Laws&url=books.nap.edu/openbook.php?record_id=9835&page=236). There is no doubt, however, that another reason for a no-talking-on-the-job rule was control. Industrial-age factory workers were often exploited, and managing work included heavy handed regulation as well as meddling in people's lives—certainly at work but, sometimes, at home as well. Henry Ford's "sociological department" (founded in 1913) developed a reputation for meddling in workers' private lives. In 1914, after the company announced a $5 per day wage, the department was responsible for establishing whether workers were leading the kinds of lives which made them eligible for full pay, meaning "they were not throwing their money away on smoking, gambling, drinking, or prostitution." Rudolph V. Alvarado and Sonya Y. Alvarado, *Drawing Conclusions on Henry Ford: A Biographical History through Cartoons* (Ann Arbor, MI: University of Michigan Press, 2001). Sweatshops still abound, especially in "cheap labor" countries, and in them you'll find, too, that workers are banned from talking on the job.

9. The preference for tools over talk spreads like a virus whenever management practices invade a particular sector. Health Management Organizations brought corporatism to health care (a misnomer if ever there was one) with administrators, who do things the MBA way, deciding how doctors will be remunerated. One result is that doctors get paid for procedures, for example running batteries of tests, presumably because when a doctor does a procedure there is tangible evidence that something has been done to someone. Lisa Sanders explains that good diagnostic practice requires doctors to listen and to talk to their patients (i.e. talk rather than tools). But in a management-oriented medical world, commonsense can't prevail. Lisa Sanders, *Every Patient Tells a Story: Medical Mysteries and the Art of Diagnosis* (New York: Random House, 2009).

10. Tom Davenport estimates that in 1995 it was a $50 billion industry. Thomas H. Davenport, "The Fad that Forgot People," *Fast Company*, October (1995).

11. See the Wikipedia entries for "business process orientation" and "business process reengineering": http://en.wikipedia.org/wiki/Business_process_orientation and

http://en.wikipedia.org/wiki/Business_process_reengineering.. The latter, although needing further refinement, deals with criticisms of BPR, as does the *Economist* article on 'Business process re-engineering' at www.economist.com/node/13130298. Evidence of the success of BPR (Texas Instruments and American Standard are given as examples) typically is anecdotal. It often comes from the purveyors of BPR (e.g. Michael Hammer, *Beyond Reengineering: How the Process-Centered Organization Is Changing Our Work and Our Lives* (New York: HarperCollins, 1996): ch. 1) with very little data to back it up. If you follow the evolution of management fads and have heard the advice of management "gurus," executives willingness to act on anecdote doesn't come as a surprise, but it is ironical given management's obsession with data. In terms of what I've said about the difference between knowledge-work and factory-work, it is also not surprising that a large percentage of the successes claimed for reengineering are in manufacturing businesses. As you would expect, given the social nature of the work, and as the JPL experience bears out, it is much harder to find a success story in knowledge organizations.

12. Davenport, "The Fad That Forgot People." Whether something is a "movement" or a "fad" depends a lot on context and timing, including the stage of the idea's life cycle that you happen to look at. Early on, it is a movement. When people have lost interest it becomes a fad.

13. Although reengineering has a longer history, *Reengineering the Corporation* by Michael Hammer and James Champy put it on the map. The book became the next blockbuster-must-read for managers and "business process orientation" become the next must-do, with the promise that corporations would enhance their competitiveness and their bottom lines, doing more, more quickly, with less. See Michael Hammer, "Reengineering Work: Don't Automate, Obliterate," *Harvard Business Review* 68, no. 4 (1990); Michael Hammer and James A. Champy, *Reengineering the Corporation: A Manifesto for Business Revolution* (New York: Harper Business Books, 1993). Bradley Jackson argues that Hammer and Champy's success, like that of management "gurus" in general, depended much more on their appealing to and polishing managers' self-images than it did on their proving that their ideas would improve the businesses bottom-lines. Managers don't need "hard facts." They are persuaded by the "soft stuff." See Bradley G. Jackson, "Re-Engineering the Sense of Self: The Manager and the Management Guru," *Journal of Management Studies* 33, no. 5 (1996): 571–90. A decade later outsourcing replaced downsizing as the next obsession for improving the bottom-line.

14. That the promises of every type of strategic initiative go unfulfilled is not an accident but a systemic problem, inherent in management practices. Large-scale mergers, for example, are usually preceded by a great deal of fanfare about "complementary organizations" and "synergy." Presumably the executives who negotiate them would like the mergers to live up to their expectations, not least because of the bonuses they stand to receive based on the combined bottom-lines. Yet, it is widely known that few merged organizations survive intact, fewer thrive, and many fail completely. Why? Because they are prefigured and then handled simplistically with tools like financial planning instruments and org charts (restructuring), with the object of "joining two organizations," rather than reorganizing.

15. The latter was certainly an important goal up to the "great contraction" of 2008 when bank failures led a large scale economic downturn. Until then, analysts had raised earnings estimates quarter after quarter, prompting an unsustainable pattern of growth.

Executives played a game of chicken with analysts, responding to those estimates as if they were mandates for action. This short-termism lead to reckless business decisions which contributed to the crash. To what extent the game will continue remains to be seen.

16. "Chainsaw Al" Dunlap, once Chairman of Sunbeam, found infamy as a ruthless and reckless corporate downsizer. The *Washington Post* Business section of May 12, 1998 describes his plans for additional downsizing at Sunbeam, a manufacturer of home appliances. Known as "Chainsaw Al" for his "propensity to slash corporate deadwood and underbrush" his practices and the attitudes are a combination of detachment, the absence of moral standards, lack of commitment, and ruthlessness. The article reports that having recently acquired other companies for $2 billion, he is now cutting 40 percent of Sunbeam's workforce and closing eight factories, equal to a third of the plants, after a first-quarter loss of $7.8 million compared with a $20.6 million profit during the same period the previous year. It quotes Dunlap as saying "the company was taking 'aggressive steps to address . . . unacceptable financial performance.' " After the sales shortfall Dunlap fired the executive vice president in charge of sales of consumer products and in the light of the cuts he promised "double-digit percentage growth in earnings and increased sales." His actions are described by a securities firm analyst as "a very well-formulated plan of attack." In summarizing Dunlap's history, the article notes that in 1983, on his first day at work at Lily-Tulip he walked into a conference room and fired all but two of the senior managers. In 1993 he laid off 10,000 employees (one-third of the workforce) at Scott Paper and, in 1996, when he joined Sunbeam, he replaced most of the executives and within three months had a plan to lay off half the workers. Although he "typically exits before the dust settles," his own position appears to be not only unharmed but also considerably strengthened in financial terms by each successive extermination he orders. The article says that "for now, he has the support of . . . [the] board and key shareholders" and he recently signed a three year contract with Sunbeam which, with stock options, was worth up to $70 million. The immediate sequel to this story, as the *Washington Post* Business section of June 16, 1998 reports, is that the Sunbeam board fired him, having "lost confidence in him and his earnings forecasts." Employees said that he had "terrorized underlings, refused to listen to suggestions . . . and adopted arbitrary rules." It is unclear whether he received severance pay, for the contract he had negotiated a month before included "a generous severance package in case of firing—$2 million a year through January 2001, plus such benefits as a country club membership and dental and health insurance for three years." Reinforcing the idea that ethical conduct is subordinate to showing the improvement in profits that was forecast, some three years later Dunlap was under investigation for being party to fraudulent accounting practices in misrepresenting Sunbeam's profits.

17. Peter J. Westwick, "Reengineering Engineers: Management Philosophies at the Jet Propulsion Laboratory in the 1990s," *Technology and Culture* 48, no. 1 (2007): 67–91.

18. Ibid.: 88.

19. Ibid.: 89.

20. Ibid.: 80.

21. See Duncan J. Watts (2004), "Decentralized Intelligence: What Toyota Can Teach the 9/11 Commission About Intelligence Gathering" (www.slate.com/id/2104808/).

22. Ronald A. Heifetz, *Leadership without Easy Answers* (Cambridge, MA: The Belknap Press of Harvard University, 1994): 22.

23. There are parallels between reorgs and any major change in an organization, including the introduction of new technologies, such as groupware (i.e. collaborative technologies). One of the best descriptions of the process and problems of groupware implementation is Wanda J. Orlikowski, "Learning from Notes: Organizational Issues in Groupware Implementation," *The Information Society* 9, no. 3 (1993). It has many of the qualities of Peter Westwick's article and reveals the problem of management myopia clearly.

24. Michael Schrage, *No More Teams: Mastering the Dynamics of Creative Collaboration* (New York: Currency Doubleday, 1995): 148–9 (my emphasis).

Chapter 9

1. The Agile Alliance's "Manifesto for Agile Software Development" (2001), reproduced here with permission, is at http://agilemanifesto.org/, where you'll also find the names of the signatories, "Twelve Principles of Agile Software," and a short explanation of the history of the Manifesto. The text is identical with the original except that I've added **bold** and *italic* font styles for emphasis.

2. On the question of what constitutes good software, I recommend Terry Winograd and Fernando Flores, *Understanding Computers and Cognition: A New Foundation for Design* (Indianapolis, IN: Addison-Wesley, 1986), which, among other things, is a treatise on human-oriented software design.

3. http://en.wikipedia.org/wiki/Waterfall_model. In common with all management practices, the waterfall method is shaped by the Western "methodological vision of development as a linear, stage-like progression through a sequence driven by a grand plan." See Martin Wood, "Cyborg: A Design for Life in the Borderlands," *Emergence* 1, no. 3 (1999): 92–104. Jeff Conklin contrasts this linear and false view of how people solve problems with the untidy, ad hoc, but ultimately practical approaches that they actually use to deal with wicked problems. See E. Jeffrey Conklin, *Dialogue Mapping : Building Shared Understanding of Wicked Problems* (Chichester, UK and Hoboken, NJ: Wiley, 2006).

4. Con Kenney, personal communication.

5. See "Agile Processes and Self-Organization," available under "Resources" in the "Scrum library" at www.controlchaos.com.

6. The word "scrum" was first used, but only in passing, by Hirotaka Takeuchi and Ikujiro Nonaka in "The New New Product Development Game," *Harvard Business Review* 64, no. 1 (1986): 137–46. See also "What is Scrum?" at www.controlchaos.com/.

7. The difference between a breakdown and a "set scrum" is that, with the latter, the form of the scrum is fixed according to the rules of the game and the referee tells the players when and where to scrum (and who will have possession of the ball at the put in) as a penalty for certain rule infringements.

8. See Ken Schwaber, "SCRUM Development Process" (n.d.) available at https://wiki.state.ma.us/confluence/download/attachments/16842777/Scrum+Development+Process.pdf; and Jeff Sutherland and Ken Schwaber, "The Scrum Papers: Nuts, Bolts, and Origins of an Agile Framework" (2011), available at http://jeffsutherland.com/ScrumPapers.pdf. I want to thank Greg Pfister, who at the time worked for Northrop-Grumman, for sharing his experience of agile methods. See also Howard Baetjer, *Software as Capital: An Economic Perspective on Software Engineering*

(Los Alamitos; CA: IEEE Press, 1997): ch. 3, which looks at software design as a social learning process. These ideas later coalesced as agile programming. From what I can gather, one of the main problems in making agile methods "stick" in organizations has nothing to do with the methods as such, but with corporate management's attitude toward developers who use them. Developers can "show results" with agile methods, but they can't overcome corporate management's aversion to them. They can't persuade management about why these methods are sensible and effective. Agile methods seem all wrong to top managers who don't understand them and are hooked on conventional management practices. See Jeremy D Miller's, The Shade Developer Blog, "Self -Organizing Teams are Superior to Command and Control Teams" (http://codebetter.com/blogs/jeremy.miller/archive/2007/04/16/ Self-Organizing-Teams-are-Superior-to-Command-n_2700_-Control-Teams.aspx).

9. See Linda Rising and Norman S. Janof, "The Scrum Software Development Process for Small Teams," *IEEE Software*, July/August (2000) and Mike Cohn, "Advice on Conducting the Scrum of Scrum Meetings" at www.scrumalliance.org/articles/ 46-advice-on-conducting-the-scrum-of-scrums-meeting.

10. Linda Rising, "Agile Meetings," *Software Testing and Quality Engineering Magazine*, May–June (2002).

11. See Jim Highsmith, "History: The Agile Manifesto" at http://agilemanifesto.org/ history.html.

12. I have Con Kenney to thank for the idea that high-control organizations infantilize people.

13. It is worth noting that it was this attitude, widespread in manufacturing, that W. Edwards Demming sought to change with his quality improvement methods that later morphed into "total quality management." His methods returned some decision-making authority to workers on the production line, giving them a reason to care about their work. Demming was an electrical engineer whose practices were based on applying statistical methods to quality control. Interestingly, his message, about hands-on decision-making from the factory floor, was more popular in Japan and other Southeast Asian countries than the United States; possibly because, being communitarian cultures, workplace relationships matter in those countries and are seen to matter. In individualist cultures, like the U.S., there is a pretense that they don't. See also, Andrea Gabor, *The Man Who Discovered Quality: How W. Edwards Deming Brought the Quality Revolution to America: The Stories of Ford, Xerox, and GM* (New York: Penguin, 1992).

14. Charles Chaplin's classic film, *Modern Times*, parodies this mindset.

15. If you think I'm exaggerating, consider that the credit card industry's name for card users who pay off their balances each month is "deadbeats." Because it's lucrative to fly them between hospitals, patients were known as "golden trout" by the helicopter program's director. See Francis Cianfrocca, "This Story Will Have Legs: Congress Takes Aim at Credit Deadbeats," *The New Ledger*, May 19, 2009 (http://newledger.com/2009/05/this-story-will-have-legs-congress-takes-aim-at-credit-deadbeats/) and Gilbert M. Gaul and Mary Pat Flahert, "The Deadly Cost of Swooping in to Save a Life," *Washington Post*, August 21, 2009: p. A01. These are just two examples of a phenomenon that is illustrated by "aggressive" marketing practices on the part of a range of industries, from finance to pharmaceuticals (e.g. the executives of bailed-out banks who paid themselves large bonuses and tried to do it surreptitiously, or the short advertising campaigns for newly invented "syndromes"

like "restless legs"). In each case they are not merely showing a lack of consideration for customers. They are actually treating them with contempt. See, for example, Carrie Johnson, "In Settlement, A Warning to Drugmakers: Pfizer to Pay Record Penalty in Improper-Marketing Case," *Washington Post*, September 3, 2009: p. A01. The whistle-blower in this case said "At Pfizer I was expected to increase profits at all costs, even when sales meant endangering lives." As usual, the settlement came without an admission of wrongdoing (i.e. without the company admitting responsibility or any personal accountability on the part of executives), which more or less guarantees that "improper practices" will continue.

16. In his journal Jeff explains that software developers' identities are closely tied to their work. If they can't do good work they see themselves as less than adequate programmers. It's the same with nurses and nursing.

17. This example came to light as the Obama Administration attempted to "reform" health care in the United States in 2009.

18. Theodore Taptiklis, *Unmanaging: Opening up the Organization to Its Own Unspoken Knowledge* (London and New York: Palgrave Macmillan, 2008): 80 (my emphasis). Patricia Benner's books include Patricia Benner and J. Wrubel, *The Primacy of Caring: Stress and Coping in Health and Illness* (Menlo Park, CA: Addison-Wesley, 1989); Patricia E. Benner, *From Novice to Expert: Excellence and Power in Clinical Nursing Practice* (Menlo Park, CA: Addison-Wesley, 1984), in which she develops a general model of professional practice based on a close study of nursing practices.

19. See Pearl M. Oliner and Samuel P. Oliner, *Toward a Caring Society: Ideas into Action* (Westport, CT: Praeger, 1995).

20. Georg Von Krogh, K. Ichijo, and Ikujiro Nonaka, *Enabling Knowledge Creation: How to Unlock the Mystery of Tacit Knowledge and Release the Power of Innovation* (New York: Oxford University Press, 2000): ch. 3.

21. Apparently, a good deal of what we think of as "management principles," including contractual labor and hierarchical, superior–subordinate relationships, were taken over from the feudal practices that accompanied the land enclosure acts in England and elsewhere, which preceded industrialization. See Peter Kriedte, Hans Medick, and Jurgen Schlumbohm, eds., *Industrialization before Industrialization: Rural Industry in the Genesis of Capitalism* (Cambridge: Cambridge University Press, 1981); Peter Kriedte, *Peasants, Landlords and Merchant Capitalists: Europe and the World Economy, 1500–1800* (Cambridge: Cambridge University Press, 1983). Art Kleiner uses the very suitable word, "vernacular," when writing about life at a time before scientific management practices were widespread. See Art Kleiner, *The Age of Heretics: A History of the Radical Thinkers Who Reinvented Corporate Management*, 2nd edn (San Francisco: Jossey Bass, 2008).

22. Henry Ford's "sociological department" (founded in 1913) developed a reputation for meddling in workers private lives. See Chapter 8, Note 8.

23. One result of this schizophrenia is that there is no contradiction, now, and no harm, in people having multiple identities. So, for example, the bankers who deceive the clients who've entrusted their money to them almost certainly care about their own families. They want their children to grow up safely in good neighborhoods and go to the best schools. If their irresponsibility eventually catches up with them they'll usually continue to live their lives more or less with impunity, unaccountable for their actions. They may even be pillars of the community, dispensing largesse, showing how much they "care," through philanthropic trusts.

Chapter 10

1. Matthew Stewart, *The Management Myth: Why the Experts Keep Getting It Wrong* (New York: W.W. Norton and Company, 2009): 56.

2. It didn't take people long to lose patience with Taylor and his methods. In spite of growing disenchantment with the man and the realization that his methods were impractical, the field of time and motion studies grew apace, as did the management consulting profession; and people remained enamored of Taylors ideas. In an exceptionally well-told story, Hugh Aitken explores Taylor's work at the Watertown Arsenal, writing about the disenchantment with his methods. See Hugh G. J. Aitken, *Scientific Management in Action: Taylorism at Watertown Arsenal, 1908–1915* (Princeton, NJ: Princeton University Press, 1985). Meg Wheatley examines the new science of quantum mechanics and complexity and explains how it changes our thinking about management. See Margaret J. Wheatley, *Leadership and the New Science: Learning About Organization from an Orderly Universe* (San Franscisco: Berrett-Koehler, 1992).

3. Jean Lave and Etienne Wenger, *Situated Learning: Legitimate Peripheral Participation* (New York: Cambridge University Press, 1991). As a book about professionals (learning) trajectories, situated learning complements the work of Patricia Benner. See Patricia E. Benner, *From Novice to Expert: Excellence and Power in Clinical Nursing Practice* (Menlo Park, CA: Addison-Wesley, 1984).

4. Etienne Wenger, *Communities of Practice: Learning, Meaning, and Identity* (New York: Cambridge University Press, 1998). Also see Wenger, "Communities of Practice: The Social Fabric of a Learning Organization," *The Healthcare Forum Journal* 39 no. 4 (1996) and "Knowledge Management as a Doughnut: Shaping Your Knowledge Strategy through Communities of Practice," *Ivey Business Journal* January/February (2004).

5. "High performance teams" (HPT) started in the emerging discipline of organization development. The term originated at the Tavistock Institute, London, with Eric Trist's ideas and practices based on his observation of self-organizing teams at work in an English coal mine. Subsequently, HPT came to be associated with the process-improvement movement ("better, quicker, cheaper") and to be seen as a management objective. See Marc Hanlan, *High Performance Teams: How to Make Them Work* (Westport, CT: Praeger Publishers, 2004).

6. On the early history of knowledge management and its antecedents, see Lawrence Prusak, "Where Did Knowledge Management Come From?" *IBM Systems Journal* 40, no. 4 (2001): 1002–6; and Patrick Lambe "The Unacknowledged Parentage of Knowledge Management," *Journal of Knowledge Management* 15, no. 2 (2011): 175–97. Both authors refer to the leading role that management consultants played in the emergence of knowledge management, while acknowledging a wider set of influences and antecedents that go back to the 1960s. It is not difficult to read into both contributions that knowledge management marks the arrival of knowledge-work and the recognition that, prior to the 1990s, neither management thinking nor practices had anything substantial to say about knowledge at work, or knowledge in work. While some writers, like Verna Allee, recognize that knowledge and knowledge-work 'changes everything,' undermining traditional management completely, the field of knowledge management today is dominated by the belief–perpetuated by consultants and vendors of IT products–that you can add knowledge (actually "information") to management

and continue to manage organizations using Taylorist principles and practices, as if nothing fundamental has changed.

7. Wenger, *Communities of Practice*: ch. 2.

8. The World Bank, for example, used the name "thematic groups." Often, a budget is what makes a group and its activities legitimate. Having a budget is evidence that, as far as top management is concerned, what they're doing is acceptable and the group has permission to exist and to operate in the organization. Without a budget, whatever they are doing isn't real work.

9. Studies include Scott D.N. Cook and John Seely Brown, "Bridging Epistemologies: The Generative Dance between Organizational Knowledge and Organizational Knowing," *Organization Science* 10, no. 4 (1999); Wenger, *Communities of Practice*; Julian E. Orr, *Talking About Machines: An Ethnography of a Modern Job* (Ithaca, NY: Cornell University Press, 1996). In order, they look at flute makers, insurance claims clerks, and technicians who service office copiers.

10. Orr, *Talking About Machines*: 17.

11. Ibid.: 23.

12. Ibid.:76–7.

13. Etienne Wenger has various, essentially similar definitions of communities of practice. I particularly like this one, from "Communities of Practice: a brief introduction"(2006), at www.ewenger.com/theory/index.htm. It is simple and elegant.

14. Asking what is "community," Zygmunt Bauman refers to the ideas of Ferdinand Tönnies and, more recently, of Göran Rosenberg: " 'Common understanding' 'coming naturally' [is] the feature which sets community apart from the world of bitter quarrels, cut-throat competition, and log-rolling . . . Human loyalties, offered and matter-of-factly expected inside the 'warm circle' [Rosenberg's expression for community], 'are not derived from external social logic or from any economic cost–benefit analysis.' " Zygmunt Bauman, *Community: Seeking Safety in an Insecure World* (Maiden, MA: Polity Press, 2001): 10. Wenger has a more technical view of what constitutes the community in a CoP, but these ideas are consistent with his emphasis on meaning making and cooperation. They also seem to be consistent with the way field-service technicians may regard their community.

15. I've borrowed the phrase from Hugo Letiche, "Meaning, Organizing, and Empowerment," in *Empowering Humanity: State of the Art in Humanistics*, eds. Annemie Halsema and Douwe van Houten (Utrecht: De Tidjstroom Uitgeverij, 2002): 217.

16. See www.ubuntu.com: "Ubuntu is a community developed, Linux-based operating system." One part of "the Ubuntu promise" is that "Ubuntu will always be free of charge, including enterprise releases and security updates."

17. Lovemore Mbigi, *Ubuntu: The African Dream in Management* (Randburg, South Africa: Knowledge Resources, 1997).

18. Allister Sparks, The Mind of South Africa: The Story of the Rise and Fall of Apartheid (London: Mandarin, 1990): 14.

19. The ethos of performance and rewards requires us to be self-centered: even though you focus on others (how well they are doing *their* work) it is ultimately because that reflects on you ("I").

Chapter 11

1. In *The Management Myth: Why the Experts Keep Getting It Wrong* (New York: W.W. Norton, 2009), Matthew Stewart does a particularly good job of highlighting the fact

that the father of scientific management's views were completely unscientific: they were just prejudices.

2. No matter how you look at it, economists' claims about the merits of competition are completely unfounded and entirely unwarranted. As neoclassical economics only has models of competition, it is impossible to compare competitive with cooperative actions. The concept of competition in economics has nothing to do with what we understand by competitive behavior: i.e. rivalry. See Mark Addleson, "General Equilibrium and 'Competition': On Competition as Strategy," *South African Journal of Economics* 52, no. 2 (1984). If this isn't enough, economists use an extraordinarily limited set of criteria to assess the goodness or effectiveness of competition. Their claims about competition, which are meant to be universal, applying to production activities in general, rest on models (e.g. "perfect competition") of cost and revenue functions of theoretical "firms" that are interpreted as industrial concerns. To make a case for the benefits of competition for society, you'd surely want to know how competition fares in other situations and you'd want to consider the consequences using a wider set of criteria than cost and revenue.

3. On the connection between the officers' training at the West Point Academy and management practices, see Keith Hoskin and Richard Macve, "The Genesis of Accountability: The Westpoint Connection," *Accounting, Organizations and Society* 13, no. 1 (1988); "Writing, Examining, Disciplining: The Genesis of Accounting's Modern Power," in *Accounting as Social and Institutional Practice*, eds. Anthony G. Hopwood and Peter Miller (Cambridge: Cambridge University Press, 1994).

4. I'm not underestimating the role of formal authority in organizing. But the value of formal authority stems largely from the combination of competition (adversarial relationships) and hierarchy. Having on your side someone whose position counts is important only as long as rank is a way of "keeping everyone in their place," separating leaders from the rank and file (or managers from workers), and determining who gets to talk to whom. One way of gauging activists' success in moving to new organizing practices is by the extent to which they've taken formal authority out of the picture.

5. In retrospect, it is clear that managers and consultants have struggled for years with the limitations of industrial era management structures; especially the linear line of authority advocated so strongly by Henri Fayol. Four of his fourteen "general principles of management" are "unity of command," "unity of direction," "centralization," and "scalar chain," leaving no doubt about the necessity of a single, clear-cut line of authority. See Henri Fayol, *General and Industrial Management*, trans. C. Storrs (London: Pitman Publishing, 1949). The "solution" to getting away from a linear chain of command, the matrix structure, created headaches all around and, with hindsight, it is relatively easy to understand why. Operating under standard rules of management, a matrix multiplies everyone's exposure to the limitations of bureaucracy, hierarchy, and competition but does nothing to change the way people think about working together and their attitudes to collaborating, sharing knowledge, and aligning.

6. Donella Meadows has an illuminating article on where to intervene in a system to produce change. Approaching this question from a systems dynamics perspective, she argues that the place of most leverage is at the level of paradigms: the way people think and see things. Unfortunately she doesn't say much about the question that plagues people advocating paradigm change: what does it take to change a paradigm and where do you begin. See Donella H. Meadows, "Places to Intervene in a System (in Increasing Order of Effectiveness)," *Whole Earth*, no. 91 (1997).

7. "Unmanaging" is Theodore Taptiklis's word. Theodore Taptiklis, *Unmanaging: Opening up the Organization to Its Own Unspoken Knowledge* (London and New York: Palgrave Macmillan, 2008).

8. This is the theme of Gordon MacKenzie's book, in which he encourages professionals to find ways to escape the "Giant Hairball" of corporate culture. See Gordon MacKenzie, *Orbiting the Giant Hairball: A Corporate Fool's Guide to Surviving with Grace* (New York: Viking, 1998).

9. I have to thank Anthony Joyce for this analogy (personal communication).

10. There may be almost as many definitions of best practice as there are best practices. This one, from Gurteen.com (www.gurteen.com/gurteen/gurteen.nsf/id/best-practice), is very similar to the definition in Wikipedia (http://en.wikipedia.org/wiki/Best_practice). The National Cancer Institute, which draws its definitions from a variety of sources that are regarded as reputable (thus employing a best practice in the use of definitions), defines "best practices" as "standard operating procedures that are considered state-of-the-science consistent with all applicable ethical, legal, and policy statutes, regulations, and guidelines" (http://biospecimens.cancer.gov/bestpractices/got/).

11. The seminal work on language, metaphor, and meaning includes contributions by George Lakoff, including George Lakoff and Mark Johnson, *Metaphors We Live by* (Chicago: University of Chicago Press, 1980) and George Lakoff, *Women, Fire, and Dangerous Things: What Categories Reveal About the Mind* (Chicago: University of Chicago Press, 1987). Although the themes have only come to prominence in the last decade or so, there is a large and growing academic literature on the importance of meaning-making, language, and stories or narratives in organizations and organizational life. Barbara Czarniawska has been a leading light in applying postmodern thinking on narrative to organizations, explaining that organizations are a web of narratives. A small sample of contributors to this field includes: Barbara Czarniawska, *Narrating the Organization: Dramas of Institutional Identity* (Chicago: University of Chicago Press, 1997); Tom W. Keenoy, Cliff Oswick, and David Grant, "Organizational Discourses: Text and Context," *Organization* 4, no. 2 (1997); Richard L. Daft and John C. Wiginton, "Language and Organization," *The Academy of Management Review* 4, no. 2 (1979); Robert Kegan and Lisa Laskow Lahey, *How the Way We Talk Can Change the Way We Work: Seven Languages for Transformation* (San Francisco: Jossey-Bass, 2001); Lloyd Sandelands and Robert Drazin, "On the Language of Organization Theory," *Organization Studies* 10, no. 4 (1989); Robert Westwood and Stephen Linstead, eds., *The Language of Organization* (London: SAGE, 2001); Bing Ran and P. Robert Duimering, "Imaging the Organization: Language Use in Organizational Identity Claims," *Journal of Business and Technical Communication* 21, no. 2 (2007); Susanne Tietze, Laurie Cohen, and Gill Musson, *Understanding Organizations through Language* (London: SAGE, 2003); David Grant, Tom W. Keenoy, and Cliff Oswick, eds., *Discourse and Organization* (London: SAGE, 1998); Cliff Oswick, Tom W. Keenoy, and David Grant, "Managerial Discourses: Words Speak Louder Than Actions?" *Journal of Applied Management Studies* 6, no. 1 (1997). See, too, the references in Chapter 6, Note 10 on the interpretive tradition in social theory.

12. As another example of how context influences people's receptiveness to a narrative, Sarah Palin and other conservatives used the slogan time "drill baby, drill" to pressure lawmakers into passing legislation that would allow companies to drill for oil in the wildlife refuge in Alaska and elsewhere. It appears that lots of people agreed with the sentiment while "dependency on foreign oil" was uppermost on their minds. When in 2010, the BP-leased drilling rig, Deepwater Horizon, exploded and sank and the

ruptured pipe spewed millions of gallons of crude oil and natural gas into the Gulf of Mexico, however, their receptiveness to this idea changed.

13. Quoted in Michael Schrage, *No More Teams: Mastering the Dynamics of Creative Collaboration* (New York: Currency Doubleday, 1995): 148–9.

14. Vuvuzelas are the plastic horns that anyone listening to or watching the 2010 World Cup football matches in South Africa got to know intimately. Although most are made in China, these have become a kind of South African national "musical" instrument because they are so popular with spectators at local soccer matches.

15. In a personal communication, Mark Leheney, a consultant, put it this way: When raising the topic of employees doing the organizing, you can feel the temperature in the room drop by 30 degrees.

16. When faced with threats that may demand quick action, the intimate relationship between language and action can be a source of inaction or an obstacle to action. The debate over "climate change" is one example of how language is called to the service of whatever cause people wish to champion. What began as concerns about "global warming" has become a minefield of language, as different sides try to portray the situation either as a potentially disastrous problem which many scientists agree needs urgent attention or as a story that has been completely overblown by irresponsible, sensation-seeking media, but which has no "hard science" to support it.

17. Perhaps one of the reasons why the field of organization development (OD) hasn't had much impact on the way organizations work is that it hasn't changed the way people think about organizations and, in fact, there hasn't been a serious effort by OD practitioners to do so.

18. David Abram explains better than anyone I know how speaking about the world— what we say and how we say it—brings it alive: that the world as we know it lives in our language and conversations. See David Abram, *The Spell of the Sensuous: Language and Perception in a More-Than-Human World* (New York: Vintage Books, 1997).

19. For more on "zing" and "zation," see Mark Addleson and Jennifer Garvery Berger, "Putting 'Zing' Back into Organizational Consulting," *Journal of Professional Consulting* 3, no. 1 (2008).

20. Peter Block makes a compelling case for stewardship over traditional leadership. Stewardship and accountability, which is another theme in his work, are closely affiliated. See Peter Block, *Stewardship: Choosing Service over Self-Interest* (San Francisco: Berrett-Koehler, 1993).

Chapter 12

1. Something that happens quite often, especially in hierarchies, is that people who wish to connect with others in order to organize, perhaps to have their questions answered by someone higher up, find they are unable to do so. For whatever reason, they are rebuffed in their effort to "open a space" with a superior, frequently by a "gate keeper" who knows nothing of the specifics of the situation and little about the interests and inclinations of either party. With their concept "peripheral participation," Jean Lave and Etienne Wenger explain why it is so important to encourage and consciously facilitate these kinds of interactions. Jean Lave and Etienne Wenger, *Situated Learning: Legitimate Peripheral Participation* (New York: Cambridge University Press, 1991).

2. See pp. 133–4.

3. The idea of social spaces helps to explain why mindsets and attitudes matter so much at work. Unfortunately, Western, post-Enlightenment thinking is inherently critical, and criticism is also the prevailing mindset in high-control management environments. You pick apart data or arguments until you have established the facts. Through scientific management, management practices inherited Cartesian rationalism and the belief that you "get to the truth" by critical analysis. Additionally, as management methods evolved in regimented, controlling environments, like military establishments and industrial-age factories, there is a pervasive attitude of "follow the rules or be punished," which is hardly conducive to creative experimentation and learning. It is a depressing attitude rather than an uplifting one. It instills fear at work rather than inspiring joy in work. See Michel Foucault, *Discipline and Punish: The Birth of the Prison* (London: Allen Lane, 1977). For some time, writers have argued for adopting an alternative, "appreciative" approach. Their concerns are valid but as the attitudes they're concerned about are inherent in management ideology, a truly appreciative workplace isn't possible without an entirely different way of organizing work. Hierarchy, competition, and compliance all have to go. They are not compatible with appreciativeness, which is closely associated with care and caring for others and for the work you do. A good deal of information on appreciative methods and the history, principles, and practices of appreciative inquiry can be found on the "Appreciative Inquiry Commons" website of Case Western University, Ohio at http://appreciativeinquiry.case.edu/. See also Tojo Thatchenkery and Carol Metzker, *Appreciative Intelligence: Seeing the Mighty Oak in the Acorn* (San Francisco, CA: Berrett-Koehler, 2006).

4. See Georg Von Krogh, K. Ichijo, and Ikujiro Nonaka, *Enabling Knowledge Creation: How to Unlock the Mystery of Tacit Knowledge and Release the Power of Innovation* (New York: Oxford University Press, 2000).

5. You don't want bridges or houses to be built to less-than-minimum specifications. In some situations, especially where standards in use are well established, matters are quite straightforward. You work with established standards. But technology moves quickly today and we are often at the edge of what is known and of established rules and standards: from nuclear energy, to the safety of drugs and aircraft design, to the impact of particular activities on the environment. At this point, whether we want to or not, we are in the process of organizing, although it might be called "policymaking" or "strategy formulation." We may be in search of answers to technical problems but the process is a social one of people making meaning together and sharing knowledge in order to find solutions. Seeing the situation as a problem to do with organizing and aligning helps us to understand why there are all the attendant problems and questions. How safe is safe? Who are the experts and whose interests do they represent? How far can established analytical and statistical methods take us in terms of providing answers? Finding answers to these reveals them to be wicked problems which interweave social—including moral—and technical considerations, which goes some way to explaining why there is an increasing awareness of the limits of human knowledge in general and the severe limitations of a "pure" technical education and of statistical tools like probability estimates, in particular, in dealing with the problems. See Langdon Winner, *The Whale and the Reactor: A Search for Limits in an Age of High Technology* (Chicago: University of Chicago Press, 1986). On the standard, probabilistic approach to risk analysis see Terje Aven, *Foundations of Risk Analysis: A Knowledge and Decision-Oriented Perspective* (Hoboken, NJ: Wiley, 2003).

6. Sometimes rules are completely inscrutable, even perhaps to the people who devised them. Here is an example that circulated on the blogsphere. The Bank of America is an American Bank which uses the American flag in its corporate logo. In September, 2009, a branch in Gaffney, SC removed American flags that had been placed along the sidewalk on a funeral route for an American Marine, Cpl Fowlkes, killed in Afghanistan. The reason, according to the branch manager, was that some might be offended by the flags. A bank spokesperson put the removal of the flags down to "an error in communication." Presumably, someone had asked and been told that it was bank policy not to have flags on the sidewalk (www.huliq.com/3257/86746/flag-scandal-begins-cost-bank-america-accounts).

7. Typically, what managers mean by "there is not enough accountability," is that they don't have a means of ensuring compliance, making certain that teams are working as effectively and efficiently as possible. They're really saying that, as it is difficult to find ways of measuring and monitoring knowledge work (which is true), they don't have the degree of control that they would like over people's work.

8. Rarely are people in charge, who are supposedly responsible for what happens, called to account when there is a spectacular business failure. For evidence, look at the organizations in headline scandals. In recent years they include Arthur Andersen (an *accounting* firm that didn't hold its employees or itself to account), WorldCom, Enron, and then AIG, Countrywide, and Merrill Lynch to name but a few. How many executives and/or employees have been "brought to account"? How much effort went into doing so? In the banking world responsibility and accountability to depositors went out of the window some time ago. Where strategies shaped by mathematical algorithms took over, these organizations lost sight of the meaning of "safe" and "sound." "Trust" doesn't enter the picture, except, ironically, that some of them still keep the word in their names. Equally glaring examples are found wherever corruption, greed, malfeasance, and incompetence become a way of life at the highest levels of government—and there are lots and lots of examples. One particular egregious one is Zimbabwe. Under Robert Mugabe, the country became a basket-case, but he continued to be feted at most assemblies of national leaders, although Britain took the minor step of stripping him of a knighthood and the title 'Sir'.

9. Douglas Stone and colleagues provide a very useful "how to" for having difficult conversations in Douglas Stone, Bruce Patton, and Roger Fisher, *Difficult Conversations: How to Discuss What Matters Most* (New York: Penguin Books, 2000).

Chapter 13

1. Eric Trist's experience with coal miners at Haigh Moor in West Yorkshire led him to the same conclusion many years ago, showing, again, that, whenever humans work with one another (which they do almost everywhere *except* on production lines in factories), they organize themselves. Organizing is universal human practice. See F.E. Emery and Eric Trist, "Socio-Technical Systems," in *Management Science, Models and Techniques*, ed. C.W. Churchman and M. Verhurst (London: Pergamon Press, 1960); E. Trist and W. Bamforth, "Some Social and Psychological Consequences of the Long Wall Method of Coal-Getting," *Human Relations* 4 (1951); E. Trist and C. Sofer, *Exploration in Group Relations* (Leicester, UK: Leicester University Press, 1959). Douglas McGregor made the same point half a century ago, long before anyone had conceived

of knowledge work. Douglas McGregor, *The Human Side of Enterprise* (New York: McGraw-Hill, 1960).

2. The amount of time and money organizations put into internal and external institutional assessments is extraordinary and confounding. Assessments are supposed to ensure quality, but, except when the object is to meet technical standards, such as those set by the International Standards Organization (see www.iso.org/iso/iso_catalogue.htm), they actually do nothing of the kind. All are prime examples of the view from the top and are relics of an empiricist belief (and industrial mindset?) that quality is measurable and that maintaining it is a technical matter not a wicked problem. It is maintained by meeting a long list of requirements, many to do with the qualifications of the people they employ and the facilities they provide. The purpose of these assessments is compliance, but it is not at all clear for whom or to what end. Their main function seems to be ritual: to show that the institutions are open to inspection, are 'clean,' and willing to show that they can satisfy a long list of requirements, no matter what their purpose.

   One example is the accreditation process that universities and similar institutions go through every five or ten years. They pay accreditation boards to certify them and this is supposed to seal their reputation, proving—for the duration of the cycle—that whatever they do is up to the mark. Like all systems of compliance, it certainly puts a dampener on innovation because standards always lag behind practices; sometimes a long way behind. The alternative to all this is mutual accountability. As long as the community of people holding each other accountable is a broad cross-section of people that includes customers or clients, whoever they happen to be, it is in their interests to have openness and maintain quality and they are the ones who are best able to define quality.

3. Peter Block, *The Answer to How Is Yes: Acting on What Matters* (San Francisco: Berrett-Koehler, 2002): 2.

4. Max Weber's ideas are still the ones to visit if you interested in the distinction between power and authority or in different types of authority. See Max Weber, *The Theory of Social and Economic Organisation*, ed. Talcott Parsons, trans. A.M. Henderson and Talcott Parsons (New York: The Free Press, 1964). There is a very large academic literature around issues of power and authority, although few of these ideas penetrate the kinds of business books you'd buy at an airport bookstore, which is what managers read. Control is one of the largely unexamined and undebated premises of the ideology of management. Perhaps because of management's industrial-age origins, controlling organizations (to make them more efficient) is implicitly a technical matter that has nothing to do with values, beliefs, and personal ambitions. The arguments for control range from "it's in the workers' self-interest" to "it's in everyone's (global) interests," and in orthodox economics there are models, which again have nothing to do with power or greed, that claim to show how and why what is good for the self is good for the globe.

5. As a corollary, everyone below the top level is supposed only to "follow orders" (the policies and priorities devised at the top) and to do so slavishly, because any deviation, being a sign of independence, would mean that lower levels, who aren't accountable to the electorate, are usurping authority.

Chapter 14

1. See Chapter 8 on change management initiatives. "Continuous change"—for its own sake—has become something of an obsession, and, when those change management

initiatives don't live up to expectation, the scapegoat, often, is "employees who resist change." Behind this familiar refrain is a peculiar assumption that, no matter why it happens, change is inevitable and everyone ought to embrace it, especially if it originates at the top. In management-speak, "change" is always an unalloyed "opportunity," and the implication is that employees often don't or won't get this. It is because they refuse to go along with them that sensible initiatives come to nothing. On the contrary, it seems pretty clear that people *don't* like change and, surely, there is no great mystery as to why they don't. We are creatures of habit, with good reason. When you feel that you know where you stand, believe you know what to do, and have a good idea about what others are likely to do, you can make sense of what is going on. This is desirable, certainly compared to the other extreme. If someone says "I've decided that it's time to change," you're likely to feel that they're pushing you in that other direction, to swap knowing for not-knowing, particularly if you've experienced a pattern of disruptive reorgs, where people lose their jobs with no noticeable improvements (or change), and it is hard to fathom out the motives behind the changes or to foresee the consequences. Who would want this? Theodore Zorn and his co-authors provide a thoughtful, critical perspective on an ideology they call "the glorification of change" in management, noting, with irony, that organizations change very little in the way they operate. T.E. Zorn, L.T. Christensen, and G. Cheney, *Do We Really Want Constant Change?* (San Francisco: Berrett-Koehler, 1999).

2. The concept of improvisation has crept into literature on management and leadership from time to time. E.g. Frank J. Barrett, "Creativity and Improvisation in Jazz and Organizations: Implications for Organizational Learning," *Organizational Science* 9, no. 5 (1998); Max De Pree, *Leadership Jazz: The Essential Elements of a Great Leader*, rev. edn (New York: Doubleday, 2008). De Pree explicitly contrasts his ideas about leadership with Peter Drucker's (earlier) view that leading an organization is like conducting a symphony orchestra. An orchestra has a formalized structure and, unlike jazz ensembles which improvise, orchestra members must stick to the score.

3. With low-control organizing, there's going to be little-to-no mention of "bosses" and "subordinates," much less emphasis on "data," "efficiency," "structures," and "control," and much more talking *to one another* about our "commitments" and "responsibilities"; about "sharing knowledge" hence "relationships," "being accountable," "being open," "being cooperative"; and about "how we are doing," "is it good work?" and "what stands in the way?" Nothing supports and reinforces the status quo of high control more than the way people are remunerated. I'm not only talking about differences in remuneration between the top and at the bottom, although, certainly, this social stratification creates boundaries to cooperation in organizations. Just as important is the "system of rewards and incentives," including pay-for-performance practices and the like. All serve to concentrate power at the top, as the top decides who gets what and why.

4. High-control systems depend on compliance (rule-following), rather than accountability or trust (interpersonal relationships). If no one can be trusted to act responsibly, the only way to ensure that people act honestly, ethically, or sensibly is to control them, by giving them rules to follow and trying to ensure that they follow them. This argument creates a logical dilemma. Where does the process of control end? If you take the argument seriously and all mortals are included, logically, everyone must answer to someone above them. Even at the top, people ought to get approval from a board or, in the case of heads of government agencies and departments, from the current

administration. In theory, the chain of command extends all the way to heaven. Presumably, though, it can stop there because we are no longer dealing with human beings and human frailties; which explains why the motto of the House of Windsor, Britain's royal family, is *Dieu et mon droit*.

5. Gordon MacKenzie, *Orbiting the Giant Hairball: A Corporate Fool's Guide to Surviving with Grace* (New York: Viking, 1998): 39.

6. Ibid.: 23.

7. Ibid.: 33.

8. Ibid.

9. A theme of Art Kleiner's book about "corporate heretics" who shaped the field and profession of organization develpment (OD) is that both work and business, which are human and social, equally are *always personal*. See *The Age of Heretics: A History of the Radical Thinkers Who Reinvented Corporate Management*, 2nd edn (San Francisco: Jossey Bass, 2008)..

10. The image of organizational change as a dance has been used before. See P. Senge, A. Kleiner, C. Roberts, R. Ross, G. Roth, and B. Smith, *The Dance of Change: The Challenges to Sustaining Momentum in Learning Organizations* (New York: Doubleday/Currency, 1999).

11. Ronald A. Heifetz, *Leadership without Easy Answers* (Cambridge, MA: The Belknap Press of Harvard University, 1994); Ronald A. Heifetz and Marty Linsky, *Leadership on the Line: Staying Alive through the Dangers of Leading* (Boston, MA: Harvard Business School Press, 2002). The distinction between balcony and dance floor may sound like the difference between the view from the top and the view from practice, but it isn't. Knowledge workers can't do the work of organizing properly without first-hand (dance-floor) knowledge of what is going on, or a view from practice. They can, in their imaginations, switch views to being observers of the action. Managers, however, who don't have that immediate experience, can't get it by imagining themselves on the dance floor. Detached from what is going on, they only have a view from the top.

12. Quite a number of writers associated with the transformation process from a rigged minority government to democratically elected majority government seem to agree that a scenario building exercise, held at Mont Fleur in the Western Cape, allowed people to imagine different futures and to see how their positions and the outcomes of multiparty deliberations could contribute to either a high-road or a low-road scenario for South Africa. Held between 1991 and 1992, the exercise produced four scenarios named "Lame Duck," "Ostrich," "Flight of the Flamingoes," and "Icarus." These were later presented to principal players and representatives of some of the major participants in the political negotiations. See le Roux, Pieter, Vincent Maphai, and a team of 23. "The Mont Fleur Scenarios: What Will South Africa Be Like in the Year 2002? With a New Introduction by Mont Fleur Facilitator, Adam Kahane," Global Business Network, *Deeper News*, 7, no. 1 (n.d.). (http://www.generonconsulting.com/publications/papers/pdfs/Mont%20Fleur.pdf).

13. See Adam Kahane, *Solving Tough Problems: An Open Way of Talking, Listening, and Creating New Realities* (San Francisco: Berrett-Koehler, 2004): 19–33.

14. Kahane (ibid.) argues strongly for the importance of *both* talking and listening as a factor in the success of negotiations.

15. The Truth and Reconciliation Commission (TRC), established in South Africa as a result of the Promotion of National Unity and Reconciliation Act of 1995, enabled

victims to tell of the often heinous crimes against them or their family members and to confront the people accused of committing the crimes (which, they often claimed, they'd done "under orders"). In a sense the TRC was an institutionalized "open" social space that allowed perpetrators to ask forgiveness from their victims for what were mostly heinous crimes on the understanding that they may be granted amnesty from prosecution. Because it provided a context where once-powerful white former senior police officers, for example, came face to face with the families of black poor and largely powerless citizens, as a social space the TRC established a form of accountability that rarely exists in any society, let alone a divided and segmented one. See Antjie Krog, *Country of My Skull* (New York, Random House, 1998).

16. See other cases in Kahane, *Solving Tough Problems*, where talks produced no positive results.

17. Robert Solomon and Fernando Flores contrast different ideas about trust, distinguishing in particular between "blind trust," which is the way followers treat a charismatic leader (and, to my mind, is a kind of false trust), and "authentic trust," which is "built" when people who are open to trusting each other are also committed to establishing a trusting relationship. The point about authentic trust is that it isn't simply there and you can't take it for granted. In the first place, it takes reciprocal commitment and effort to establish trust and care to maintain it. This kind of trust can be broken through carelessness, as a result of all kinds of actions. It can also be rebuilt if the people concerned are willing to work at it. Robert C. Solomon and Fernando Flores, *Building Trust: In Business, Politics, Relationships, and Life* (New York: Oxford University Press, 2001).

18. Implicitly I'm distinguishing between a capacity that has been called "emotional intelligence" and technical competence. Emotional intelligence derives from Howard Gardener's work. See Howard Gardner, *Frames of Mind: The Theory of Multiple Intelligences* (New York: Basic Books, 1983). On emotional intelligence see Daniel Goleman, *Emotional Intelligence: Why It Matters More Than I.Q.* (New York: Bantam, 1995) and —"What Makes a Leader?," *Harvard Business Review* 76, no. 6 (1998). The short history of emotional intelligence illuminates the pathological treatment of new ideas in management. Once announced to the world, usually in a book, word gets round that the ideas being offered are a "must have" (or "must do") if you want to be a good manager and/or leader. This idea is a kind of miracle cure that will make everything better. You'll be a better manager/leader, your organization will function better, and, all in all, the world will be a better place if only . . . With hordes of people waiting to cash in on the next fad, in no time a dozen books are published and an entire industry of consultants springs up around the fad with tools to sell you or your organization. Then, sooner or later the noise dies down and everyone is off after the next big idea. It is one thing to draw attention to emotions. Like feelings and relationships, they are "part" of our work, although they have been excised from left-brain management thinking and practices. But, apart from general over-exposure to the idea and the implication that only people with the right training are capable of emotional intelligence, some of the most important questions, like why have emotions been missing for all this time, never get asked. Matthew Stewart writes entertainingly and with conviction and insight about the phenomena I've described while laying bare the pathologies of the management consulting industry. Matthew Stewart, *The Management Myth: Why the Experts Keep Getting It Wrong* (New York: W.W. Norton, 2009). On a slightly different tack, Antonio Damasio writes from a neuroscientist's

perspective on why mind (reason) and emotion are inseparable. See Antonio Damasio, *Descartes' Error: Emotion, Reason, and the Human Brain* (New York: Putnam, 1994).

19. Contrasting formal and informal organization was quite popular among writers on organizations in the 1950s and 1960s. See Peter M. Blau and Scott W. Richard, *Formal Organizations: A Comparative Approach* (San Fransisco: Chandler, 1962). Clay Shirky has some useful examples of how social networking technologies, including cellphones, enable people to organize spontaneously, "without organizations." His premise that they are doing this without organizations, however, is misleading. Although their roles in the work of organizing are largely hidden, organizations, like telephone companies and internet service providers, are important in terms of providing the means for people to network and self-organize. Clay Shirky, *Here Comes Everybody: The Power of Organizing without Organizations* (New York: The Penguin Press, 2008).

20. Jennifer Reingold and Jia Lynn Yang, "The Hidden Workplace," *Fortune*, July 23, 2007; Marshall Goldsmith and Jon Katzenbach, "Navigating the 'Informal' Organization," *BusinessWeek*, February 14, 2007 (www.businessweek.com/print/careers/content/feb2007/ca20070214_709560.htm), my emphasis. See also Beyer, Damon, Nico Canner, Jon Katzenbach, Zia Khan, et al. *The Informal Organization: A Report by Katzenbach Parters*. USA: Katzenbach Partners LLC, 2007.

21. ERP systems began to be widely used in the 1990s. They were originally created for manufacturing enterprises. Now used in government and other large service organizations such as universities, in addition to industry, these are described as "integrating and automating most business processes as well as sharing data and practices across the enterprise and producing and accessing information in real time." See Fiona Fui-Hoon Nah, Janet Lee-Shang Lau, and Jinghua Kuang, "Critical Factors for Successful Implementation of Enterprise Systems," *Business Process Management Journal* 7, no. 3 (2001) and Deloitte Consulting, "ERP's Second Wave: Maximizing the Value of ERP-Enabled Processes," report published by Deloitte Consulting. NY: 1999. Portals have names like "EDGE" for "Enterprise Data and Global Exchange" and are applications that are supposed to give employees inside the organization, or contractors or clients who are outside, access to all the information, both internal and external, that they may need. As one vendor describes them in their product brochure, portals "serve as a single and unified gateway to a company's information and knowledge base for employees, shareholders, customers and vendors, compris[ing] the building blocks of a collaborative and knowledge sharing infrastructure to enable information exchange." The vendor in question is TMS; the product is EKP.

22. The expression "interactive media" can be confusing, like many newly coined terms related to computer technologies. It generally means technologies which allow, even require, some kind of user input: from speaking to pressing buttons to imitating the motions of playing a guitar (e.g. the video game "Guitar Hero"). The other, more important, meaning is media that enable people to interact with *each other*. Web-based video games and more complex virtual environments, like Second Life, "where participants' avatars 'live' together in a virtual setting" represent one type. Social networking sites, like Facebook, are another type, where the participants can leave messages or any kind of digital record for others to see, read, hear, and respond to.

23. See www.virtualadjacency.com/.

24. Wanda J. Orlikowski, "Learning from Notes: Organizational Issues in Groupware Implementation," *The Information Society* 9, no. 3 (1993). Lotus Notes was subsequently purchased by IBM. (www-01.ibm.com/software/lotus/products/notes/).

25. On cloud computing, see "Computing Heads for the Clouds," *Bloomberg Business Week*, November 16, 2007 (www.businessweek.com/technology/content/nov2007/tc20071116_379585.htm). On open source software see The Open Source Initiative (www.opensource.org/). On smart phones, see "What Makes a Smartphone Smart?" by Liane Cassavoy, About.com Guide (http://cellphones.about.com/od/smartphonebasics/a/what_is_smart.htm). On Web 2.0, see the essay by Paul Graham on the three elements of Web 2.0 at www.paulgraham.com/web20.html.

26. See Dan Baum, "Battle Lessons: What the Generals Don't Know," *New Yorker*, January 17, 2005. They made the decision despite the fact that the U.S. military has been a pioneer in knowledge management and a forerunner in sharing knowledge through lessons learned, having instituted after action reviews quite some time ago.

27. Unfortunately, the management mindset that puts tools ahead of talk reinforces the idea that it's acceptable, even desirable, for people to work online when they could just as easily do so face to face.

28. Presence has a shadow as well. It isn't always good behavior that emerges, but as we expect good behavior, when it's just the opposite and someone murders or tortures, in explaining this antisocial behavior we typically "take away" their personal responsibility for it and look for a pathology ("he is a sociopath") or an external influence ("she was ordered to do it" or "she was treated cruelly as a child").

29. See Jean Lave and Etienne Wenger, *Situated Learning: Legitimate Peripheral Participation* (New York: Cambridge University Press, 1991). They were examining what later came to be called "communities of practice" not the kinds of networks of organizers that I'm writing about.

Chapter 15

1. Taught to believe in the sanctity of numbers, we learn that these are "objective facts." There is, however, a long, solid, academic tradition that explains the social nature of accounting and the social construction of accounts. Accounts, as the word suggests, are narratives used to tell a story of an organization. To many, accounts are an important story, so they are written and manipulated, for marketing purposes, by accountants and other "experts," to give the most favorable impression to particular audiences of how organizations are doing. See, for example, Ylan Qui, "SEC Charges Former IndyMac Executives with Fraud," *Washington Post*, February 11, 2001 (www.washingtonpost.com/wp-dyn/content/article/2011/02/11/AR2011021106210.html). The scandal surrounding Enron that rocked the big accounting firms a few years ago and led to the demise of Arthur Andersen, together with the "financial meltdown" of 2008, when Lehmann Brothers and other firms collapsed, has given the public a limited but better view of just how accounting stories are constructed. "Financial wizards" found ways of putting liabilities on the books as assets whenever their accounts were due to be scrutinized by the public or a government agency responsible for oversight. Calling financial instruments (actually data entries derived from mathematical algorithms) "securities" is a way of conjuring "assets" out of thin air. Their values, of course, are anything but secure. On the social construction of accounts see Anthony G. Hopwood and Peter Miller, *Accounting as Social*

and Institutional Practice (Cambridge: Cambridge University Press, 1994); Don Lavoie, "The Accounting of Interpretation and the Interpretation of Accounts: The Communicative Function of 'the Language of Business,'" *Accounting, Organizations and Society* 12, no. 6 (1987); Gareth Morgan, "Accounting as Reality Construction: Towards a New Epistemology of Accounting Practice," *Accounting Organizations and Society* 13, no. 5 (1988); Marilyn Neimark and Tony Tinker, "The Social Construction of Management Control Systems," *Accounting, Organizations and Society* 11, nos. 4/5 (1986).

2. Matthew Crawford, *Shop Class as Soulcraft* (New York: Penguin Books, 2009).
3. Ibid. 14–15 and 73 (my emphasis).
4. Ibid. 25. See also ch. 4.
5. I'm identifying humanness and the humanness of work with one's sense of being in it, being constituted by the situation and the doing—Martin Heidegger's *Dasein*, which Herbert Dreyfus calls "being-in-the-world." See Hubert L. Dreyfus, *Being-in-the-World: A Commentary on Heidegger's Being and Time, Division I* (Cambridge, MA: MIT Press, 1991).
6. For an overview of the ISO 9000 family of standards, see Wikipedia, http://en.wikipedia.org/wiki/ISO_9000.
7. Wikipedia has articles on "lean manufacturing", "Six Sigma," and "quality management". See, http://en.wikipedia.org/wiki/Lean_manufacturing, http://en.wikipedia.org/wiki/Six_Sigma, and http://en.wikipedia.org/wiki/Quality_management_system.
8. It appears Taylor's views sparked the attitude that, as John P. Hoerr notes, "wage workers and their representatives lacked the competence to handle complex issues that required abstract knowledge and analytical ability." Quoted in Mike Rose, *The Mind at Work: Valuing the Intelligence of the American Worker* (New York: Viking, 2004): xxi.
9. Matthew Stewart, *The Management Myth: Why the Experts Keep Getting It Wrong* (New York: W.W. Norton, 2009): 28.
10. The question of whether gods work is interesting at an intellectual level and possibly from a theological point of view too. The Greek gods presumably did, as they had to deal with all kinds of vicissitudes. Perhaps the point is that when there are many, competing gods something like work has to be part of the picture. When you have one, omnipotent god, it does not.
11. The image in Figure 12.1, loosely based on a pyramid maze puzzle marketed by Loncraine Broxton, is used with permission of the Lagoon Trading Co. Ltd.
12. What would it be like inside the pyramid? Your experience might be similar to playing a shoot-'em-up computer game, like Halo[TM], Quake[TM], or Counter-Strike[TM], written to create the illusion of a first-person perspective. You'd have to "explore" the terrain to find the passages and identify dead ends. This isn't really a human perspective, or the view from practice, because you're in a ready-made world, where your actions are limited and the "future" is already decided. You and others can't shape it. All you can do is make your way through it by trial and error selecting from a set of predetermined moves. As seasoned gamers know, you have the option of stopping or going back. From a human standpoint, time marches on inexorably and there is no going back to do again what you've already tried to do. The fact that you've tried changes the course of history and the options that are open.
13. David Abram, *The Spell of the Sensuous: Language and Perception in a More-Than-Human World* (New York: Vintage Books, 1997): 50 (my emphasis).

14. Henri-Louis Bergson, *Time and Free Will: An Essay on the Immediate Data of Consciousness*, trans. F.L. Pogson (New York: Dover, 2001).

15. See Julia Preston, "Homeland Security Cancels 'Virtual Fence' After $1 Billion Is Spent," *New York Times*, January 14, 2011 (www.nytimes.com/2011/01/15/us/politics/15fence.html).

16. On the nature of derivatives see Cris Sholto Heaton's prophetic article, 'The dangers of derivatives,' in *MoneyWeek*, Sep 27, 2006 (http://www.moneyweek.com/investments/stock-markets/the-dangers-of-derivatives).

17. It appears that this is exactly what financial institutions which used algorithms to create derivatives *wanted* people to believe. Perhaps their employees also deluded themselves into believing that by using sophisticated mathematical formulae they'd actually be able to conquer uncertainty, making present and future seem like one.

18. Hedge-fund managers who bet on the housing bubble bursting earned "more money than god," as Sebastian Mallaby puts it. See Sebastian Mallaby, *More Money than God: Hedge Funds and the Making of a New Elite* (New York: Penguin Press, 2010).

19. Matthew Crawford, *Shop Class as Soul Craft*: 55–6.

20. In the 1930s, Frank Knight, a University of Chicago economist, introduced the important distinction between risk, which can be calculated, and uncertainty, which cannot. To calculate the probability of something occurring, the event must fall into the same category as the throw of a dice to satisfy the requirements of statistical theory (i.e. it must be random and repeat). Events in business, which are unique, are uncertain. People who claim to be able to predict their likelihood have either forgotten the distinction or, more likely, simply choose to ignore it. See F.H. Knight, *Risk, Uncertainty and Profit* (London: London School of Economics and Political Science, 1933).

21. The congressional investigation in the US into the disaster at the BP well noted poor management decisions in the days before the explosion of the *Deepwater Horizon* drilling rig; decisions that were driven by considerations of time and money. See Steven Mufson and Anne E. Kornblut, "Lawmakers Accuse BP of Taking 'Shortcuts,' " *Washington Post*, June 15, 2010: A01. An operations drilling engineer emailed a colleague a few days before the explosion. Referring to the fact that the steel pipe had not been properly centered in the drill hole, he said, "Who cares, it's done, end of story . . . ?"

22. In testimony before Congress, in June 2010, the CEO of BP, Tony Hayward, said "safety was uppermost in our minds." If, by this, he meant it was the company's top priority, he was being disingenuous, as internal emails and and other sources have subsequently confirmed. Except after an accident, or when the industry is threatened with new regulations, safety is not a big topic of conversation in executive suites. In BP, like other corporations, executives, who've been raised to think the MBA way, are primarily after "results." Faithful to Milton Friedman's myopic dictum that "the business of business is business," by which he meant making more money, they are busy dealing with the challenges of "doing business," which, in the case of multinational oil companies, includes negotiating contracts with foreign governments who have their own ways of doing business and fending off the growing numbers of "environmentalists" who want to limit the use of hydrocarbon-based sources of energy.

23. The statement "What's good for General Motors is good for the country" is evidently a misquotation of something C.E. Wilson, GM's president, said in testifying before the Armed Services Committee in 1953. See "History of General Motors" at http://en.wikipedia.org/wiki/History_of_General_Motors.

24. See "The Ritalin Explosion" at www.pbs.org/wgbh/pages/frontline/shows/medicating/ experts/explosion.html, part of a *Frontline* television program, "Medicating Kids," first aired in 2001.

25. Margaret Talbot, "Brain Gain: The Neuroenhancer Revolution," *The New Yorker*, April 27, 2009: 32–43 (www.newyorker.com/reporting/2009/04/27/090427fa_fact_talbot).

26. Pleading with Franklin D. Roosevelt to support Britain's fight against Nazi Germany, Winston Churchill, the British Prime Minister, said this in a radio speech.

27. Two recent books, with some similar themes, trawl history, ancient and more recent, for evidence of humans' failure to see the impacts of actions (and, possibly, to listen to their inner voices) which devastated their environments, resulting in environmental collapses and the destruction of whole societies. You have to conclude that humans often aren't at all reason-able (i.e. able to reason intelligently) and "progress" is by no means either linear or assured. See Jared Diamond, *Collapse: How Societies Choose to Fail or Succeed* (New York: Viking Penguin, 2005); Ronald Wright, *A Short History of Progress* (New York: Carroll and Graf, 2004). Ian McCallum explores the idea of "ecological intelligence," the "act of weaving and unweaving our reflections of ourselves on Earth." The issues I've raised echo themes in this marvelous book. See Ian McCallum, *Ecological Intelligence: Rediscovering Ourselves in Nature* (Cape Town: Africa Geographic, 2005).

28. The expression "small people" received lots of attention, when used, tellingly, by Carl-Henric Svanberg, Chairman of BP. He was referring to the fishermen and many others whose livelihoods, together with the fishing industry in large areas along the coast of the Gulf of Mexico, were destroyed by the *Deepwater Horizon* disaster in 2010.

29. One of the enduring narratives in management, possibly a hand-me-down from Taylor's distaste for workers, is that "people don't like hard work." I regard this as a myth. What people don't like is work that is demeaning and/or degrading and/or mind numbingly boring. Because the management mindset doesn't recognize that work can be demeaning, degrading, mind numbing, or all three, perhaps it is not surprising that management practices often make work so.

References

Abram, David. *The Spell of the Sensuous: Language and Perception in a More-Than-Human World*. New York: Vintage Books, 1997.

Addleson, Mark. "General Equilibrium and 'Competition': On Competition as Strategy." *South African Journal of Economics* 52, no. 2 (1984): 156–71.

Addleson, Mark, and Jennifer Garvery Berger. "Putting 'Zing' Back into Organizational Consulting." *Journal of Professional Consulting* 3, no. 1 (2008): 7–18.

Aitken, Hugh G. J. *Scientific Management in Action: Taylorism at Watertown Arsenal, 1908–1915*. Princeton, NJ: Princeton University Press, 1985.

Aldrich, Mark. *Safety First: Technology, Labor and Business in the Building of Work Safety, 1870–1939*. Baltimore: Johns Hopkins University Press, 1997.

Allee, Verna. "Knowledge Networks and Communities of Practice." *OD Practitioner* 32, no. 4 (2000).

Alvarado, Rudolph V., and Sonya Y. Alvarado. *Drawing Conclusions on Henry Ford: A Biographical History through Cartoons*. Ann Arbor, MI: University of Michigan Press, 2001.

Alvesson, Mats, and Hugh Willmott, eds. *Critical Management Studies*. London: SAGE Publications, 1992.

Aven, Terje *Foundations of Risk Analysis: A Knowledge and Decision-Oriented Perspective*. Hoboken, NJ: Wiley, 2003.

Baetjer, Howard *Software as Capital: An Economic Perspective on Software Engineering*. Los Alamitos, CA: IEEE Press, 1997.

Barley, Stephen, and Gideon Kunda. "Bringing Work Back In." *Organization Science* 12, no. 1 (2001): 76–95.

Barrett, Frank J. "Creativity and Improvisation in Jazz and Organizations: Implications for Organizational Learning." *Organizational Science* 9, no. 5, (1998): 605–22.

Barrett, Frank J. "Living in Organizations: Lessons from Jazz Improvisation." In *The Social Construction of Organization*, edited by D.M Hosking and Sheila Mc Namee. Malmö, Sweden: Liber and Copenhagen Business School Press, 2006: 269–77.

Baum, Dan. "Battle Lessons: What the Generals Don't Know." *New Yorker*, January 17, 2005.

Bauman, Zygmunt. *Community: Seeking Safety in an Insecure World*. Maiden, MA: Polity Press, 2001.

Bell, Daniel. *The Coming of Post-Industrial Society: A Venture in Social Forecasting*. New York: Basic Books, 1973.

Benner, Patricia E. *From Novice to Expert: Excellence and Power in Clinical Nursing Practice*. Menlo Park, CA: Addison-Wesley, 1984.

Benner, Patricia, and J. Wrubel. *The Primacy of Caring: Stress and Coping in Health and Illness*. Menlo Park, CA: Addison-Wesley, 1989.

Berger, Peter, and Thomas Luckmann. *The Social Construction of Reality.* London: Allen Lane, 1967.

Bernstein, R.J. *Beyond Objectivism and Relativism: Science, Hermeneutics and Praxis.* Oxford: Basil Blackwell, 1983.

Bergquist, William. *The Postmodern Organization: Mastering the Art of Irreversible Change.* San Francisco: Jossey-Bass, 1993.

Bergson, Henri-Louis. *Time and Free Will: An Essay on the Immediate Data of Consciousness* Translated by F.L. Pogson. New York: Dover, 2001.

Beyer, Damon, Nico Canner, Jon Katzenbach, Zia Khan, et al. *The Informal Organization: A Report by Katzenbach Partners.* New York: Katzenbach Partners LLC, 2007.

Blackler, Frank. "Knowledge, Knowledge Work and Organizations: An Overview and Interpretation." *Organization Studies* 16, no. 6 (1995): 1021–46.

Blackler, Frank, Michael Reed, and Alan Whitaker. "Knowledge Workers and Contemporary Organizations." *Journal of Management Studies* 30, no. 6, (1993): 851–62.

Blau, Peter M., and Scott W Richard. *Formal Organizations: A Comparative Approach.* San Fransisco: Chandler Publishing, 1962.

Block, Peter. *Stewardship: Choosing Service over Self-Interest.* San Francisco: Berrett-Koehler Publishers, 1993.

Block, Peter. *The Answer to How Is Yes: Acting on What Matters.* San Francisco: Berrett-Koehler, 2002.

Boje, D.M., R.P. Gephardt, and T.J. Thatchenkery, eds. *Postmodern Management and Organization Theory.* Thousand Oaks; CA: SAGE Publications, 1996.

Breiger, Ronald. "The Analysis of Social Networks." In *Handbook of Data Analysis*, edited by Melissa Hardy and Alan Bryman. London: SAGE Publications, 2004: 505–26.

Brown, John Seely, and Paul Duguid. "Organizing Knowledge." *California Management Review, Special Issue on "Knowledge and the Firm"* 40, no. 3 (1998): 90–111.

Brown, John Seely, and Paul Duguid. *The Social Life of Information.* Boston, MA: Harvard Business School Press, 2000.

Brown, Phil. "Popular Epidemiology and Toxic Waste Contamination: Lay and Professional Ways of Knowing." *Journal of Health and Social Behavior* 33, no. 3 (1992): 267–81.

Bryan, Lowell L., and Claudia Joyce. "The 21st Century Organization." *The McKinsey Quarterly*, no. 3 (2005): 24–33.

Burns, Tom, and G.M. Stalker. *The Management of Innovation.* 3rd edn. Oxford: Oxford University Press, 1961. Reprint, 1994.

Camillus, John C. "Strategy as a Wicked Problem." *Harvard Business Review* 86, no. 5 (2008): 98–106.

Catmull, Ed, "How Pixar Fosters Collective Creativity," *Harvard Business Review* 86, no. 9 (2008): 64–72.

Chaplin, Charles. "Modern Times." United States of America: United Artists, 1936.

Chia, Robert. "From Modern to Postmodern Organizational Analysis." *Organization Studies* 16, no. 4 (1995): 508–604.

Conklin, E. Jeffrey. "Wicked Problems and Social Complexity." (http://cognexus.org/wpf/wickedproblems.pdf).

Conklin, E. Jeffrey. *Dialogue Mapping: Building Shared Understanding of Wicked Problems.* Chichester, UK ; Hoboken, NJ: Wiley, 2006.

Conklin, E. Jeffrey, and William Weil. "Wicked Problems: Naming the Pain in Organizations." Washington, DC: Group Decision Support Systems (n.d.) [ca. 1992].

Cook, Scott D.N., and John Seely Brown. "Bridging Epistemologies: The Generative Dance between Organizational Knowledge and Organizational Knowing." *Organization Science* 10, no. 4 (1999): 381–400.

Cooper, Gail. "Frederick Winslow Taylor and Scientific Management," in *Technology in America: A History of Individuals and Ideas*. Edited by C.W. Pursell. Cambridge, MA: MIT Press, 1990.

Cooper, Robert, and Gibson Burrell. "Modernism, Postmodernism and Organizational Analysis: An Introduction." *Organizational Studies*. 9, no. 1 (1988): 91–112.

Crainer, Stuart. *The Management Century: A Critical Review of 20th Century Thought and Practice*. San Francisco: Jossey-Bass Publishers, 2000.

Crawford, Matthew. *Shop Class as Soulcraft*. New York: Penguin Books, 2009.

Cross, Robert, and Andrew Parker. *The Hidden Power of Social Networks: Understanding How Work Really Gets Done in Organizations*. Boston, MA: Harvard Business School Press, 2004.

Czarniawska, Barbara. *Narrating the Organization: Dramas of Institutional Identity*. Chicago: University of Chicago Press, 1997.

Daft, Richard L., and John C. Wiginton. "Language and Organization." *The Academy of Management Review* 4, no. 2 (1979): 179–91.

Damasio, Antonio. *Descartes' Error: Emotion, Reason, and the Human Brain*. New York: Putnam Publishing, 1994.

Davenport, Thomas H. "The Fad That Forgot People." *Fast Company*, October 1995.

Dear, Peter. *Revolutionizing the Sciences: European Knowledge and Its Ambitions, 1500–1700*. Princeton, NJ: Princeton University Press, 2001.

Deloitte Consulting, "ERP's Second Wave: Maximizing the Value of ERP-Enabled Processes," report published by Deloitte Consulting. NY: 1999.

De Pree, Max. *Leadership Jazz: The Essential Elements of a Great Leader*. Revised edn. New York: Doubleday, 2008.

Descartes, Rene. *Meditations on First Philosophy*. Translated by J. Cottingham. Cambridge: Cambridge University Press, 1996.

Diamond, Jared. *Collapse: How Societies Choose to Fail or Succeed*. New York: Viking Penguin, 2005.

Dombrowski, Paul M. "*Challenger* through the Eyes of Feyerabend." *Journal of Technical Writing and Communication* 24, no. 1 (1994): 7–18.

Doray, Bernard. *From Taylorism to Fordism: A Rational Madness*. London: Free Association Books, 1988.

Dreyfus, Hubert L. *Being-in-the-World: A Commentary on Heidegger's Being and Time, Division I*. Cambridge, MA: MIT Press, 1991.

Drucker, Peter F. *Landmarks of Tomorrow : A Report on the New "Post-Modern" World*. New York: Harper Colophon Books, 1959.

Drucker, Peter F. *The Age of Discontinuity: Guidelines to Our Changing Society*. New York: Harper and Row, 1969.

Drucker, Peter F. *The Practice of Management*. New York: Harper and Row, Publishers, 1986 [1954].

Drucker, Peter F. "The Age of Social Transformation." *The Atlantic Monthly* 274, no. 5 (1994): 53–80.

Drucker, Peter F. "Management's New Paradigms." *Forbes* 162, no. 7 (1998): 152–77.

Elkington, John. "Towards the Sustainable Corporation: Win–Win–Win Business Strategies for Sustainable Development." *California Management Review* 36, no. 2 (1994): 90–100.

Emery, F.E., and Eric Trist. "Socio-Technical Systems." In *Management Science, Models and Techniques*, edited by C.W. Churchman and M. Verhurst. London: Pergamon Press, 1960: 83–97.

Fayol, Henri. *General and Industrial Management*. Translated by C. Storrs. London: Pitman Publishing, 1949.

Fineman, Stephen, Daniel Sims, and Yannis Gabriel. *Organizing and Organizations*. 2nd edn. San Francisco: SAGE Publications, 2000.

Foucault, Michel. *The Archaeology of Knowledge*. London: Routledge, 1972.

Foucault, Michel. *Discipline and Punish: The Birth of the Prison*. London: Allen Lane, 1977.

Freidman, Susan Stanford. "Definitional Excursions: The Meanings of Modern/Modernity/Modernism." *Modernism/Modernity* 8, no. 3 (2001).

Gabor, Andrea. *The Man Who Discovered Quality : How W. Edwards Deming Brought the Quality Revolution to America : The Stories of Ford, Xerox, and GM*. New York: Penguin, 1992.

Gadamer, Hans-Georg. *Truth and Method*. Translated by G. Barden and J. Cumming. New York: Seabury Press, 1975.

Galbraith, John Kenneth. *The New Industrial State*. Boston: Houghton Mifflin, 1967.

Gardner, Howard *Frames of Mind: The Theory of Multiple Intelligences*. New York: Basic Books, 1983.

Goldsmith, Marshall, and Jon Katzenbach. "Navigating the 'Informal' Organization." *BusinessWeek*, February 14, 2007.

Goldstein, Jeffrey. "Emergence as a Construct: History and Issues," *Emergence: Complexity and Organization* 1 (1999): 49–72

Goleman, Daniel. *Emotional Intelligence: Why It Matters More Than I.Q.* New York: Bantam Publishers, 1995.

Goleman, Daniel. "What Makes a Leader?" *Harvard Business Review* 76, no. 6 (1998): 93–102.

Grant, David, Tom W. Keenoy, and Cliff Oswick, eds. *Discourse and Organization*. London: SAGE Publications, 1998.

Growler, Dan, and Karen Legge. "The Meaning of Management and Management of Meaning." In *Understanding Management*, edited by S. Linstead, R.G. Small and P. Jeffcutt. London: SAGE Publications, 1996.

Habermas, Jurgen. *Knowledge and Human Interests*. Boston: Beacon Press, 1971.

Hamel, Gary. "Moon Shots for Management: What Great Challenges Must We Tackle to Reinvent Management and Make It More Relevant to a Volatile World?" *Harvard Business Review* 87, no. 2, (2009): 91–98.

Hamel, Gary, and Bill Breen. *The Future of Management*. Cambridge, MA: Harvard Business School Press, 2007.

Hammer, Michael. "Reengineering Work: Don't Automate, Obliterate." *Harvard Business Review* 68, no. 4 (1990): 104.

Hammer, Michael. *Beyond Reengineering: How the Process-Centered Organization Is Changing Our Work and Our Lives* New York: HarperCollins, 1996.

Hammer, Michael, and James A. Champy. *Reengineering the Corporation: A Manifesto for Business Revolution*. New York: Harper Business Books, 1993.

Hanlan, Marc. *High Performance Teams: How to Make Them Work*. Westport, CT: Praeger Publishers, 2004.

Harvey, David L. *The Condition of Postmodernity: An Enquiry into the Origins of Cultural Change*. Oxford: Oxford University Press, 1989.

Heidegger, Martin. *Being and Time*. Translated by J. Macquarrie and E. Robinson. New York: Harper and Row, 1962.

Heifetz, Ronald A. *Leadership without Easy Answers*. Cambridge, MA: The Belknap Press of Harvard University, 1994.

Heifetz, Ronald A., and Marty Linsky. *Leadership on the Line: Staying Alive through the Dangers of Leading*. Boston, MA: Harvard Business School Press, 2002.

Helgesen, Sally. *The Web of Inclusion: A New Architecture for Building Great Organizations*. New York: Currency/Doubleday, 1995.

Hindle, Tim. "The New Organization." *The Economist*, January 21, 2006.

Hofstede, Geert. "Cultural Constraints in Management Theories." *The Executive* 7, no. 1 (1993): 81–94.

Holzman, Lois. "Lev Vygotsky and the New Performative Psychology: Implications for Business and Organizations." In *The Social Construction of Organization*, edited by D.M and Mc Namee Hosking, S. Malmö, Sweden: Liber and Copenhagen Business School Press, 2006: 254–68.

Homer-Dixon, Thomas. *The Ingenuity Gap: Facing the Economic Environmental, and Other Challenges of an Increasingly Complex and Unpredictable World*. New York: Vintage Books, 2002.

Hopwood, Anthony G., and Peter Miller. *Accounting as Social and Institutional Practice*. Cambridge: Cambridge University Press, 1994.

Hoskin, Keith, and Richard Macve. "The Genesis of Accountability: The Westpoint Connection." *Accounting, Organizations and Society* 13, no. 1 (1988): 37–73.

Hoskin, Keith, and Richard Macve. "Writing, Examining, Disciplining: The Genesis of Accounting's Modern Power." In *Accounting as Social and Institutional Practice*, edited by Anthony G. Hopwood and Peter Milller, Cambridge: Cambridge University Press, 1994: 67–97.

Husserl, Edmund. *The Crisis in European Science and Transcendental Phenomenology: An Introduction to Phenomenological Philosophy*. Translated by Carr D. Evanston, IL: Northwestern University Press, 1970.

Ichijo, Kazuo, and Florian Kohlbache. "Tapping Tacit Local Knowledge in Emerging Markets – the Toyota Way." *Knowledge Management Research & Practice* 6 (2008): 173–86.

Institute on Medicine, Board on Health Sciences Policy, Committee to Assess Training Needs for Occupational Safety and Health Personnel in the United States. *Safe Work in the 21st Century: Education and Training Needs for the Next Decade's Occupational Safety and Health Personnel*. Washington, DC: National Academy Press, 2000. (www.nap.edu/openbook.php?isbn=0309070260).

Jackson, Bradley G. "Re-Engineering the Sense of Self: The Manager and the Management Guru." *Journal of Management Studies* 33, no. 5 (1996): 571–590.

Kahane, Adam. *Solving Tough Problems: An Open Way of Talking, Listening, and Creating New Realities*. San Francisco: Berrett-Koehler Publishers, 2004.

Kamoche, Ken, Miguel Pina e Cunha, and João Vieira da Cunha. "Towards a Theory of Organizational Improvisation: Looking Beyond the Jazz Metaphor." *Journal of Management Studies* 40, no. 8 (2003): 2023–51.

Kanigel, Robert. *The One Best Way: Fredrick Winslow Taylor and the Enigma of Efficiency*. New York: Viking, 1997.

Keenoy, Tom W., Cliff Oswick, and David Grant. "Organizational Discourses: Text and Context." *Organization* 4, no. 2 (1997): 147–57.

Kegan, Robert, and Lisa Laskow Lahey. *How the Way We Talk Can Change the Way We Work: Seven Languages for Transformation*. San Francisco: Jossey-Bass, 2001.

Kleiner, Art. *The Age of Heretics: Heroes, Outlaws, and the Forerunners of Corporate Change*. New York: Currency Doubleday, 1996.

Kleiner, Art. "Karen Stevenson's Quantum Theory of Trust." *Strategy+Business*, no. 29 (2002): 3–14.

Knight, F.H. *Risk, Uncertainty and Profit*. London: London School of Economics and Political Science, 1933.

Knight, Louise, and Annie Pye. "Multiple Meanings of 'Network': Some Implications for Interorganizational Theory and Research Practice." In University of Bath School of Management Working Paper Series # 2006.12. Claverton Down, Bath, 2006.

Kriedte, Peter. *Peasants, Landlords and Merchant Capitalists: Europe and the World Economy, 1500–1800*. Cambridge: Cambridge University Press, 1983.

Kriedte, Peter, Hans Medick, and Jurgen Schlumbohm, eds. *Industrialization before Industrialization: Rural Industry in the Genesis of Capitalism*. Cambridge: Cambridge University Press, 1981.

Krog, Antjie. *Country of My Skull* New York: Random House, 1998.

Lachmann, Ludwig M. "Austrian Economics in the Present Crisis of Economic Thought," in Ludwig M. Lachmann, *Capital, Expectations and the Market Process: Essays in the Theory of the Market Economy*, edited by Walter E. Grinder, Kansas City, KS: Sheed Andrews and McMeel Inc, 1977.

Lakoff, George. *Women, Fire, and Dangerous Things: What Categories Reveal About the Mind*. Chicago: University of Chicago Press, 1987.

Lakoff, George, and Mark Johnson. *Metaphors We Live By*. Chicago: University of Chicago Press, 1980.

Lambe, Patrick. "The Unacknowledged Parentage of Knowledge Management." *Journal of Knowledge Management* 15, no. 2 (2011): 175–97.

Lang, Fritz. "Metropolis." Germany: UFA, 1927.

Lave, Jean, and Etienne Wenger. *Situated Learning: Legitimate Peripheral Participation*. New York: Cambridge University Press, 1991.

Lavoie, Don. "The Accounting of Interpretation and the Interpretation of Accounts: The Communicative Function of 'the Language of Business.'" *Accounting, Organizations and Society* 12, no. 6 (1987): 579–604.

Le Roux, Pieter, Vincent Maphai, and a team of 23. "The Mont Fleur Scenarios: What Will South Africa Be Like in the Year 2002? With a New Introduction by Mont Fleur Facilitator, Adam Kahane." Global Business Network, *Deeper News*, 7, no. 1 (n.d.). (http://www.generonconsulting.com/publications/papers/pdfs/Mont%20Fleur.pdf).

Letiche, Hugo. "Meaning, Organizing, and Empowerment." In *Empowering Humanity: State of the Art in Humanistics*, edited by Annemie Halsema and Douwe van Houten. Utrecht: De Tijdstroom uitgeverij, 2002: 211–27.

Linstead, Stephen, Robert Grafton Small, and Paul Jeffcutt, eds. *Understanding Management*. London: SAGE Publications, 1996.

Lynn, Barry C. *The End of the Line: The Rise and Coming Fall of the Global Corporation*. 1st paperback edn. New York: Currency Doubleday, 2005.

MacKenzie, Gordon. *Orbiting the Giant Hairball: A Corporate Fool's Guide to Surviving with Grace*. New York: Viking, 1998.

Maier, Mark. "A Major Malfunction: The Story Behind the Space Shuttle Challenger Disaster." Binghamton, NY: Research Foundation of the State University of New York, 1992. VHS Videorecording with supplemental materials.

Mallaby, Sebastian. *More Money Than God: Hedge Funds and the Making of a New Elite*. New York: Penguin Press, 2010.

Mayntz, Renate. "Modernization and the Logic of Interorganizational Networks." In *Societal Change between Market and Organization*, edited by John Child, Michael Crozier, Renate Mayntz et al.. Aldershot, UK: Ashgate Publishing, 1993: 3–18.

Mbigi, Lovemore. *Ubuntu: The African Dream in Management*. Randburg, South Africa: Knowledge Resources, 1997.

McCallum, Ian. *Ecological Intelligence: Rediscovering Ourselves in Nature*. Cape Town: Africa Geographic, 2005.

McDermott, Richard. "Knowing Is a Human Act." *Upgrade* 3, no. 1 (2002): 8–10.

McGregor, Douglas. *The Human Side of Enterprise*. New York: McGraw-Hill, 1960.

Meadows, Donella H. "Places to Intervene in a System (in Increasing Order of Effectiveness)." *Whole Earth*, no. 91 (1997): 78–84.

Meadows, Donella H and Peter Marshall. "Dancing with Systems." *Whole Earth*, no. 106 (2001): 58–63. Also at www.sustainabilityinstitute.org/pubs/Dancing.html.

Merleau-Ponty, Maurice. *The Phenomenology of Perception*. London: Routledge and Kegan Paul, 1962.

Mintzberg, Henry. *Managers Not MBAs: A Hard Look at the Soft Practice of Managing and Management Development*. San Francisco: Berrett-Koehler, 2004.

Morgan, Gareth. "Accounting as Reality Construction: Towards a New Epistemology of Accounting Practice." *Accounting Organizations and Society* 13, no. 5 (1988): 477–85.

Nah, Fiona Fui-Hoon, Janet Lee-Shang Lau, and Jinghua Kuang. "Critical Factors for Successful Implementation of Enterprise Systems." *Business Process Management Journal* 7, no. 3 (2001): 285–96.

Neimark, Marilyn, and Tony Tinker. "The Social Construction of Management Control Systems." *Accounting, Organizations and Society* 11, nos. 4/5 (1986): 369–95.

Nonaka, Ikujiro, and N. Konno. "The Concept Of 'Ba': Building a Foundation for Knowledge Creation." *California Management Review* 40, no. 1, Special Issue on "Knowledge and the Firm" (1998): 40–54.

Oliner, Pearl M., and Samuel P. Oliner. *Toward a Caring Society : Ideas into Action*. Westport, CT: Praeger, 1995.

Orlikowski, Wanda J. "Learning from Notes: Organizational Issues in Groupware Implementation." *The Information Society* 9, no. 3 (1993): 237–50.

Orr, Julian E. *Talking About Machines: An Ethnography of a Modern Job*. Ithaca, NY: Cornell University Press, 1996.

Orton, James Douglas, and Karl E. Weick. "Loosely Coupled Systems: A Reconceptualization." *Academy of Management Review* 15, no. 2 (1990): 203–23.

Oswick, Cliff, Tom W. Keenoy, and David Grant. "Managerial Discourses: Words Speak Louder Than Actions?" *Journal of Applied Management Studies* 6, no. 1 (1997): 5–12.

Pink, Daniel H. *A Whole New Mind: Moving from the Information Age to the Conceptual Age*. New York: Riverhead Books, 2005.

Polanyi, Michael. *Personal Knowledge: Towards a Post-Critical Philosophy*. London: Routledge and Kegan Paul, 1973.

Prusak, L. "Where Did Knowledge Management Come From?" *IBM Systems Journal* 40, no. 4 (2001): 1002–6.

Ran, Bing, and P. Robert Duimering. "Imaging the Organization: Language Use in Organizational Identity Claims." *Journal of Business and Technical Communication* 21, no. 2 (2007): 155–87.

Reich, Robert. *The Work of Nations: Preparing Ourselves for 21st Century Capitalism.* New York: Alfred A. Knopf, 1991.

Rich, Ben R., and L. Janos, *Skunk Works: A Personal Memoir of My Years at Lockheed.* New York: Back Bay, 1994.

Rising, Linda. "Agile Meetings." *Software Testing and Quality Engineering (STQE) Magazine*, May–June (2002): 42–6.

Rising, Linda, and Norman S. Janof. "The Scrum Software Development Process for Small Teams." *IEEE Software*, July/August (2000).

Rittel, Horst, and Melvin Webber. "Dilemmas in a General Theory of Planning." *Policy Sciences* 4 (1973): 155–69.

Roethlisberger, Fritz. J., William J. Dickson, and Harold A. Wright. *Management and the Worker: An Account of a Research Program Conducted by the Western Electric Company, Hawthorne Works, Chicago* (Cambridge, MA: Harvard University Press, 1939).

Romzek, Barbara S., and Melvin J. Dubnick. "Accountability in the Public Sector: Lessons from the Challenger Tragedy." *Public Administration Review* 47, no. 3 (1987).

Rose, Mike. *The Mind at Work: Valuing the Intelligence of the America Worker.* New York: Viking, 2004.

Rosner, David, and Gerald Markowitz, eds. *Dying for Work: Workers Safety and Health in Twentieth Century America.* Bloomington: Indiana University Press, 1987.

Sandelands, Lloyd, and Robert Drazin. "On the Language of Organization Theory." *Organization Studies* 10, no. 4 (1989): 457–77.

Sanders, Lisa. *Every Patient Tells a Story: Medical Mysteries and the Art of Diagnosis.* New York: Random House, 2009.

Sandow, Dennis, and Ann Murray Allen. "The Nature of Social Collaboration: How Work Really Gets Done." *Reflections: The SoL Journal* 6, nos. 4–5 (2005): 1–14.

Schön, Donald. *The Reflective Practitioner: How Professionals Think in Action.* New York: Basic Books, 1983.

Schrage, Michael. *No More Teams: Mastering the Dynamics of Creative Collaboration.* New York: Currency Doubleday, 1995.

Schutz, Alfred. *The Phenomenology of the Social World.* Translated by G. and F. Lehnert Walsh. London: Heinemann Educational Books, 1972.

Schwaber, Ken. "SCRUM Development Process." n.d. (https://wiki.state.ma.us/confluence/download/attachments/16842777/Scrum+Development+Process.pdf).

Senge, P., A. Kleiner, C. Roberts, R. Ross, G. Roth, and B. Smith. *The Dance of Change: The Challenges to Sustaining Momentum in Learning Organizations.* New York: Doubleday/Currency, 1999.

Shirky, Clay. *Here Comes Everybody: The Power of Organizing without Organizations.* New York: The Penguin Press, 2008.

Solomon, Robert C., and Fernando Flores. *Building Trust: In Business, Politics, Relationships, and Life.* New York: Oxford University Press, 2001.

Sparks, Allister. *The Mind of South Africa: The Story of the Rise and Fall of Apartheid.* London: Mandarin, 1990.

Spretnak, Charlene. *The Resurgence of the Real: Body, Nature, and Place in a Hypermodern World*. Reading, MA: Addison-Wesley, 1997.

Stewart, Matthew. *The Management Myth: Why the Experts Keep Getting It Wrong*. New York: W.W. Norton and Company, 2009.

Stone, Douglas, Bruce Patton, and Roger Fisher. *Difficult Conversations: How to Discuss What Matters Most*. New York: Penguin Books, 2000.

Sutherland, Jeff, and Ken Schwaber, "The Scrum Papers: Nuts, Bolts, and Origins of an Agile Framework." 2011 (http://jeffsutherland.com/ScrumPapers.pdf).

Szulanski, Gabriel. "Exploring Internal Stickiness: Impediments to the Transfer of Best Practice within the Firm." *Strategic Management* 17, Special Issue (1996): 27–43.

Takeuchi, Hirotaka and Ikujiro Nonaka, "The New New Product Development Game," *Harvard Business Review* 64, no. 1 (1986): 137–46.

Taptiklis, Theodore. *Unmanaging: Opening up the Organization to Its Own Unspoken Knowledge*. London and New York: Palgrave Macmillan, 2008.

Taylor, Fredrick Winslow. *The Principles of Scientific Management*. New York: W.W. Norton, 1911. Reprint, 1967.

Taylor, Frederick Winslow. "The Principles of Scientific Management." *Bulletin of the Taylor Society*, December (1916).

Thatchenkery, Tojo, and Carol Metzker. *Appreciative Intelligence: Seeing the Mighty Oak in the Acorn*. San Francisco, CA: Berrett-Koehler Publishers, 2006.

Tietze, Susanne, Laurie Cohen, and Gill Musson. *Understanding Organizations through Language*. London: SAGE Publications, 2003.

Trist, E., and W. Bamforth. "Some Social and Psychological Consequences of the Long Wall Method of Coal-Getting." *Human Relations* 4 (1951): 3–38.

Trist, E, and C. Sofer. *Exploration in Group Relations*. Leicester, UK: Leicester University Press, 1959.

Truzzi, Mario, ed. *Verstehen: Subjective Understanding in the Social Sciences*. Reading, MA: Addison-Wesley, 1974.

Vaughan, Diane *Lessons Learned in the Challenger Launch Decision: Risky Technology, Culture, and Deviance at NASA*. Chicago, IL: The University of Chicago Press, 1996.

Von Krogh, Georg, K. Ichijo, and Ikujiro Nonaka. *Enabling Knowledge Creation: How to Unlock the Mystery of Tacit Knowledge and Release the Power of Innovation*. New York: Oxford University Press, 2000.

Warnke, Georgina. *Gadamer: Hermeneutics, Tradition and Reason*. Cambridge: Polity Press, 1987.

Watts, Duncan J. "Relationship Space: Meet Your Network Neighbors." *Wired* 11.06 (2003).

Watts, Duncan J. "Decentralized Intelligence: What Toyota Can Teach the 9/11 Commission About Intelligence Gathering." (www.slate.com/id/2104808/).

Weber, Max. *The Theory of Social and Economic Organisation*. Translated by A.M Henderson and Talcott Parsons. Edited by Talcott Parsons. New York: The Free Press, 1964.

Weber, Max. "Objectivity in Social Science and Social Policy." In *Understanding and Social Inquiry*, edited by F.R Dallmayr and T.A. McCarthy. Notre Dame: University of Notre Dame Press, 1977: 24–37.

Weick, Karl E. "Educational Organizations as Loosely Coupled Systems." *Administrative Science Quarterly* 21, no. 1 (1976): 1–19.

Weick, Karl E. *Sensemaking in Organizations*. Thousand Oaks, CA: SAGE Publications, 1995.

Wenger, Etienne. "Communities of Practice: The Social Fabric of a Learning Organization." *The Healthcare Forum Journal* 39 no. 4 (1996): 20–5.

Wenger, Etienne. *Communities of Practice: Learning, Meaning, and Identity*. New York: Cambridge University Press, 1998.

Wenger, Etienne. "Knowledge Management as a Doughnut: Shaping Your Knowledge Strategy through Communities of Practice." *Ivey Business Journal*, January/February (2004): 1–8.

Westwick, Peter J. "Reengineering Engineers: Management Philosophies at the Jet Propulsion Laboratory in the 1990s." *Technology and Culture* 48, no. 1 (2007): 67–91.

Westwood, Robert, and Stephen Linstead, eds. *The Language of Organization*. London: SAGE Publications, 2001.

Wheatley, Margaret J. *Leadership and the New Science: Learning About Organization from an Orderly Universe*. San Franscisco: Berrett-Koehler Publishers, 1992.

Willmot, Hugh. "Bringing Agency (Back) into Organizational Analysis: Responding to the Crisis of (Post)Modernity." In *Towards a New Theory of Organizations*, edited by John Hassard and Martin Parker. London and New York: Routledge, 1994: 87–130.

Winner, Langdon *The Whale and the Reactor: A Search for Limits in an Age of High Technology*. Chicago: University of Chicago Press, 1986.

Winograd, Terry, and Fernando Flores. *Understanding Computers and Cognition: A New Foundation for Design*. Indianapolis, IN: Addison-Wesley, 1986.

Wood, Martin. "Cyborg: A Design for Life in the Borderlands." *Emergence* 1, no. 3 (1999): 92–104.

Wright, Ronald. *A Short History of Progress*. New York: Carroll and Graf, 2004.

Zorn, T.E., L.T. Christensen, and G. Cheney. *Do We Really Want Constant Change?* San Francisco: Berrett-Koehler, 1999.

Index

Note: page number followed by *n* means the entry is in the notes at the end of the book.

of communities of practice are special, 131
reflect participants' beliefs, feelings,
emotions 76
virtual spaces are impersonal ones, 192
see also space between
space between, the
is where you'll find knowledge-work, in the
middle of conversations, 73
meaning resides in, 227*n*
the title of a song by the Dave Matthews
Band, 73
see also social spaces
Stewart, Matthew, critiquing Fredrick Taylor's
ideas on management, 126, 205, 233*n*,
242*n*
synergy, 27, 47, 76, 146, 221*n*

tacit knowledge, 35, 44, 222*n*
talk
among field service technicians, the, 130–1
anathema to management, 22
and listening are the means of aligning, 22
builds relationships, 183
complements tools, 109, 168
contrasted with tools, 57–9, 99–100
is meaning making, 14; how people share
knowledge, 17
is real when people are fully engaged, 102
is the heart of knowledge-work, organizing,
20, 38–9, 77, 98, 11
is the way to take charge at work, 144, 179,
195
is work, action, 20, 71, 100
management practices discourage it, 22
sometimes it is hard to tell tools from, 59
the kind that is the focus of work (work talk),
62, 67, 150
see also tools
Taptiklis, Theodore, writing about care, 123
Taylor, Frederick
his "science" failed, 98–9; success based on
stories, 99, 205
had no regard for workers, 127, 136, 205
legacy in the language of work, 62
management paradigm, 14, 99
obsession with measurement/data, 62–3, 98,
205, 220*n*
teams
collaboration is the key, 46
in the view from the top, 19–20
knowledge workers are commonly organized
into, 11
members' contributions inevitably vary, 196

members perform an intricate dance, 43
often exist in name only, 11, 219*n*
synergy is often what separates great from
mediocre, 27
take pride in what they do, 52, 129
why you shouldn't expect consensus in, 96
see also project teams
telecommuters as typical knowledge workers 65
how this work differs from
factory-work, 65–7
tools
allure of, 99–100
alone won't change practices, 138
contrasted with talk, 57–9, 99–100
don't do the work of organizing, 109
kinds used by managers, 58, 87, 99, 101, 102,
106, 190, 214
management relies almost exclusively on, 57,
98, 102, 234*n*
prevent us from seeing what matters, 100, 103
symbiotic relationship with talk, 59, 102, 183
that treat time as continuous and
homogeneous, 108
trapeze, metaphor for moving beyond
management, 138–42, 145, 172

ubuntu (Southern African humanistic
philosophy)
humanity has to do with relationships, 133
openness is compatible with, 160
organizing captures the spirit of, 134, 140
values not found in management practices,
134
Uluru, also known as *Ayers Rock*, a place sacred
to Aborigines in Australia, 74
uncertainity, contrast to risk, 208–9, 246*n*, 255*n*

view from practice
defined and described, 7, 20–2, 56, 250*n*
hierarchy is relationships, not structure, with
a, 182
is about getting things done, 7
needed to understand knowledge-work and
organizing, 7
what matters to project teams, 52
view from the top
concept of quality belongs to, 205
defined and described, 6–7, 15, 18–20, 52,
54–5, 218*n*, 221*n*, 250*n*
focuses on the organization and tools, ignores
organizing, 6, 107
has everyone looking the wrong way, thinking
about the wrong things, 15